Martin Luther on Reading the Bible as Christian Scripture

Princeton Theological Monograph Series

K. C. Hanson, Charles M. Collier, D. Christopher Spinks,
and Robin A. Parry, Series Editors

Recent volumes in the series:

Stanley S. MacLean
Resurrection, Apocalypse, and the Kingdom of Christ:
The Eschatology of Thomas F. Torrance

Brian Neil Peterson
Ezekiel in Context: Ezekiel's Message Understood in Its Historical
Setting of Covenant Curses and Ancient Near
Eastern Mythological Motifs

Amy E. Richter
Enoch and the Gospel of Matthew

Maeve Louise Heaney
Music as Theology: What Music Says about the Word

Eric M. Vail
Creation and Chaos Talk: Charting a Way Forward

David L. Reinhart
Prayer as Memory: Toward the Comparative Study of Prayer
as Apocalyptic Language and Thought

Peter D. Neumann
Pentecostal Experience: An Ecumenical Encounter

Ashish J. Naidu
Transformed in Christ:
Christology and the Christian Life in John Chrysostom

Martin Luther on Reading the Bible as Christian Scripture

The Messiah in Luther's Biblical Hermeneutic and Theology

WILLIAM M. MARSH

Foreword by Robert Kolb

PICKWICK *Publications* · Eugene, Oregon

MARTIN LUTHER ON READING THE BIBLE AS CHRISTIAN SCRIPTURE
The Messiah in Luther's Biblical Hermeneutic and Theology

Princeton Theological Monograph Series

Pickwick Publications
An Imprint of Wipf and Stock Publishers
199 W. 8th Ave., Suite 3
Eugene, OR 97401

www.wipfandstock.com

PAPERBACK ISBN: 978-1-60608-000-9
HARDCOVER ISBN: 978-1-4982-8822-4
EBOOK ISBN: 978-1-4982-8212-3

Cataloguing-in-Publication data:

Names: Marsh, William M., author | Kolb, Robert, 1941–, foreword.

Title: Martin Luther on reading the Bible as Christian scripture : the Messiah in Luther's biblical hermeneutic and theology / William M. Marsh, with a foreword by Robert Kolb.

Description: Eugene, OR: Pickwick Publications, 2017 | Includes bibliographical references.

Identifiers: ISBN: 978-1-60608-000-9 (paperback) | ISBN: 978-1-4982-8822-4 (hardcover) | ISBN: 978-1-4982-8212-3 (ebook).

Subjects: Luther, Martin, 1483-1546 | Hermeneutics | Messiah—History of doctrine | Jesus Christ—History of doctrines.

Classification: BR333.5 C4 M37 2017 (print) | BR333.5 (ebook)

Manufactured in the U.S.A. 07/14/17

To My Family

Contents

Foreword

MARTIN LUTHER WAS LISTENING MORE THAN HE WAS LOOKING AS HE APproached Holy Scripture. That is, he took the position that God was addressing him from and in the words of the prophets and apostles; he wanted to listen to what God had to say to him. Of course, as a professor of Bible at the University of Wittenberg, he looked at the text as well. He practiced his exegesis with all the tools and skills provided him by God: his own linguistic and analytical gifts combined with the historical tradition of interpretation and the new humanist explorations of the ancient languages in which the biblical texts were written. But Luther found not just the writers' clues and observations regarding what God is about in dealing with sinners in their words. He heard the Holy Spirit engaging him and all other readers with the words of God, with the voice of Christ, as he studied the Holy Scriptures. In them Jesus had promised that he was to be found (John 5:39), even by the son of a smelter, by a monk, by a professor, by an excommunicated outlaw.

In this volume William Marsh explores the manner in which Luther listened to and conveyed to others this conviction that God converses with his people in and through The Book. Marsh concludes that Luther did not find Christ to be the center of biblical revelation because of a dogmatic presupposition that compels the reader to place him there. Instead, the Reformer's experience in the texts with which he had wrestled in his search for peace with God and a way to deal with God's just wrath drove him to an ever more careful hearkening to and immersion in the text of the biblical writers. There the voice and the message of the Lord himself, the savior of sinners, struck him as he read the ancient prophets of Israel as well the evangelists and apostles of Christ's own time. Luther devoured their conversation with the Creator and Redeemer as they brought him into the exchange as well. He listened to the Lord's call to repentance and faith, and he experienced the power of the Holy Spirit in their words as they all concentrated on what God had to say to humankind. Luther found that the writers of both Old and New Testaments were talking about Jesus, *in spe* and then *in re*, day in and day out.

Marsh's use of the Wittenberg professor's prefaces to books of the Bible as a key point for ascertaining how Luther constructed and conveyed his keys to the Sacred Scriptures, his principles of biblical interpretation, is in line with the Reformer's own application of this long-standing genre as a guide for students of Scripture to move them into the text. In his prefaces to the books of the Bible Luther spelled out what God had to talk about with his people. It was their straying from him, their rebellion against him, that preoccupied the Creator in every age. The writers who recorded what he had to say to humankind were presenting, Luther perceived, from Genesis 3:15 on, God's solution to this problem: the Lord Jesus, the incarnate second person of the Trinity, the promised Messiah, as the substance of the divine solution to human rejection of their Creator and Lord and the means of the execution of that solution as well. Marsh argues effectively that Luther actually did what he said he was doing as he lectured and preached: he was not impressing New Testament concepts on the Old Testament texts, but he was following the New Testament writers who claimed that what they were witnessing and experiencing exposed the true significance of Old Testament texts that had placed Israel's and the world's hope in the coming of Jesus the Messiah and his creation of the new Israel.

This volume leads readers into one of the many exciting paths where Luther found the action of the Holy Spirit engaging his people as the professor used the form of the introductory preface to explain to students and lay readers of the Bible how best to grasp what God had to say to them in the writing of one particular author. Marsh effectively helps his readers work through the thought of the Reformer as he repeats the message of the prophets and apostles in their presentation of Jesus Christ. In this way Luther leads all his readers ever deeper into the text of Scripture itself. A rewarding read indeed!

Robert Kolb
Wolfenbüttel, August 14, 2016

Preface

THIS MONOGRAPH SEEKS TO DEMONSTRATE THAT LUTHER BELIEVES CHRIST to be the *sensus literalis* of Scripture on the basis of the Bible's messianic promise. This claim asserts that Luther's scriptural exegesis of the Bible's "letter" is responsible for his designation of Christ as its literal sense.

Chapter 1 introduces the scholarship on Luther as a biblical interpreter and reviews various assessments of his "christocentric" perspective on the Bible. The main criticism leveled against Luther to which this study seeks to respond is that of "Christianization."

Chapter 2 sets forth the preface-genre as a literary practice within the Medieval and Reformation periods where holistic statements of one's hermeneutic and biblical theology are commonly expressed. Next, the chapter embarks upon an in-depth analysis of Luther's prefaces to the *Deutsche Bibel* in order to manifest the Reformer's unified vision of Christ as Scripture's *sensus literalis* because of the Bible's preoccupation with the promise and fulfillment of the messianic hope.

Chapter 3 explores central components of the hermeneutical implications of chapter 2's examination of the Bible-prefaces that play a fundamental role for Luther in the establishment of Christ as the literal sense of Scripture. These three key aspects of his biblical interpretation are: the Messiah in the OT, authorial intention, and the relationship between the Old and New Testaments.

Chapter 4 features an excursus on the treatise, *On the Last Words of David* (1543). The goal of this chapter is to investigate a non-preface writing from Luther's corpus that shares similar intentions of prescribing and demonstrating his approach to reading the Bible with the conviction that Christ is its *sensus literalis* based upon Scripture's witness to the Messiah in its "letter." This analysis seeks to evaluate the significance of the three "hermeneutical implications" (chapter 3) derived from the prefaces to the Bible (chapter 2) for Luther's "Christological" interpretation of the OT in

On the Last Words of David with the aim of discerning a core hermeneutic in Luther's approach to Scripture.

Chapter 5 summarizes the conclusions derived from this study and suggests prospects for further research directly related to Luther's hermeneutic and biblical theology.

Acknowledgments

THIS BOOK IS THE CULMINATION OF A JOURNEY THAT BEGAN IN THE FALL OF 2000 when I entered my first semester of college as a "Christian Studies" major. For someone who only a few months prior had decided to apply for college to have completed a doctoral program, and now to see his dissertation published is its own proof that God still performs miracles. This monograph is a revised version of my dissertation, "Martin Luther's Messianic Rationale for Christ as the *Sensus Literalis* of Scripture in His Prefaces to the Books of the Bible" presented to the School of Theology at Southwestern Baptist Theological Seminary, Fort Worth, Texas.

Many people have been the Lord's instruments along the way without whom I would never had reached this point. The faithful discipleship I received from Steve Lee, my home church pastor at Mt. Olivet Baptist Church in Camden, South Carolina, was the starting point for any aspirations I had towards vocational Christian ministry and Christian education. I will always be indebted to his selfless shepherding. I would also like to express thanks to Dr. Walter Johnson, Dr. Pete Wilbanks, and Dr. David Haynie, who impacted my life and thought significantly during my undergraduate studies. It was under their tutelage especially that I witnessed the embodiment of ministry and academics, whereby the Lord cultivated in my heart a desire to pursue the recovery of the pastor-theologian role through further education at the seminary level.

Heartfelt gratitude must also be expressed to Dr. Jason Lee, my *Doktorvater*. I am deeply blessed for his mentorship in and outside the classroom. God has greatly used his life and ministry to shape me. I am thankful for all of his wisdom and careful guidance throughout every stage of this project.

Additionally, I have benefited from several others who have read and commented upon this work. I would like to express my gratefulness to Dr. Kevin Kennedy for his in-depth and valued feedback. Also, Dr. Ched Spellman, with whom I have shared many hours of "table talk" about Luther over the years, has caused this work to be sharpened in several respects. My colleague and fellow medievalist, Dr. John Gilhooly, read it with interest and guided me to places in need of precise edits. And last, I have been overwhelmed by the tremendous generosity of Dr. Robert Kolb, who graciously read various portions of the work at different stages and offered invaluable insight over the last several years in the midst of his busy schedule. I am honored and humbled by his willingness to contribute the Foreword to this book.

At last, thanks must be accorded to my parents, Phil and Gloria Marsh. They have supported and walked me with me every step of my spiritual and educational journey. I hope that this work is an honor to them for the path they set me on so long ago by the Lord's grace. The final expression of sentiment is reserved for my wonderful wife, Kim, and three precious children, Wyatt, Logan, and Layla. Kim challenged this reluctant student from the start that graduate school needed to end with a PhD. Her unwavering love and support have made this achievement just as much hers as mine. To my boys, you have no idea how much our vigorous wrastlin' matches kept me going. And to Layla, who was born a month after I completed this project, what better gift could a father be given when coming up out of the trenches of a dissertation.

Abbreviations

LW   *Luther's Works*. Edited by Jaroslav Pelikan (vols. 1–30), Helmut
        T. Lehman (vols. 31–55), and Christopher B. Brown (vols.
        56–75). St. Louis: Concordia; Philadelphia: Fortress, 1955–.

WA   *D. Martin Luthers Werke: Kritische Gesammtausgabe: Schriften.*
        65 vols. to date. Weimar: Hermann Böhlaus Nachfolger, 1883–.

WA, *Br*   *D. Martin Luthers Werke: Kritische Gesammtausgabe: Briefwech-*
        sel. 18 vols. Weimar: Hermann Böhlaus Nachfolger, 1930–85.

WA, *DB*   *D. Martin Luthers Werke: Kritische Gesammtausgabe: Deutsche*
        Bibel. 12 vols. Weimar: Hermann Böhlaus Nachfolger, 1906–61.

I

Introduction

INVESTIGATIONS INTO MARTIN LUTHER'S BIBLICAL INTERPRETATION OR his doctrine of Scripture have consistently recognized his christocentric reading of the Bible as one of the primary components of his hermeneutical method. The "Christ-centered" nature of Luther's approach to Scripture can take many forms, yet among them, one aspect stands as foundational for this manner of reading the Bible, that is, Luther's notion of Christ as the *sensus literalis*[1] of Scripture. As a biblical interpreter, Luther's propensity to read Christ in all the Scriptures ought to be perceived as a resultant practice derived from the textual warrant he finds in Scripture's own ontological purpose to bear witness to Christ within its "letter." Since Luther has no single definitive work or treatise devoted to prescribing principles for biblical interpretation, scholars recognize that Luther's hermeneutic must be studied from all genres of his corpus. In particular, his prefaces to the various books and portions of the Bible prove themselves to be perhaps the most suitable sources for discerning the essence of Luther's approach to Scripture, for in them, he instructs everyday Christians on how they should read and understand the Bible as the Spirit's inspired, two-Testament witness to Jesus Christ.

---

1. Various definitions of "literal sense" exist throughout the history of biblical interpretation; however, this study will adopt Luther's own definition in association with the term's development in the Late Middle Ages explicated below in subsequent sections. A working definition at this point could be: the *sensus literalis* is an author's intention discerned through literary (textual) analysis. On a grander scale, to speak of the *sensus literalis* of Scripture as a whole is to acknowledge that the Bible is a unified text divinely inspired and written to testify to a prime subject matter. On either the micro- or the macro-level, the literal sense is identified with the ultimate intention/ meaning communicated through an author's writing.

Statement of Research Problem and Thesis

Although many factors constitute Luther's "Christ-centered" interpretation of Scripture, his messianic interpretation of the Old and New Testaments is the main rationale for the "later" Luther's insistence that Jesus is the literal sense of Scripture. The acceptance of this claim has significant implications for current conceptions of the place of Christ in Luther's exegetical method. Many of Luther's interpreters argue that Luther's designation of Christ as the essence of Scripture is the result of, for instance, his doctrine of the Word or his theology of the cross; however, these perspectives bypass the textual basis upon which Luther rests the entire structure of the way he conceives of Christ as Scripture's literal sense. Because these alternatives place a doctrinal position as the starting point for the Reformer's scriptural interpretation, it comes as no surprise, then, when they conclude that Luther is forcing his Christian dogmatic lens onto the Bible to produce meanings that supposedly are not latent within the biblical texts already.

This study seeks to make the opposite claim, namely, that Luther's construal of Christ as Scripture's *sensus literalis* is not foremost a dogmatic conviction brought to bear upon biblical texts. Rather, it is a reflection of what he believes is textually present in Scripture due to authorial intention. Luther roots his appropriation of Christ as the *sensus literalis* of the Bible in his belief that Scripture is supremely a book about the Messiah. This reasoning makes his interpretive approach foremost a hermeneutical conclusion reached from the exegetical interpretation of biblical text(s) rather than a confessional re-reading of the OT in light of the NT or the Christian faith. To frame the situation another way, if Luther did not regard the OT as having a messianic *telos* communicated through the authorial purposes of its writers/prophets (e.g., Moses, David, Isaiah), then Luther's Christ-centered approach to Scripture would be emptied of its *raison d'être*. Study of the "prefaces," then, will serve to present Luther offering a guide for reading the Bible grounded upon the character of both Testaments as Christian Scripture inspired by the Holy Spirit who spoke through the prophets and apostles for the ultimate purpose of bearing witness to, on the one hand, the coming Messiah, and on the other hand, Jesus of Nazareth as this promised Christ, the resurrected Son of God and Son of Man.

Methodology

This study will seek to contribute to the field of historical theology within the realm of Luther studies. Luther's "prefatory" writings as they pertain to introducing books or portions of the Bible have been chosen as the primary source material for substantiating this study's claim. The main selection of prefaces under review will be the "prefaces" that Luther wrote for inclusion with his German translation of the Bible. Other genres in Luther's works feature similar "prefaces" such as his *Church Postils* and his lectures/commentaries. Since certain prefaces to books of the Bible are related across genres in terms of form and content, all "prefaces" directly associated with a book or a collection in Scripture regardless of genre will be treated as primary source material for analysis. Priority, however, will be allotted to those accompanied with Luther's *Deutsche Bibel*.[2] The broader backdrop of Luther's writings will be utilized for supplemental and evidential support.

The rationale for analysis of Luther's various prefaces to books or portions of the Bible comes with several presuppositions in anticipation for what the source material can afford. First, with the earliest of the prefaces under review dated at 1521, the chronology of the prefaces as a whole begins subsequent to the occurrence of an alleged "shift" in Luther's hermeneutic.[3] The prefaces, then, should contain established elements of Luther's "new hermeneutic" in a relatively matured form that would allow founded observations to be made concerning his most consistent approach to interpreting Christ as the literal sense of Scripture. Second, the nature of a "preface" lends itself both to summary and to theory. It seeks to be instructive and succinct while emphasizing the essential tools requisite to give its subject a fair reading. Luther's prefaces offer a rich, yet concise guide for understanding Holy Scripture. Therefore, the prefaces provide a unique opportunity to mine Luther's thoughts on how to read (hermeneutics) and what to expect (purpose/doctrine/theology) from the individual books of the Bible and Scripture as a whole.[4] Together, Luther's prefaces are a definitive source for

---

2. What is labeled as the "Prefaces to the Bible" in *Luther's Works*, vol. 35, is the collection of the prefaces Luther wrote to serve as introductions to the individual books of the Bible in his German translation of Scripture. A few of these prefaces were meant to introduce groupings in Scripture such as the *Preface to the Old Testament* (the Pentateuch) and the *Preface to the New Testament* (the Gospels and Acts). Luther authored other prefaces to have a similar function such as *A Brief Instruction on What to Look for and What to Expect in the Gospels*, which circulated with his *Church Postils*; in addition, Luther generated similar prefaces to introduce his lectures on various books of the Bible.

3. The dating of the "early" Luther's hermeneutical shift has not found a consensus in scholarship. The period from 1513 to 1519 is the locus of various theories on when and if a shift took place in Luther's approach to Scripture. Some evaluation of this debate will be covered below. Whatever the case may be, this "shift" would be antecedent to Luther's Bible-prefaces.

4. More rationale for granting primacy to the prologue-genre will be supplied

the core elements of his biblical theology, a biblical theology borne from the Reformer's extensive exegetical, hermeneutical, and translational labors over Scripture as the Word of God.

Luther's Bible-prefaces are not the only sources where the messianic dimension of Luther's construal of Christ as the literal sense of Scripture can be found. In chapter 4, Luther's treatise *On the Last Words of David: 2 Samuel 23:1–7* will be evaluated in light of the hermeneutical conclusions reached from the analysis of the "prefaces." Chapter 4 serves two primary goals: (1) to undergird the main claim for which chapters 2 and 3 on the "prefaces" contend; and (2) to demonstrate the presence and consistency of this claim in a different, yet fitting genre from Luther's corpus.

Starting Points

Luther, Letter, Law, Literal

The concept of the *sensus literalis* was not foreign to Luther's career as a biblical interpreter. He maintained an ongoing interrelationship between the *sensus literalis* and Jesus Christ from his beginnings as a Doctor of Holy Scripture to his final years as a seasoned Reformer. On the other hand, the christological interpretation of Scripture's relation to the *sensus literalis* experienced variant expressions at different stages of Luther's hermeneutical development.[5] Perhaps the earliest and most explicit encounter with Luther's

---

below in the opening sections of chapter two. In the meantime, a basic deduction could be made from another of Luther's prefaces. To borrow from *A Brief Instruction*, one can find a clear explanation of the purpose of Luther's "Prefaces to the Bible" in the writing's full title, *A Brief Instruction on What to Look for and Expect in the Gospels*. Notice three essential elements: (1) the preface is meant to be didactic (i.e., *A Brief Instruction*); (2) the preface then instructs the reader in his or her "reading" of the Gospels (i.e., "What to Look for"); and (3) the preface summarized what one should anticipate to be the theme or message of the Gospels (i.e., "What to Expect").

5. In his quest for the "original Luther," Hagen discourages use of terms like "hermeneutics," "system," or "method" in reference to the Reformer because he believes the scientific disciplines to which these terminologies belong originated in the nineteenth century as products of the Enlightenment. For Hagen, Luther is not the first modern, but rather is foremost a Medieval-Catholic, who approaches Scripture as the *sacra pagina*. In contrast to modern hermeneutics that assumes distance between the ancient text and the contemporary reader, Hagen reminds Luther's interpreters that he worked from within the monastic tradition, "where theology was practiced, prayed, sung, proclaimed, worked, copied, and edited, [it] viewed theology as grounded in sacred Scripture (the sacred page). In this tradition of *sacra pagina*, the canon of Scripture was the rule of faith, and theology was the discipline of the sacred page." Hagen, *Luther's Approach to Scripture*, 17. This study largely concedes Hagen's

promotion of Jesus Christ as the Bible's literal sense can be observed in the three prefaces he attached to the *Dictata super Psalterium* (hereafter *Dictata*), Luther's first lectures on the Psalter from 1513–15. These prefaces reveal Luther employing the christological interpretation of Scripture within the bounds of the *Quadriga*:[6] (1) *Preface to the Glosses*;[7] (2) *Preface of Jesus Christ*;[8] and (3) *Preface to the Scholia*.[9] These prefaces provide critical insight into the early state of Luther's exegetical approach and view of the OT. Through them Luther instructs his audience on how to apply the fourfold approach to the Psalms, though the literal sense is divided into "historical" and "prophetic" and the anagogical sense is downplayed.[10]

Although these prefaces are from the "early" Luther (this study will investigate the "later" Luther per the discussion below) and are intended to introduce his lectures rather than his later translation of the Psalter into

---

point; nevertheless, words such as "hermeneutics" or "method" will be utilized as interchangeable with Hagen's preference for phrasing similar to his work's title, "Luther's *approach* to Scripture." To speak of Luther's "hermeneutic(s)" in this study simply represents the components or principles Luther employed to hear or to understand the living Word of God in Scripture. See also Hagen's valuable entry in the *Dictionary of Major Biblical Interpreters* for a condensed version of his views on Luther as a biblical interpreter and theologian of the *sacra pagina*. Hagen, "Luther, Martin," 687–94.

6. The *Quadriga*, or the fourfold method of Medieval biblical exegesis, affirmed multiple senses in the meaning of a biblical text: (1) the literal sense as the historical-grammatical meaning; (2) the allegorical sense as the spiritual or theological meaning; (3) the tropological sense as the moral meaning; and (4) the anagogical sense as the eschatological or future-oriented meaning. See David Steinmetz's highly influential essay for an introductory explanation of the *Quadriga* and the method's prospect for ongoing relevance in biblical hermeneutics, Steinmetz, "The Superiority of Pre-Critical Exegesis," 3–14. For in-depth historical analyses of the fourfold method throughout the Middle Ages see the seminal works of Smalley, *The Study of the Bible in the Middle Ages* and Lubac's multivolume, *Medieval Exegesis*.

7. *LW* 10:3–5; WA 55.1:1–5.

8. *LW* 10:6–7; WA 55.1:6–11.

9. *LW* 10:8–10; WA 55.2:25–27.

10. The *Preface to the Glosses* includes the anagogical sense in its illustrations of the fourfold method applied to the Psalms, but in the *Preface of Jesus Christ*, Luther omits it altogether. The *Preface to the Scholia* mentions neither the literal nor the anagogical, nor does it give a full-length demonstration of the *Quadriga* as do the other two. This inconsistency seems to be a result of Luther's presentation of the literal sense in each one. In the *Preface to the Glosses*, Luther orients the literal sense as the historical sense, though it can be interpreted "spiritually." His practice in the *Preface of Jesus Christ*, on the other hand, is to treat the literal sense as the literal-prophetic sense that has an eschatological dimension to it. Luther's neglect of the anagogical meaning in the *Preface of Jesus Christ* is most likely due to his formulation of the literal sense as the prophetic sense (i.e., future-oriented). *LW* 10:3–10; WA 55.1:1–11; 55.2:25–27.

German for the *Deutsche Bibel*, the purpose they serve here is to demonstrate that at the forefront of the "early" Luther's concern for a proper reading of the Psalms was how one should understand the interpretive significance the biblical text's literal sense meaning in correlation to the person and work of Jesus Christ. This interpretive aim can be witnessed in Luther's formulaic prescription in the *Preface of Jesus Christ*: "Every prophecy and every prophet must be understood as referring to Christ the Lord, except where it is clear from plain words that someone else is spoken of."[11] As one can see, Luther's central interest as he embarks upon interpreting the Psalter is to bring it into connection with Christ. So, from the earliest examples of Luther as a biblical interpreter, the question of the relationship of Jesus to Scripture is primary.

Another writing that lends significant insight into the state of Luther's conception of the *sensus literalis* by the time of the penning of his "prefaces" to the *Deutsche Bibel* is, *Answer to the Hyperchristian, Hyperspiritual, and Hyperlearned Book by Goat Emser in Leipzig—Including Some Thoughts Regarding his Companion, the Fool Murner* (hereafter *Hyperchristian*). On March 29, 1521, Luther sent his third reply against Emser to the printing press. The exchange between the two had already become quite vitriolic.[12] What prompted *Hyperchristian* was Emser's total repudiation of *To the Christian Nobility of the German Nation Concerning the Reform of the Christian Estate* (1520), which he considered Luther's complete subversion of the Roman Catholic Church.[13] Given the featured theme of the priesthood in *To the Christian Nobility*, Luther attacked Emser in *Hyperchristian* once more concerning his stance on ecclesiastical authority in that Rome had wrongly subjected Scripture to the papacy's supremacy. In the reply's central section "On the Letter and the Spirit," Luther sought to undo Emser's entire case for Rome's clerical hierarchy by way of dismantling the interpretive method which Luther held as responsible for producing the scriptural and theological support for such a system of church offices. The import of *Hyperchristian* for this study is that it reflects Luther's theology and interpretive approach to Scripture contemporaneous to his work on the *Deutsche Bibel* and the development of its "prefaces."

As is customary for Medieval or Reformational commentary on the nature of "the letter and the Spirit," Luther begins with a glance at Paul's words in 2 Corinthians 3:6 when the Apostle posits, "For the letter kills, but

---

11. *LW* 10:7; WA 55.1:6, "Omnis prophetia et omnis propheta de Christo domino debet intelligi, nisi ubi manifestis verbis appareat de alio loqui."

12. Brecht, *Martin Luther: His Road to Reformation*, 332–35.

13. Ibid., 377–79.

the Spirit gives life." Luther accuses Emser of committing the same error as did Origen, Jerome, and Dyonisius by assuming a twofold meaning in Scripture, an external and a hidden one, or rather, a literal and a spiritual meaning.[14] Luther's critique comes from his own evolved interpretive position wherein he now understands Paul's antithesis of "letter and Spirit" in terms of "law and gospel."[15] This advancement is a sign of hermeneutical growth compared to the manner in which he exposited the Psalms in the *Dictata* where, as Gerhard Ebeling has argued, Luther still stood within a traditional formulation of "the letter and the Spirit," even if the *Dictata* may have revealed to some degree a "hermeneutical shift" away from the typical Medieval fourfold method.[16]

In place of the classic "letter/Spirit" division of scriptural meaning, Luther declared the *sensus literalis* as "the highest, best, strongest, in short, the whole substance, nature, and foundation of Holy Scripture. If one abandoned it, the whole Scripture would be nothing."[17] Later he adds that "Scripture cannot exist without the [literal] meaning."[18] The literal sense is what ensures meaning in scriptural interpretation according to Luther. To say that the "letter" is nothing more than a graceless literalistic sense of Scripture is to cause the Bible to "give up the Ghost" so to speak. Luther's conviction is that the old "letter/Spirit" separation of historical and theological meaning empties Scripture as an inspired *text* of its certainty and ground for imparting divine truth.[19] Under this assumption, Luther believes that

---

14. *LW* 39:175; WA 7:647.

15. In Ebeling, *Luther: An Introduction to His Thought*, 93–124, Ebeling traces the move from what began as "the letter and the Spirit" divide in Luther's earlier writings to its later transformation into the Reformer's classic "law and gospel" distinction. Cf. Randall Gleason's more recent thesis in, "'Letter' and 'Spirit' in Luther's Hermeneutics," that sees the law/gospel formulation at the core of the letter/Spirit contrast in Luther's thought.

16. See the section below on the "Early Luther" for further discussion on Luther's "hermeneutical shift."

17. *LW* 39:177; WA 7:649, "das ist, Emsers geystlicher vorstand gillt nichts, dießer gober der höhiste, beste, sterckiste und kurtz umb die gantz substanz, weßen und grund der heyligen schrifft ist also, das, wo man den abethet, were die gantze schrifft schon nichts."

18. *LW* 39:178; WA 7:650, "[S]o man yhm allein anhangt und den schrifftlichen faren lesset, besser were eyttell Poeten fabell dafur geleßen, den er ist ferlich und on yhn besteht die schrifft, aber on yhenen kan sie nit bestehen."

19. "Now see how well Emser rides along with his twofold Bible. The result [of his effort] is that *nothing remains certain*" (italics mine); *LW* 39:179; WA 7:651, "Nu sihe, wie feyn Emser mit seyner zwispeltigen Biblie daher ferett, macht, das keynis nit gewiß bleybett."

a proper understanding of the *sensus literalis* guards biblical hermeneutics from interpretive relativism.

Throughout "On the Letter and the Spirit," Luther offers brief moments of definitional clarity for what he envisions as the Bible's *sensus literalis*. In an early instance, he asserts, "Only the true principle meaning which is provided by the letters can produce good theologians."[20] From a more elaborative passage, Luther suggests that using the label "literal meaning" is perhaps not as beneficial as supposed since the concept has been so variously conceived within the history of biblical interpretation. Instead, he proposes the descriptor of the "grammaticum, historicum sensum," that is, the grammatical-historical sense and/or meaning.[21] Luther explains that "grammatical-historical" represents the pursuit of scriptural meaning achieved through grasping the *usus loquendi*, or as he defines it, the "meaning of the tongue or of language."[22] What seems to be Luther's point is that the "verbal sense" (i.e., grammatical-historical, *sensus literalis*) communicates the "spiritual" sense.[23] Not that the two senses are opposed to one another and that the reader must break through the mere "grammatical" barrier of a passage in order to discover the theological and spiritual meaning that is supposedly entrenched somewhere beneath or behind word symbols and syntax. If this method were the appropriate one, then once an interpreter located the "spiritual" sense, its grammatical conveyance would become obsolete and would have no role to play as an arbiter of a text's right understanding. The verbal entry point would be nothing more than simply a gateway to true scriptural meaning somewhere beyond the actual text wherein abiding theological and spiritual significance of the written Word would alone reside.

However, Luther argues that a proper rendering of the *sensus literalis* as the "grammatical-historical" sense does not allow for, on the one hand, a wooden literalistic translation of verbal meaning, and on the other hand,

20. *LW* 39:178; WA 7:650, "Es muß der eynige rechte herubt synn, den die buchstaben geben, alleine thun."

21. *LW* 39:181; WA 7:652.

22. *LW* 39:181; WA 7:652, "das man yhn nennet der tzungen oder sprachen sinn."

23. "Verbal sense" may be used interchangeably with "literal sense" and can be defined as interpretation of the "sense" or "meaning" of the author's words/writing as a part of the whole received biblical text. For a helpful discussion on the "verbal sense's" relatedness to the concept of the "literal sense," one may consult Greene-McCreight, *Ad Litteram*, 21–22; Greene-McCreight, "Literal Sense, 455–56. A simple attempt at definition can be seen also in Kevin Vanhoozer's explanation of the "literal" primarily as a literary sense, "If the author's intention is embodied in the text, then the ultimate criterion for right or wrong interpretation will be the text itself, considered as a literary act." Vanhoozer, *Is There A Meaning in This Text?*, 303.

an ahistorical determination of a supposed "hidden" or "spiritual" sense far removed from the basic interpretation of a text at its grammatical level. As evidence, he enlists Paul's allegory of Abraham's two sons from Galatians 4:21–31. Luther explains that the "grammatical-historical" meaning of the OT texts that recount Abraham having two sons from two wives mean what they say, both grammatically and historically, and that any suggestion of understanding this familial circumstance in an allegorical fashion must be an interpretive move explicitly prompted by the Holy Spirit, which obviously takes place in the inspired mind of the Apostle Paul in Galatians 4. Nevertheless, Luther's point is that without the basic "grammatical-historical" reality of Abraham and his family in the OT text there would be no ground for the Spirit's disclosure of the passage's "hidden" or allegorical meaning.[24]

Luther views Paul's allegory in Galatians 4 as an exceptional case in Scripture; it is not to become the norm. Because the Holy Spirit serves as the ultimate author of the Bible, who is also the "simplest writer and adviser in heaven and on earth," a text should have "no more than the one simplest meaning which we call the written one, or the literal meaning of the tongue."[25] It is helpful when Luther makes the distinction between mere "grammatical" interpretation and how language or the "spoken" tongue is used. Luther's understanding of the doctrine of inspiration reorients the *sensus literalis* with authorial intent because the Spirit supplies "divine" meaning by way of the human writer's *usus loquendi*. The breakdown of scriptural meaning into "letter" and "Spirit" as divisions between "human" and "divine" intentions in the text has no place in Luther's expression of biblical interpretation since the Spirit communicates the literal sense of a

24. In this section of "On the Letter and the Spirit," Luther responds to the tradition that affirms a separate "spiritual" meaning in Scripture. He says that what others have called *anagogas*, or other times "allegory," the Apostle Paul regards as *mysteria*. Using 1 Corinthians 14:2 (i.e., one who utters "the mysteries of the Spirit"), Luther denies that the "tongue" or a person's "manner of speaking" can carry a "secret" or separate "spiritual" meaning unless the Spirit himself identifies it as a revealed *mysteria* such as Ephesians 5:32 (Christ and the church union), or in this case, Paul's Spirit-prompted and inspired allegorical interpretation of Sarah and Hagar in Gal 4:24. Note Luther's caveat, "But here it is necessary that no one invent mysteries on his own, as some people have done and are still doing. *The Spirit himself must do it*—or else one must prove it with Scripture." Italics mine; *LW* 39:181; WA 7:652. Outside of these rare occurrences, Luther assigns the locus of the theological/spiritual meaning to the literal sense (i.e., the grammatical-historical meaning), where the divine author is communicating his intent to the reader through the human author's literary acts.

25. *LW* 39:178; WA 7:650, "Der heylig geyst ist der aller eynfeltigst schreyber und rether, der ynn hymell und erden ist, drumb auch seyne wortt nit mehr den eynen einfeltigsten synn haben kunden, wilchen wir den schrifftlichen odder buchstabischen tzungen synn nennen."

text through the human agent's authorial communicative act. Understood in this way, Luther's claim for Scripture to have a "single" or "one" meaning should not be regarded as reductionist. Instead, Luther's outlook on textual meaning is a holistic one whereby to understand a biblical writing's authorial intent in the context of dual authorship (human and divine) does not necessitate the division of "letter" from "Spirit" to arrive at Christian Scripture's *sensus literalis*.

The purpose of this brief exposition of Luther's sentiments about the literal sense of Scripture in his third letter to Emser is to emphasize how the traditional viewpoint of Scripture's twofold meaning underneath the titles of "letter and Spirit" becomes an obsolete hermeneutic for Luther at this stage of his interpretive journey. "Law and gospel" replaces the former articulation as a manner of perceiving the "use" or "experience" of Scripture depending upon a reader or hearer's spiritual condition. For Luther, Scripture's *sensus literalis* is a unified meaning accessed through "grammatical-historical" interpretation and analysis of the author's *usus loquendi* for the purpose of determining the essential "spiritual" and/or theological meaning of the divinely inspired biblical text. Signification is not a practice Luther wishes to perpetuate.[26] He desires to avoid fanciful exegesis or any attempts at assigning a supposed "spiritual" sense to a passage that was not gained by identifying that to which the author's words themselves refer. As he asserts, "Likewise, even though the things described in Scripture mean something further, Scripture should not therefore have a twofold meaning. Instead it should retain the one meaning to which the words refer."[27]

Survey of Scholarship on Luther's Hermeneutic Pertaining to the *Sensus Literalis* and the Christological Interpretation of Scripture

This study will focus on the period of the "later" Luther which most scholars identify as the segment of Luther's life beginning in 1521 post-Diet of Worms

---

26. The practice of "signification" is what lies at the heart of the fourfold method of biblical interpretation. Augustine set the trajectory for the development of the *Quadriga* in the Middle Ages, when he prescribed the base rule for "signification" in his treatise, *On Christian Teaching*, as "Words, for example: nobody uses words except in order to signify something. From this it may be understood what I mean by signs: those things which are employed to signify something." Augustine, *On Christian Teaching*, 9.

27. *LW* 39:179; WA 7:651, "[A]lso ob wol die ding, ynn der schrifft beschrieben, etwas weytters bedeutten, soll nit darumb die schrifft tzwispeltigen synn habenn, ßondern den eynigen."

and lasting until his death in 1546.[28] In his article from 1982, "Interpreting

28. When speaking of the "early/young" or "later/older" Luther one should keep in mind that these descriptors represent the state of his career as a Reformer and the stage of his theological development more so than as a reflection on his age. The dating of an "early/young" or "later/older" Luther is without exactness in Luther scholarship. Broad periodizations have found somewhat of a consensus, and this point is perhaps truer for the chronological boundaries of the "early/young" Luther than the "later/older" division. Heinrich Boehmer's *Die Junge Luther* (1925)—the long-time standard-bearer for the biography of Luther's beginnings—could be held responsible for defining the period from Luther's birth to 1521 as the time of the "young" Luther. Bornkamm desired to continue Boehmer's work in *Luther in Mid-Career, 1521–1530*, which was left incomplete due to his death, and was posthumously published under the editorial care of his daughter Karin Bornkamm (Bornkamm, *Luther in Mid-Career*, xi–xv). Bornkamm had wished to take his biography one step further into 1531, the year of the Nuremberg Truce, because he believed this event signified a critical turning point in the Reformer's life (Bornkamm, xi). Unfortunately, his death in 1977 at the age of seventy-five left his vision unrealized. Still in pursuit of a complete biography of Luther, Jünghans edited a collaborative anthology published in 1983, *Leben und Werk Martin Luthers vom 1526 bis 1546*. This collection of independent essays from an array of authors sought to fill the void of a standard biographical source on the "older" Luther, since Boehmer's and Bornkamm's contributions had stopped short of Luther's final years. Most recently, Brecht's massive three-volume chronicle of Luther's entire life has superseded its predecessors, and now is considered in both German and English scholarship the definitive biographical source(s) on Luther. Brecht presents Luther's life in three periods: 1483–1521 (vol. 1); 1521–32 (vol. 2); and 1532–46 (vol. 3). Brecht intended his first volume to replace Boehmer's *Der Junge Luther* as it modeled Boehmer's study by ending with the Diet of Worms in 1521, not to mention borrowing essentially the same English subtitle to Boehmer's for his own English translation: *Road to Reformation* (Brecht, *Martin Luther: His Road to Reformation*, ix–xi; cf. Boehmer, *Road to Reformation: Martin Luther to the Year 1521*). For both biographers, the year 1521 clearly marked the latest point in the Reformer's life where the descriptors "early" and/or "young" could be appropriately utilized to identify the state of Luther's life and thought. Brecht's second volume paralleled Bornkamm's *Luther in Mid-Career*, except Brecht was able to offer a complete account that made its way into the events of 1532. Although Brecht published a third volume on the final fourteen years of Luther's life from 1532–46, this last periodization ought not to be solely characterized as the "later/older" Luther as if the years 1521–32 constituted a "middle" Luther. In his "Foreword" to volume 2, it seems that Brecht envisioned the last book in this series as simply a continuation of the general trajectory Luther's life took following the Diet of Worms in 1521 and his return from the Warburg Castle in 1522 (Brecht, *Martin Luther: Shaping and Defining the Reformation*, xii). In this way, it seems that one could interpret the second and third volumes of Brecht's biography as the "later" Luther "part one" and part two" respectively. Helmar Jünghans, in his essay, "Interpreting the Old Luther," 272–74, contends that the designation of the "older" Luther should be attributed to the rest of the Reformer's life subsequent to the Diet of Speyer in 1526. Jünghans sees the Diet of Speyer as a monumental event in which the Reformation found support through imperial policy. With this occasion, the Reformation reached a significant milestone insofar as through the endorsement

the Old Luther," Helmar Jünghans reflected on how the study of the "young" or "early" Luther predominated Luther scholarship in the twentieth century.[29] This same observation can be similarly made when considering the contributions to scholarship on Luther as a biblical interpreter. Apart from Heinrich Bornkamm's *Luther and the Old Testament*, the major studies on Luther's hermeneutic and biblical interpretation center on Luther's "early" career from 1513–19.[30] The case could even be made that scholars have paid the most attention to Luther's *Dictata super Psalterium*, since some authors regard these lectures as where Luther's fundamental break with the fourfold Medieval method of interpretation takes place, or at the least, finds its catalyst until it comes to completion by 1519.

The "Early" Luther

Studies on the "early" Luther's hermeneutic cover many aspects of the Reformer's developing approach to Scripture as it slowly distances itself from the Medieval norm. The two basic questions posed to this period of the Reformer's hermeneutical development are: (1) When did Luther's so-called "hermeneutical shift" away from traditional usage of the *Quadriga* occur? And (2), what is the intersection between Luther's conception of the *sensus literalis* and his christological interpretation of Scripture? Gerhard Ebeling's seminal article, "Die Anfänge von Luthers Hermeneutik," published in 1951 and later translated into English in 1993 by Richard B. Steele, represents the traditional perspective on the formation of the "young" Luther's hermeneutical and interpretive method.[31]

---

of the German princes a new evangelical church achieved special organization never before experienced. In short, this summary on the divisions of Luther's life seems to show that one has reached the "later/older" Luther when he or she has journeyed with the German Reformer past his *Tumerlebnis*, his posting of the Ninety-Five Theses in 1517, and his trial at the Diet of Worms in 1521. With all of these tumultuous incidents behind him, Luther appears to have attained a level of maturity in his career and Reformation theology during the 1520s that represents a "stabilized Luther," one worthy of being set apart from an earlier personality that was still undergoing considerable shaping and formation until he was forced to make seemingly his final stand before the church, the Emperor, and God in the city of Worms.

29. Jünghans, "Interpreting the Old Luther," 271–72.

30. Bornkamm admits that his study is on the "mature" Luther as opposed to seeking to add his voice to the ongoing debates concerning the state of Luther's early hermeneutics. Bornkamm, *Luther and the Old Testament*, viii; 285n1.

31. Ebeling, "Die Anfänge von Luthers Hermeneutik," 172–230; Ebeling, "The Beginnings of Luther's Hermeneutics," 129–58, 315–38, 451–68; Ebeling, "The New Hermeneutics and the Early Luther," 34–46.

Ebeling argued that in his first set of lectures on the Psalter (1513–15), *Dictata super Psalterium*, Luther still engaged in the fourfold Medieval approach to biblical interpretation, but in a modified form.[32] Luther remained "under the spell" of the traditional *Quadriga* until the end of the *Dictata*, yet what *did* change was the new foundation from which Luther expounded the four senses.[33] That "new foundation" was none other than the christological meaning of the Psalms.[34] Because Luther regarded the Psalms's prophetic character as ultimately referring in every instance to Christ, the fourfold method's starting point was entirely christological.[35] The "hermeneutical shift" at this point, according to Ebeling, is that Luther joined Faber Stapulensis in defining the literal sense as the prophetic sense; however, where Luther diverges from Faber is that this new method becomes the platform from which the *Quadriga* is explicated rather than the means of its silencing.[36]

By the end of his study, Ebeling concluded that Luther's major hermeneutical achievement in the *Dictata* was his fastening together the literal-prophetic (christological) sense with the tropological. Ebeling saw Luther transforming the tropological meaning into an existentialist interpretation of the Psalms insofar as God's activity through His Word is always causative and cognitive, reorienting a person's self-understanding to its proper place in relation to God and Christ.[37] The tropological sense, therefore, became something more than mere moral application; it had become "faith," the appropriate application of the end goal of Christ as the literal-prophetical meaning of Scripture.[38] In sum, Ebeling reckoned that Luther envisioned the tropological sense as the ultimate and principal meaning of Scripture even above the literal.

Ebeling's work on Luther's early hermeneutic was the standard until James Preus issued a challenge to the consensus beginning with his 1967 preliminary article, "Old Testament *Promissio* and Luther's New Hermeneutic," and then definitively in 1969 with the publication of his book, *From Shadow to Promise: Old Testament Interpretation from Augustine to the Young Luther*.[39] Preus set himself apart from Ebeling's proposal in several ways. First,

32. Ebeling, "The Beginnings of Luther's Hermeneutics," 451.

33. Ibid., 452.

34. Ibid., 453.

35. Ibid., 454.

36. Ibid., 455–56. On Faber's influence upon Luther, see Hahn, "Faber Stapulensis und Luther," 356–432.

37. Ebeling, "The Beginnings of Luther's Hermeneutics," 463.

38. Ibid., 464.

39. Preus, *From Shadow to Promise*; and Preus, "Old Testament *Promissio* and

Preus strove to make the case for a more defined "hermeneutical shift" from the Medieval system of interpretation than Ebeling allowed. Even though Ebeling acknowledged that by the end of the *First Lectures on the Psalms* Luther had fused together the literal-prophetic (christological meaning) with the tropological sense in a manner distinct from his Medieval forbearers, Ebeling did not believe Luther completely abandoned the traditional usage of the *Quadriga*, and especially allegory, until 1519.[40] Preus, on the other hand, upheld that Luther made a more pronounced break with the fourfold method sometime in the spring of 1515.[41] Whereas Ebeling placed Luther alongside Faber affirming a double-literal sense in the Psalms, one being literal-historical and the other literal-prophetic with the "prophetic" sense serving as access to the spiritual meaning, Preus claimed that Luther's significant "hermeneutical shift" consisted of linking the spiritual meaning of the Psalms with their literal-historical sense.[42]

According to Preus, Luther's key concept responsible for this shift was *promissio*. In "Part One" of *From Shadow to Promise*, Preus traced the development of Medieval hermeneutics beginning with Augustine up to Luther. His intent for revisiting this historical terrain was to make the claim that Medieval interpreters bypassed the theological significance of the literal-historical sense of the OT text, thus perpetuating the faulty hermeneutical division of "letter" and "Spirit." Consequently, this model pitted the actual text of Scripture against its own theological, spiritual meaning. Preus

---

Luther's New Hermeneutic." Preus continued to expound upon his approach to Luther in two subsequent articles. In "Luther on Christ and the Old Testament," he restated his main thesis in *From Shadow to Promise*, but then tested it against some of Luther's reflections from his writings on the NT as well as extending his argumentation to the "later" Luther. Next, Preus moved beyond his case for Luther's "hermeneutic shift" as from "shadow" to "promise" by analyzing how the Reformer, then, progressed from "promise" to "presence" in his perspective of the relation between the OT saints and Christ in "From Promise to Presence." In short, Preus observed a sacramental aspect to Luther's interpretation of "promise" in the OT wherein saints hoped for a *future* messiah, yet in their faith Christ was really *present*.

40. Ebeling, "The Beginnings of Luther's Hermeneutics," 131.

41. Preus, *From Shadow to Promise*, 169; Preus, "Old Testament *Promissio* and Luther's New Hermeneutic," 152.

42. Preus analyzes the Penitential Psalms and believes to have discovered the first instance of Luther locating the spiritual meaning in the literal-historical sense in Psalm 101, where "the psalmist's own word, spoken out of his own circumstances, is the basis for the theological interpretation ... Now Christ, rather than being the 'prophetic-literal' sense, that is, the point of departure for a spiritual exegesis, becomes the goal or *telos* of the whole exegesis. And the *applicatio* springs not from the Christian's likeness to Christ, but from his likeness to the Old Testament speaker, with whom he shares the anticipation of the Coming One." Preus, *From Shadow to Promise*, 171.

argued that Luther's discovery of the *promissio* concept in the Psalms during his *Dictata* was the solution to this breakdown. *Promissio* stood for God's promise to send the Messiah for the sake of His people's salvation. Therefore, as Luther lectured on the Psalms, his reading transformed into one that considered the OT's own history as the place where the people of God were consciously striving to live by faith in the covenant-promise of God to send the Messiah as the answer to their current fallen human condition and existence *coram Deo*.[43] In this way, the OT's "letter" no longer needed to be treated as mere *figura* or shadows that required a prophetic reference to Christ in order to acquire a spiritual-theological meaning and application. Rather, Christ was already promised (*promissio*) in the actual words and historical occasion of the OT text, and so Luther was able to link the NT Church with the OT "faithful synagogue" through its own literal-historical circumstance.[44]

Preus regarded Ebeling's thesis of the union of the christological-prophetic and tropological sense in the *First Lectures* as the interpretive method that Luther actually had to overcome in order to rediscover the theological value of the OT.[45] This "rediscovery" of *promissio* in the OT's "letter" was what Preus attributed as the principal cause for Luther's later Reformation breakthrough. If the Psalms's literal sense was primarily a prophetic reference to Christ, then the tropological meaning was the "faith of Christ"; however, this hermeneutic "worked against the development of [Luther's] Reformation theology" in Preus's view.[46] Instead, Preus contended that at some point during the *Dictata*, Luther recognized that God's promises were not being made to Christ, but to Israel. The *promissio* present in the OT "letter" was directed to the people who were hearing it.[47] In sum, "It was the word of promise, not *conformitas Christi* via tropological signification, that led Luther away from Medieval theology to the exclusive '*sola* fide' and '*solo* verbo' of Reformation theology."[48]

Despite Preus's rigorous efforts, Ebeling's original perspective on the state of the "young" Luther's hermeneutic remains the dominant position on the topic. Moreover, leading Luther scholars have heavily critiqued Preus's thesis. In a scathing review, Reformation historian Gordon Rupp dismissed Preus's claims at every point until finally remarking, "For Dr. Oberman to

43. Ibid., 4.
44. Ibid.
45. Ibid., 226–27.
46. Ibid., 248–49.
47. Ibid., 246.
48. Ibid., 268.

say of this work that it is 'the best Luther study since World War II' is, we may hope, an example of a teacher doing his best for his brilliant pupil."[49] In 1974, Scott Hendrix rejected Preus's position on the "faithful synagogue" in the OT in his book *Ecclesia in Via*. For Hendrix, Preus did not give attention to the apparent distinction Luther draws in the *Dictata* between OT and NT faith. Hendrix conceded that the two periods of faith were related, but he rejected their equivocation. According to Hendrix, Luther preferred to describe the coming Christ in the OT as the *fides revelanda*.[50] The "faith which is to be revealed" is not the same revealed faith of the NT; instead, Hendrix described it as a depth perception awarded to the prophets and only to some of the people of the OT to recognize the prefiguring of the future things in "the significative character of the Old Testament words and promises."[51] OT faith, then, is a "proleptic" faith where messianic insight is progressively granted mainly to the prophets and to a minor few of the OT saints. Hendrix believed Preus misunderstood Luther's approach to the OT insofar as Luther had not rediscovered the correct nature of the OT in the *promissio*, but instead, he was reading it with an over-realized NT theology.[52] In short, Hendrix's main critique of Preus was for seeing in Luther's interpretation a more "revealed" faith present in the Psalms than Luther himself had really discerned.[53]

49. Rupp, Review of *From Shadow to Promise*, 278.

50. Hendrix, *Ecclesia in Via*, 269.

51. Ibid., 269.

52. Ibid., 271.

53. Preus's thesis on the "hermeneutical shift" of the "early" Luther sparked ongoing discussion. In 1970, John Pilch offered a critical reflection, denying that Preus's analysis of the Penitential Psalms provided any conclusive evidence of a "shift," but instead simply highlighted Luther's tendency to "vacillate" between a spiritual (christological sense) or a literal (historical) reading of the Psalms, which Pilch regarded as true of the Reformer throughout his life. Pilch, "Notes and Observations: Luther's Hermeneutical 'Shift,'" 447–48. Then, Darrell Reinke in 1973 proposed a nuanced thesis that accepted Preus's basic case for Luther's movement away from "allegory" or a "spiritual" reading of Scripture, but suggested that Luther's alleged "shift" was due to the psychological effect resultant from his disengagement with the monastic tradition, where "Scripture, then, is not a devotional book, but a self-contained metaphor; its meaning is not spiritual experience or self-consciousness, but the past historical Christ—and Christ alone. The art of reading is not *meditatio*, but *explicatio*." Reinke, "From Allegory to Metaphor: More Notes on Luther's Hermeneutical Shift," 390. A final example is John R. Wilch, who attempted to unravel how Luther preached Christ from the OT by covering the "early" Luther's hermeneutical development and outlining typical key components of Luther's principles of biblical interpretation in the short span of seven pages. For the most part, Wilch largely channeled Preus without any substantive distinction. Wilch, "Luther as Interpreter: Christ and the Old Testament,"

The "Later" Luther

As previously noted, the beginnings of Luther's "new hermeneutic" dominated scholarship on "Luther the biblical interpreter" in the twentieth
century. When one seeks to discover the official position on Luther's hermeneutics beyond his early years, Heinrich Bornkamm's classic study, *Luther
and the Old Testament*, stands virtually alone. Bornkamm did not wish to
revisit the hermeneutical development of the "early" Luther since the subject
had undergone already considerable treatment. Instead, his purpose was "to
clarify Luther's theological concept of the Old Testament."[54] The relevance
of Bornkamm's monograph to this study is fundamental. Bornkamm has
much to say regarding Luther's notion of the literal sense and his christological interpretation of Scripture, and in many cases, Bornkamm works
from the prefaces to the various books of the Bible to substantiate his claims.
Despite these commonalities, this study will seek to highlight the shortcom-
ings of Bornkamm's insights in order to submit an alternative proposal on
the orientation of Luther's view of Christ as the literal sense of Scripture as
evidenced in his "prefatory" writings affiliated with the Bible.

Bornkamm has famously labeled Luther's approach as "Christocentric
interpretation" as opposed to a "Christological-prophetic" method.[55] The
former, as Bornkamm defines it, prompts the interpreter to read the OT
as a Christian, that is, with a Christian lens, "enlightened through the New
Testament, to illumine the situation of man and his encounter with God on
the manifold Old Testament levels."[56] In other words, Luther's christocentric interpretation of the OT is an example of reading the NT back into the
Old. As for the opposing method, Bornkamm asserts that a "Christological-
prophetic" interpretation "is forced to carry the concepts of the New Testament revelation into the Old Testament and put them in the mouths of the
patriarchs and writers."[57] For Bornkamm, this type of approach cannot be
considered "a truly historical exegesis," and thus cannot survive the severest
historical research on Scripture.[58]

Near the beginning of chapter 4, "The Old Testament as Word of God,"
Bornkamm stands in line with Ebeling by affirming that Luther followed
Faber through adoption of the literal-prophetic sense as the true literal

---

3–9.

54. Bornkamm, *Luther and the Old Testament*, vii.

55. Ibid., 121, 263.

56. Ibid., 26.

57. Ibid.

58. Ibid.

meaning of Scripture.[59] Likewise, Bornkamm suggests that the literal-prophetic sense served as the catalyst for what would become Luther's main exegetical goal: "to make Christ, the content of Scripture, present for the individual in judgment and grace."[60] It appears that Bornkamm allowed this perspective to norm his understanding of the "mature" Luther's interpretation of Christ in the OT. When recounting Luther's repudiation of allegory, Bornkamm remarks that Luther only employed it later in life as "an exception to the comprehensive *prophetic application of the Old Testament to Christ*."[61] This "prophetic application" is what Bornkamm intends with his "Christocentric" title. In essence, Luther "applies" the NT Christ to OT texts—texts which do not speak of Christ in their literal-historic meaning—in order to find "secret [prophetic] references to Christ" all throughout Scripture.[62] Moreover, Bornkamm posits that Luther's "prophetic application" of Christ in the OT was an implication of the Reformer's christological understanding of the doctrine of the Word. Christ as the eternal Word, therefore, was awaiting "discovery in Scripture" in Luther's exegetical method.[63]

In a subsection within chapter 4 titled "Predictions of Christ and the Trinity," Bornkamm set out to juxtapose the difference between interpreting the OT as direct prediction of Christ and the more indirect manner of seeing how the NT gospel permeates OT interpretation.[64] From the outset, Bornkamm asserts that the direct application of OT texts to Jesus Christ was the predominant practice in Luther's interpretive approach to the OT. Bornkamm then progresses to show how Luther acknowledged the customary "messianic" passages such as Genesis 3:15 and Deuteronomy 18:15. Next, he quickly moves past these "direct" occurrences, and attempts to demonstrate how Luther used his "prophetic application" of Christ to non-messianic passages like Exodus 33–34 and David's "last words" in 2 Samuel 23:1–7 to prove that they contained christological "promises."[65] At the end of this section, Bornkamm maintains his initial conviction that Luther is re-reading the OT with NT concepts and categories. In fact, Bornkamm goes so far as to say that "the Old Testament made no essential independent contribution" towards Luther's christological-trinitarian evidence in the OT.[66]

59. Ibid., 88.

60. Ibid., 89.

61. Ibid., 96; italics original.

62. Ibid.

63. Ibid.

64. Ibid., 101.

65. Ibid., 102.

66. Ibid., 119.

The claim that Luther did not have an independent use of the OT for the development of Christian doctrine pinpoints the problem that this study wishes to identify and to address through analysis of Christ as the literal sense of Scripture in Luther's prefaces to the various books of the Bible.

In her essay, "Luther's Trinitarian Hermeneutic and the Old Testament," Christine Helmer critiques Bornkamm at this juncture and laments the unfortunate tendency among Luther's interpreters to regard the OT's prophetic references to Christ as "proclamation" instead of "prediction."[67] Although Helmer is concerned with Luther's trinitarian hermeneutic instead of the christological, her overall aim is pertinent to this study because she is responding to the denial of the OT as a legitimate source for informing Christian dogma in its own right. Modern theology, in Helmer's estimation, allowed historical criticism to reject the validity of even proposing Christ to be the direct reference of the letter of the OT.[68] Instead, only the NT can speak appropriately on matters of Christian theology on the basis of historical grounds. Hence, for the OT to have theological significance and authority for the development of Christian doctrine, the NT would need to be read back into the OT for the sake of a fresh interpretation. Helmer does not accept this paradigm, and so she makes the purpose of her essay "to orient the discussion to Luther's explication of the trinitarian doctrine and its exegetical foundation in the Hebrew text of the Old Testament."[69] To state it another way, Helmer contends that Luther's exposition of the Trinity in the OT is not the mere infusing of NT and confessional theology into the OT's "letter," but instead, it is the product of a hermeneutic that is rooted deeply in the actual Hebrew text, that is, in its words, grammar, and syntax, all joined together with a trinitarian semantics.[70]

As she recounts the dire situation in modern theology's view of the OT's place in the Christian Bible, Helmer identifies the work of Bornkamm and Preus as two Luther scholars who sought to revisit the Reformer's appropriation of the OT's *sensus literalis* with some hope of revitalizing the relationship between the OT's "letter" and its coherence with NT theology and the early church's trinitarian and christological dogmas. Her assessment of Bornkamm's efforts has already been discussed above, and unfortunately, her reflection on Preus is brief with only the mention of the topic of his study and its restriction to the "pre-Reformation Luther."[71] Ironically, Pre-

67. Helmer, "Luther's Trinitarian Hermeneutic and the Old Testament," 66n12.
68. Ibid., 50.
69. Ibid.
70. Ibid., 50, 65.
71. Ibid., 66n12.

us's main agenda for demonstrating that Luther recaptured the theological value of the OT for the Christian faith at the level of its literal-historical sense is quite similar to the end goal of Helmer's essay. Preus sought to counter the consensus that Luther's vision of Christ as the literal sense of Scripture was a NT reading of the OT. Rather, Preus contended that Luther had rediscovered the true theological meaning of the OT in its own literary and historical sense. If the criticisms are true that Preus has incorrectly interpreted Luther's hermeneutics in the *Dictata*, perhaps his crime is that he read the "older" Luther's hermeneutics into the Reformer's early years. Nevertheless, it does not seem that the final word has been spoken on how one should understand Luther's christological interpretation of Scripture.

Modern Assessments of Luther's Christological Interpretation of Scripture

Luther's view of Christ as the literal sense of Scripture is central to his hermeneutics, a commonly-noted aspect of Luther's role as a biblical interpreter in the history of interpretation. Yet a quick sampling of some of the modern assessments of this feature assume that Luther is forcing Christ upon the OT either due to the Reformer's doctrine of the Word or exegesis ruled by the Christian faith. If Luther's messianic reading of the OT is considered, it is done so cursorily.

For example, characteristic of many treatments of Luther's hermeneutical method, Raymond Surburg primarily spoke of Luther's christological approach to Scripture as a principle by which the Reformer established the theological unity of the whole Bible.[72] Still, Surburg intimated that contrary to "modern higher criticism . . . , Luther . . . accepted the interpretation of Christ and the Apostles, which clearly portrayed the Old Testament as speaking and prophesying about the Messiah."[73] Unfortunately, Surburg omitted an explanation of how Luther understood the OT's "speaking" and "prophesying" of Christ, and ended his article only one paragraph later. Later in 1963, Paul Althaus emphasized how Luther saw Christ as the essential theme or subject matter of Scripture.[74] Similar to Bornkamm, Althaus stated that "Christocentric interpretation for Luther thus means gospel-centered interpretation, understood in terms of the gospel of justification

72. Surburg, "The Significance of Luther's Hermeneutics for the Protestant Reformation," 257.

73. Ibid., 258.

74. Althaus, *The Theology of Martin Luther*, 74.

by faith alone."[75] In other words, Althaus believed Luther found Christ in the OT because he read it with gospel-centered presuppositions.

In 1984, David Dockery devoted an article to "Martin Luther's Christological Hermeneutics" in which he evaluated Luther's "Christological principle" for contemporary evangelical hermeneutics.[76] Like Surburg and Althaus, Dockery readily acknowledged that Luther saw Christ as the heart of the Bible.[77] He also posited that there was no difference for Luther between the christological principle and grammatical-historical meaning.[78] Moreover, he described Luther's christological approach as theoretical/exegetical and practical/theological.[79] Even though Dockery highlighted key points of Luther's view of Christ as the *sensus literalis*, he did not shy away from concluding that Luther's reading of the Trinity and Christ into the OT was a method "rejected hundreds of years earlier by the School of Antioch."[80] Dockery continued to point out the weaknesses of Luther's approach in that "it [veiled] the historicity of the OT" and "led to a forced interpretation of the passage."[81] Dockery also accused Luther of frequently reading a NT meaning into an OT text.[82] The only real strengths that Dockery ascribed to Luther's christological interpretation of Scripture was that it led to a distrust of allegory and a dismantling of the fourfold method.[83] Because Dockery saw Luther's "christological principle" for the most part as a violation of the history of an OT text, his estimation of its present-day value was that evangelicals should regard it as a canonical or theological principle utilized to move a step beyond the grammatical-historical level of meaning.[84] This assessment commits the same error that Helmer assigned to Bornkamm where such conclusions fail to recognize what Luther saw in the actual text of Scripture. Even though certain manifestations of Luther's christological interpretation of Scripture throughout his writings may fit nicely into the category of a second or third order "theological principle," the starting point for his conviction of Christ as the literal sense of Scripture resides in the

---

75. Ibid., 79.
76. Dockery, "Martin Luther's Christological Hermeneutics," 189.
77. Ibid., 191.
78. Ibid., 192.
79. Ibid.
80. Ibid., 193.
81. Ibid.
82. Ibid.
83. Ibid., 194.
84. Ibid., 203.

actual words, intent, and semantic reference of the biblical texts. To put it another way, the *verbum*, for Luther, contains the *res*.

Luther scholar Kenneth Hagen forcefully echoed this sentiment in his 1993 study *Luther's Approach to Scripture as Seen in His "Commentaries" on Galatians, 1519–1538*. Hagen's main contention was that Luther's approach to Scripture should not be characterized by post-Enlightenment, modern concepts such as "hermeneutics" or "method," which were born out of the nineteenth century. Instead, Luther read Scripture consistent with his Medieval, monastic tradition, which regarded the Bible as the *sacra pagina* (sacred page).[85] Scripture as the *sacra pagina* is not a mere "letter" to be consumed for sapiential wisdom.[86] The "sacred page" is from God to promote God and his gospel.[87] As Hagen summarized:

> The text of Scripture for Luther was the result of God in Christ as Word (*Verbum*), who proclaimed the words (*verba*) of the Gospel, repeated by Paul, and written down as text (*textus*). Luther was primarily interested in the Word, *Christus*. *Christus* is not a *sensus*, a meaning; he is the *res*, the reality of the truth of God. He is the thing itself (*res*), not the occasion for questions.[88]

In this selection, Hagen appears to come close to Bornkamm's "christological-prophetic" model where "The Christ, who is the eternal Word, awaits discovery in Scripture (John 5:39)."[89] Yet, Hagen resisted being categorized in "prophetic" terms because he considered Luther's understanding of "promise" and "Christ" not as multiple levels of meaning, but instead posited, "They are the very thing itself of God."[90] So, though at first glance Hagen may seem to follow in Bornkamm's footsteps, he quickly distinguishes his perspective because of his position that Luther was consciously a reader of the *sacra pagina*, where the single, simplest sense—the grammatical sense—was the means of interpreting the *verba* in order to encounter the *Verbum* (*res*).[91] The grammatical-historical meaning is inseparable from the *res* because, "For Luther, the proper use of Scripture is to gain access to

85. Hagen, *Luther's Approach to Scripture*, 15–17.
86. Ibid., 10.
87. Ibid., 16.
88. Ibid., 18.
89. Bornkamm, *Luther and the Old Testament*, 96.
90. Hagen, *Luther's Approach to Scripture*, 18.
91. Ibid.

the *res.*"⁹² Hagen, therefore, can say of Luther's approach, "the grammatical meaning and theological meaning are the same."⁹³

At this point, Hagen is beneficial to this study's thesis because of his strong assertion that Luther's christological interpretation of Scripture is text-oriented, even though Luther's take on the messianic hope is not in the purview of his work. Like Hagen, the conviction of this work is that in Luther's construal of the *sensus literalis*, the grammatical-historical (i.e., letter/text) and the theological (i.e., spiritual) meaning find union. Despite Hagen's suspicion of the relevance of speaking of "senses" in reference to Luther's interpretation of the Bible, Luther is still a beneficiary of the Medieval interpretive tradition, and therefore, would have been mindful of his place within the history of exegesis. That Luther was cognizant of his relationship to the practice of the *Quadriga* even after his so-called "shift" can be seen in various writings where he disavows allegory while upholding his notion of the literal sense as the grammatical-historical meaning.⁹⁴ Nevertheless, Hagen primarily affirms Christ as the center of Scripture in Luther's thought because "Christ is the eternal Word of God, *present* in the Old Testament, [and] . . . *present* in the New Testament."⁹⁵ Thus, it seems that Hagen would argue that the ultimate rationale for Luther's vision of Christ as the *sensus literalis* of Scripture is due to the Reformer's doctrine of the Word of God rather than at root an exegetical conclusion.

Another prominent perspective on Luther's view of Jesus and Scripture comes from Siegfried Raeder, who has formulated the matter as "evangelio-centric" (gospel-centered) interpretation rather than christological.⁹⁶ Raeder's conclusions are mainly derived from his study on Luther's second series of lectures on the Psalter, *Operationes in Psalmos* (1519–21).⁹⁷ Raeder observed that in the *Operationes*, Luther interpreted the Psalms more in re-

92. Ibid.

93. Hagen, "Luther, Martin," 691.

94. *LW* 1:232–33, 27:311; WA 42:173, 2:551.

95. Hagen, "Luther, Martin," 691; italics mine. One can hear in Hagen's word choice of "present" a sacramental perspective on how Christ, the Word of God, is *in* all the Scriptures akin to what Preus hinted at in his aforementioned essay, "From Promise to Presence," 100–125. To hear the liturgical language of "presence" brought to bear upon Luther's "contemporaneous" vantage point in his interpretation of both the Old and New Testaments, see Maschke, "Contemporaneity: A Hermeneutical Perspective in Martin Luther's Work," 165–82.

96. Reader, "The Exegetical and Hermeneutical Work of Martin Luther," 377. See also his older contribution, "Luther als Ausleger und Übersetzer der H. Schrift," 1:153–278, 2:800–805.

97. WA 5:26–673.

lation to the gospel of Christ than to the person of Christ.[98] In other words, Luther explained the Psalms "in the light of faith," whereas in the *Dictata* he strove to understand them prophetically about Christ.[99] Yet, similar to Hagen, Raeder desires to do justice to Luther as a biblical interpreter to avoid glossing him simply as a dogmatic theologian reading the New Testament into the Old.

This concern can be discerned in Raeder's assertion, "For Luther the hermeneutical key to open the door to the Old Testament is the fact that God has revealed himself in Christ. Therefore linguistic findings are subordinated to the Gospel of Christ. Luther will not hurt the grammatical rules, but he knows that they have their limits."[100] Again, Raeder's point coheres with Hagen's view that the "words" are relevant insofar as they are the means for an encounter with the "reality" behind them. Hence, Hagen's claim, "*Christus* is not a *sensus*, a meaning; he is the *res*, the reality of the truth of God."[101] Ultimately, Raeder adopts this position because of Luther's side note in his exposition of Psalm 22:17 in the *Operationes* that the "words" (*verba*) must submit to the "substance/reality" (*rebus*), the "letter" (*litera*) follows the "spirit" (*spiritum*).[102] The logic of Luther's approach to Scripture in this setup holds "faith" (*res*) as the starting point, though the grammar (*verba*) must yield to it when exegesis is taking place.[103]

98. Raeder, "The Exegetical and Hermeneutical Work of Martin Luther," 377.

99. Ibid.

100. Ibid.

101. Hagen, *Luther's Approach to Scripture*, 18.

102. "Sola ergo superest grammatica, quam decet Theologiae cedere, cum non res verbis, sed verba rebus subiecta sint et cedant, et vox merito sensum sequatur et litera spiritum." WA 5:634.

103. Mattox mirrors this sequencing in his analysis of Luther's reading of the Trinity in the OT as worded in his essay's title, "From Faith to the Text and Back Again: Martin Luther on the Trinity in the Old Testament," 281–303. Mattox's thesis—which he would also apply to Luther's christological interpretation of Scripture—is that "Luther's trinitarian reading of the Old Testament . . . was not grounded in grammatical or historical interpretation, but in a distinctive use of the *regula fidei*, that is, in the exegetical application of the faith which grasps and knows the Triune God" (ibid., 301–2). Similar to Raeder, Mattox sees the *regula fidei* as the "*res* that controls the understanding of the *verba*, for right interpretation depends in the first place on the right knowledge of the God revealed in the words of Scripture" (302). Yet to say that the *res* has so ruled Luther's approach to Scripture that either his trinitarian or christological reading of the OT cannot be attributed to the grammatical-historical method appears to misunderstand the nature of the *regula fidei*. The purpose of the "rule of faith" must not be diminished to the form of a simple retelling or condensed version of Christian doctrine produced by tradition. What is often missed is how the "rule of faith" exists because Jesus Christ is the one who is in accordance with the Scriptures (the Old

On the other hand, it seems Raeder was hesitant to fall into nice agreement with Bornkamm's final conclusion in *Luther and the Old Testament* that, "[Luther's] work Christianized the Old Testament."[104] Raeder questioned the justification for Bornkamm's critique, since it led to the assumption that whether in exegesis or in translation, Luther introduced foreign "Christian" elements into the OT.[105] Luther's christological sense, Raeder admitted, was not always the "original" sense, "But apart from that we are allowed to ask the question, whether it is right—so to speak—to lock up the message of the Old Testament in the limits of its original meaning, scrutinized by historians."[106] As it appears, Raeder's dilemma is that he wishes to avoid accusing Luther of "Christianizing" the OT, yet he regards it as "no longer possible to find texts in the Old Testament, which must be related to Christ directly as prophecies" in the vein of Luther's interpretation.[107] Perhaps Raeder's notion of direct "prophetic" reference is also in line with Bornkamm's concept of the OT's "prophetic application" to Christ, which in itself is still a method for forcing a confessional "Christian" reading onto the grammatical-historical sense of the OT's "letter."[108] This assessment seems

---

Testament) and who is one with the Triune God revealed and borne witness to by a two-Testament, singular Word of God. Said differently, Luther's move "from faith to text" occurs because the "from faith" is "from the text" (in "accord"; 1 Corinthians 15:3–4). If the *regula fidei* is solely envisioned as the product of NT theology, then certainly, the OT's grammatical-historical meaning cannot contribute to confessional, Christian dogma, and Luther has duly violated the OT's "letter." On the other hand, if the "rule of faith" is understood to have arisen because NT believers received the OT as equally Christian Scripture as that which proves the apostolic writings, then the trinitarian God and his Christ serve as the same reality witnessed to by the Holy Spirit's speaking through the prophets (OT) and the apostles (NT). Seitz summarizes the issue well when he writes, "In our view, this is the chief concern of an appeal to a rule of faith, that is, demonstrating that the God of the Scriptures and Jesus Christ are one, and active together in the selfsame witness. Prior to the existence of a second canonical witness, the first is doing primary theological work of an incipiently trinitarian sort, and the cruciality of that is undiminished by the existence of apostolic writings" (Seitz, *The Character of Christian Scripture*, 194).

104. Bornkamm, *Luther and the Old Testament*, 266.

105. Raeder, "The Exegetical and Hermeneutical Work of Martin Luther," 405.

106. Ibid.

107. Ibid., 394.

108. Bornkamm sees Luther following Stapulensis's practice of a "literal-prophetic sense," which as Bornkamm defines it, is "the interpretation speaking out of the spirit of the prophets which pointed to the coming Christ" (Bornkamm, *Luther and the Old Testament*, 88). Before Bornkamm, Ebeling also acknowledged Luther's implementation of Faber's literal-prophetic sense. Ebeling explains, "The literal-prophetic sense is the mystical sense of the literal-historical sense. The historical becomes a sign and

evident in Raeder's statement, "The Reformer's understanding of certain texts as explicit prophecies about Christ is no longer acceptable; but his principal standpoint cannot be given up, namely, that the Old Testament is focused towards the New Testament. This principle is grounded on the very centre of Christian faith."[109]

Raeder's proposition for the appropriation of Luther's presupposition that "the Old Testament is focused towards the New Testament" sounds like a claim about the OT's "letter." If the post-Enlightenment's configuration of the OT's "historical" sense (i.e., original meaning) prohibits the legitimacy of direct reference to Christ, and if to do Christian theology from the OT as a confessional, Christian theologian is to "Christianize" it, then in what other way(s) could it be conceived that the OT has the NT in its horizon? On the surface, Raeder appears to be more gracious with Luther than Bornkamm's forthright accusation of "Christianization" when he ends his essay on the note that Luther's exegesis and translation must be understood from two perspectives: "On the one hand, it is qualified and limited by conditions of a time, when the method of investigating the Bible in a historical and critical way had not yet arisen. On the other hand, his translation of the Bible is based on the principal conviction, being as old as Christianity itself, that the Old Testament comes to its fulfillment in Jesus Christ."[110] This appraisal, however, leaves the problem at an impasse. If Luther's interpreters must regard his pre-critical approach as ignorant of proper scientific, historical exegesis of the biblical text while simultaneously hearing the exhortation not to abandon the Reformer's "principle conviction" of reading the OT as a Christian theologian of the church's faith where the Old Testament comes to fulfillment in the New, how is one left to interpret the OT at any Christianly level without the charge of "Christianization" if assigning a christological sense to the OT's grammatical-historical meaning is off limits?

In essence, this query is the dilemma within Luther scholarship on Luther's christological interpretation of Scripture that this study wishes to address and offer a possible solution. By demonstrating through the

---

parable which points beyond itself" (Ebeling, "The Beginnings of Luther's Hermeneutics," 455). Ebeling observes that the prophetic meaning is interchangeable with the text's spiritual sense. The spiritual sense is a mystical sense because it is deeply hidden beneath the plain words of the prophet. Therefore, the Spirit must illumine the reader to the prophet's true, literal meaning (i.e., literal-prophetic sense) that corresponds to the divine intent. "Prophetic application," thus, is not grammatical-historical "prediction"; it is a "hidden" meaning dislocated from the surface literary level of the biblical text.

109. Raeder, "The Exegetical and Hermeneutical Work of Martin Luther," 394.

110. Ibid., 406.

prefaces to the Bible Luther's commitment to the messianic hope of the OT and the proclamation of its fulfillment in the NT as a first order concern in his biblical theology, it will become clear that the impetus for Luther's construal of Christ as the Bible's *sensus literalis* is an exegetical rationale derived from Scripture's "letter" at the grammatical-historical level achieved with the assumption of fidelity to a unified view of divine and human authorial intention.

The next chapter will seek to show why the "prefaces" are suitable primary source writings to represent Luther's hermeneutic and biblical theology, followed by an in-depth analysis of Luther's "prefaces" to the various books and groupings of the Bible to substantiate the claim that Luther's messianic reading of the Bible lies at the core of his conviction that Christ is the literal sense Scripture.

2

Christ as the *Sensus Literalis* of Scripture in Luther's Prefaces to the Bible

The Preface-Tradition in the History of the Christian Bible

THE CREATION OF PREFACES TO INTRODUCE INDIVIDUAL OR GROUPS OF books within Scripture is not novel to Luther. The main progenitor of this practice can be traced back to Jerome in his production of a new translation of the Latin Bible (*Vetus Latina*) in the fourth and fifth centuries that came to be known as the *Vulgate*.[1] The publication and widespread use of Jerome's *Vulgate* standardized the place of the prefaces as a literary feature to be perpetually included with the Bible as a *text*. Jerome authored many of the prefaces himself; however, he did not generate a prologue for every book of the Bible. The *Vulgate*'s full set of prefaces, though primarily belonging to Jerome, was the result of multiple different authors, some of which had their origin in heretical traditions such as Marcionite and Pelagian prologues to the Pauline epistles and Monarchian prefaces to the Gospels.[2]

---

1. Commissioned in AD 382 by Pope Damasus, Jerome at first set out only to revise the Latin translations of the Gospels and the Psalter from the existing *Vetus Latina* Bible. Over time, Jerome decided to work towards a brand new translation of the OT based upon the proto-Masoretic text. Jerome's pursuit of a fresh translation from the Bible's original languages mainly centered upon the OT. His work on the NT did not reach beyond the revisions of the *Vetus Latina*'s fourfold Gospel. For a concise account of the *Vulgate*'s history, one may consult, Van Liere, *An Introduction to the Medieval Bible*, 80–109.

2. Schild, *Abendländische Bibelvorreden bis zur Lutherbibel*, 71–95.

From the time of their formalization in Jerome's *Vulgate*, Bible-prefaces have had a specific audience in view: the biblical reader.[3] Even though distance between the clergy and the laity increased throughout the Middle Ages, the prefaces still represented, at some level, the desire to make the Bible accessible to the untrained reader.[4] Scribal transmission of the *Vulgate* consisted of more than the biblical text; extrabiblical accompaniments were also copied. These paratextual components included elements such as a table of contents, section/chapter headings, chronological tables, dictionaries, and also prefaces.[5] Together, these extrabiblical features functioned as interpretive aids for reading and comprehending Scripture with all sorts of students of the Bible in mind.[6]

The Bible-preface as a paratextual pretext to individual books or groups of books in Scripture signaled not only the concern to equip readers, but also pointed to the development of the close relationship between Scripture and interpretation in the Middle Ages. Christopher Ocker recognizes this dynamic, when he writes, "Medieval scholars knew that these texts [prologues] were not scripture, even if they did not know the unorthodox origins of some of them, and they took this material critically. But the physical form of the Bibles they used nevertheless displays well the intimate connection of scripture and interpretation in their minds."[7] "The physical form of the Bible" is a means of study that can open a significant window into others's view and use of Scripture.[8] As it regards the Medieval period, it was a

---

3. Ibid., 12.

4. "Die Bibelvorreden zeigen ja, daß gewisse Leute sich doch für den Leser interessierten. Dies waren immer Leute, für die die Schrift etwas Besonderes zu bedeuten begonnen hatte, und die dies mitzuteilen für entscheidend hielten. So geht es in den Bibelvorreden, ob ausdrücklich oder nicht, immer um den Leser." Ibid.

5. Van Liere, *An Introduction to the Medieval Bible*, 104.

6. Ibid.

7. Ocker, *Biblical Poetics before Humanism and Reformation*, 9. See also Ocker's essay, "Medieval Exegesis and the Origin of Hermeneutics," 328–45. Although he re-packaged this material for part of his chapter 1 in *Biblical Poetics before Humanism and Reformation*, the stand-alone essay has a stronger emphasis on the thesis that the Medieval period ought not to be eclipsed by the patristics or the Reformation as early moments of modern hermeneutics. Medieval exegetical literature exhibits the collapse of isolating exegesis from understanding and/or from application. In Ocker's view, if any period within the history of biblical interpretation ought to be seen as the proper forerunner for modern questions about the interpretation of Scripture in relation to understanding, it is the Middle Ages, contrary to many modern assumptions, of which Ocker sets forth Wilhelm Dilthey and Hans-Georg Gadamer as representative.

8. Light has demonsrated this methodology with meticulous detail in her several studies on the "Paris Bible" from the thirteenth century. The "Paris Bible" is an

time of innovation insofar as many interpretive resources and supplements for Bible study first came to be during this era. The *Glossa Ordinaria*, Peter Comestor's *Historia scholastica*, the beginnings of the *Postillae* popularized by Nicholas de Lyra, concordances, and chapter divisions, all originated in the span of the Middle Ages, and became "the chief tools of scholastic exegesis" leading up to the Reformation.[9] Prologues to the Bible preceded and endured these developments to facilitate interpretation of the biblical text, and together with them, represent the church's attempt to grow in its ability to read *and* to understand Holy Scripture.

A more direct connection can be made for the relevancy of utilizing Luther's own prefaces in a study that seeks to uncover the heart of his perspective on the *sensus literalis* of Scripture. Alastair Minnis, in his seminal work, *Medieval Theory of Authorship*, has put forward the prologue genre as the prime setting for the emergence of a distinct concept of authorship combined with a sophisticated readership in pursuit of a definite intention.[10] Scriptural prefaces, in particular to commentaries, incorporated essential aspects such as the title of the work, name of the author, the subject matter, its didactic method, its branch of learning, and most importantly, the author's intention.[11] By the thirteenth century, Medieval exegetical practice

important test case from which to glean insight on the development of the production of the Bible as a text because, in addition to being the first truly "pocket Bible" as a small, pandect (single volume containing OT and NT), it was reduplicated in great quantities, and later became the source for Gutenberg's Bible as well as the Sixto-Clementine Bible of 1592, which was officially adopted by the Roman Catholic Church at the Council of Trent, lasting until 1979. Light makes careful observations both of the actual scriptural text and the "Paris Bible's" paratextual elements, which consists of prefaces, *capitula* lists, chapter divisions, and on occasion, an addendum on the *Interpretation of Hebrew Names*. See Light, "The Bible and the Individual: The Thirteenth-Century Paris Bible," 228–46; Light, "French Bibles c. 1200–30: A New Look at the Origin of the Paris Bible," 155–76; Light, "The Thirteenth Century and the Paris Bible," 380–91.

9. Ocker, *Biblical Poetics before Humanism and Reformation*, 15.

10. Minnis, *Medieval Theory of Authorship*, 40–72. See also the anthology of Medieval prologues in Minnis and Scott, *Medieval Literary Theory and Criticism, c. 1100–c. 1375: The Commentary Tradition*. Whereas Minnis's research centers on prologues to commentaries on Scripture for the purpose of tracking the Medieval development of *auctores* and *auctoritas*, Dunn has conducted a broader study on other types (nonscriptural) of prefaces to see how this literary practice contributed to the increased individualism and self-established (i.e., justification) authority of an author. His historical period of interest is the Renaissance; however, he does manage to recognize Luther's own significant contribution to the prologue-genre. See Dunn, *Pretexts of Authority*, 27–50.

11. In Minnis's study, he categorizes Medieval prologues into three types. The third

declined in its search for the spiritual or "hidden" meaning of the divine author in favor of locating the biblical text's meaning within the literal sense of the human author.[12] "As a result," Minnis notes, "the exegetes' interest in their texts became more literary."[13] The prologues were purposefully crafted to introduce the reader to the textually discerned (i.e., literary analysis) literal sense of the biblical author, which could be accepted as the divine author's inspired meaning.[14]

Humanism continued the practice of preface-writing into the sixteenth century as exemplified in the contributions of Erasmus of Rotterdam. With the publication of his Greek and Latin edition of the NT in 1516, Erasmus also wrote the *Paraclesis*, his classic statement on the "philosophy of Christ," as a prologue to the entire NT, though he probably had the Gospels mainly in view.[15] Additionally, Erasmus penned prefaces for individual writings of

---

type—"Type C"—became the standard approach to scriptural prologues for what Minnis calls, "the exposition of *auctores*." See the following for a breakdown of each of the literary components that constitute a "Type C" prologue applied to biblical commentaries. Minnis, *Medieval Theory of Authorship*, 19–25.

12. Ibid., 73–159.

13. Ibid., 5.

14. A qualification should be made at this point. Commentators who developed the thirteenth-century prologue came to adopt the Aristotelian theory of causality. God was the primary "efficient cause" who used inferior "efficient causes" to move from potentiality to action. Human authors were instrumental "efficient causes" empowered to impart the intent of the divine First Mover. Thus, as Minnis observes, "In the world of 'Aristotelian prologue,' the divine omnipotence no longer interfered with the integrity of the human *auctor*." Ibid. Ocker adds further insight as he reflects upon Minnis's evidence for the importance of the "efficient cause" in the Medieval conception of authorship in the Late Middle Ages. He notes, "The efficient cause was conceived in such a way that it included divine agency and remained congruent with the other causes. Theologians believed that efficient causality of any kind was ultimately attributable to God, who nevertheless set in motion intermediate powers that exercised their own effects." Ocker, *Biblical Poetics before Humanism and Reformation*, 131. Although Luther's prefaces do not speak of Aristotle's four causes, his goal, nevertheless, is to understand what the Holy Spirit has said via the biblical author's own language and literary style. At many points throughout the prefaces, both for his *Deutsche Bibel* and his lectures on books of the Bible, Luther reiterates his plea for the grammatical-historical approach, which in its explication of textual meaning, displays similarities to the Medievals's use of Aristotelian causality to explain biblical inspiration as divine intent imparted through human authorship mediated in literary communication.

15. Erasmus, "The *Paraclesis*," 97–108. Erasmus's partiality for Jerome should be noted. One of Erasmus's main goals was the emendation of Jerome's writing, a task achieved in September 1516 that was printed in nine folio volumes. Erasmus considered Jerome a model Christian scholar, and sought revival of his writings as a means

the NT, including Acts and many of the Pauline epistles.[16] Whereas the *Paraclesis* cast a vision for renewed study of Scripture and Christianity, the aim of the individual prologues was to identify the biblical author's *argumentum*, that is, the writing's prime subject matter or *sensus literalis*.[17] Likewise, Timothy Wengert has detected in Philip Melanchthon the employment of the same humanist method in service of rhetorical analysis applied to biblical books. Melanchthon utilized the *argumentum* to preface his *Annotations on Romans* (1522), wherein he sought to uncover Paul's central theological issue, i.e., the *scopus* or the *summa*.[18] As one can see, when Luther joined the ranks of preface-writers, he would have been aware of this genre's long and substantial heritage in association with the history of the Christian Bible. Moreover, he would have known that the prologue afforded a special opportunity for him to communicate not only the literal sense of each individual book, but also to set it within the grand scope of the *sensus literalis* of all of Scripture.[19] And last, given Minnis's contention that the Late Middle Ages ushered in an approach to the prologue that assigned primacy to literary analysis of a biblical author's writing as well as the Humanists's approach

for true theology's retreival. Furthermore, there can be no doubt that Erasmus's own preface-writing to the NT was a conscious effort to emulate a tradition established by the patristic figure he so greatly admired. Olin, *Christian Humanism and the Reformation*, 8–19; see also Ocker, *Biblical Poetics before Humanism and Reformation*, 199–201, who recounts Erasmus's affinity for Jerome, particulary with respect to Erasmus's prologues and the *Paraclesis*.

16. Schild, *Abendländische Bibelvorreden bis zur Lutherbibel*, 151–65.

17. "Diese Schriftstücke sind meist länger als die entsprechenden der Vulgata. Er greift dabei auf die Grundbedeutung des Begriffes 'argumentum' zurück, im Sinne von Inhalt, Gegenstand. Ihn will er kurz herausstreichen, damit der Leser ein erstes Verständnis des Briefes erhält." Ibid., 155.

18. Wengert, "Philip Melanchthon's 1522 Annotations on Romans and the Lutheran Origins of Rhetorical Criticism," 125–31; Wengert, "The Rhetorical Paul: Philip Melanchthon's Interpretation of the Pauline Epistles," 146–49. In the latter essay, Wengert raises a question worth pursuing concerning Melanchthon's influence upon Luther's own *Preface to Romans*. Melanchthon's procedure for the introduction to his commentaries on Romans included the *argumentum* along with an elaborate definition of key terms. This same practice is unique to Luther's *Preface to Romans*, and is not found in his other prologues. In the *Preface to Romans*, Luther devotes a lengthy opening section to provide definitions to Paul's most important theological vocabulary such as "law," "sin," "righteousness," and "faith." Wengert believes that Luther's famous *Preface to Romans* shows clear signs of Melanchthon's fingerprints. I am indebted to Dr. Robert Kolb for directing me to these two essays by Timothy Wengert.

19. This point is manifest in the robust presentations of his biblical theology and expressions on the relationship between the Old and New Testaments found in his *Preface to the New Testament* (1522) and *Preface to the Old Testament* (1523) discussed below.

to scriptural introductions in the *argumentum*, its comes as no surprise to witness Luther setting himself apart from allegorical abuses in promotion of his grammatical-historical approach for discerning the Holy Spirit's divine intention within the human author's literary practices.

The Significance of the Prefaces for Understanding Luther's Biblical Hermeneutic

In the "preface" to his own collection of Luther's prefaces to the Bible, Heinrich Bornkamm suggests, "As Luther has called the Psalter 'a short Bible' in which we possess 'almost the entire *Summa*, composed in a small booklet,' one might call his prefaces to the Holy Scriptures a short summary of his entire theology."[20] Even more pertinent is the additional claim Bornkamm makes that "Here is Luther's understanding of Scripture spread out, rich and alive as in nowhere else."[21] As previously noted, a single treatise devoted to the principles of biblical interpretation or the doctrine of Scripture is absent from Luther's corpus. Bornkamm's statement encapsulates the contention of this study that the prefaces as a composite whole can provide a holistic account of the essence of Luther's approach to Scripture.

Others have also noted the importance of Luther's prefaces. Adolf Harnack ended his magisterial *History of Dogma* in the seventh volume with the declaration, "The history of dogma comes to a close with Luther."[22] He continues with this query, "How can there be a history of dogma in Protestantism *after Luther's Prefaces to the New Testament*, and after his great Reformation writings?"[23] An answer to Harnack's question is most likely bound up with the role of faith in Luther's thought and the concretization of his definition of the gospel for Protestantism. Whatever the case may be, Harnack recognizes the significance of the prefaces for Luther's theology. In addition, NT scholar Werner Kuemmel acknowledges inevitable disagreements with Luther, nonetheless, if contemporary scholarship is to gain anything, "we must learn from Luther's prefaces that we ought to be eager to learn where

---

20. "Wie Luther den Psalter 'eine kurze Biblia' genannt hat, in der wir 'fast die ganze Summa, verfasset in ein klein Büchlein,' besitzen, so möchte man seine Vorreden zur heiligen Schrift eine kurze Summe seiner ganzen Theologie nennen." Bornkamm, *Luthers Vorreden zur Bibel*, 11.

21. "Hier ist Luthers Schriftverständnis, reich und lebendig wie sonst nirgends, ausgebreitet." Ibid., 11.

22. Harnack, *History of Dogma*, 268.

23. Ibid., 269; italics mine.

the *central* message of the New Testament is to be found."[24] Furthermore, Kurt Aland, the renowned NT textual critic, applauds Luther's promotion of the study of biblical languages and the necessity of painstaking exegesis, but then also endorses Luther's pursuit of the essence of Scripture.[25] Where is the ideal place to discover this approach in Luther's writings? Aland says none other than the prefaces. He writes, "Here also we possess a complete group of utterances by Luther from which we can read his meaning in its context. I refer to his prefaces to the separate books of the Bible which he gradually added between 1522 and 1534 to his different editions of the Bible in German to assist the Church in their Bible study."[26] Aland, then, regrets, "Unfortunately far too little attention is paid to Luther's prefaces, . . ."[27]

In short, Luther's prefaces for his German translation of the Bible are indispensible source material to comprehend this Reformer's thought, and taken together, they form a holistic picture of Luther's essential theology of Scripture *and* his view of Scripture's theology.[28] More specifically, his prefaces are the prime literary medium through which he can convey his understanding of Christ as the Bible's literal sense.[29] And how he does so is now the direction to which this study will turn.

24. Kuemmel, "The Continuing Significance of Luther's Prefaces to the New Testament," 581.

25. Aland, "Luther as Exegete," 47.

26. Ibid.

27. Ibid.

28. This twofold distinction is borrowed from Ebeling's essay on "biblical theology," where he distinguishes defining the term as, on the one hand, "a theology of the Bible," and, on the other hand, a theology that coheres with the "Bible's theology." Ebeling, "The Meaning of 'Biblical Theology'," 79.

29. The influence of Luther's prefaces during the time of the Reformation and afterwards would be a worthwhile study. In particular, British Reformer William Tyndale utilized (oftentimes copied) many of Luther's writings, including his prefaces, for his own works. See Schild on Tyndale's incorporation of Luther's prologues from the *Deutsche Bibel* for his English NT, "A Translator Interprets: Luther's Prologues in Tyndale's New Testament," 149–60; in addition, see Werrell, "Tyndale's Disagreement with Luther in the Prologue to the Epistle to the Romans," 57–68, for an evaluation of where Tyndale might have diverged from Luther's theology in his adaptation of the *Preface to Romans*.

Chronological Study of Luther's Prefaces to the Bible (1521–46)

The aim of this section is to observe how the "prefaces" support the conclusion that Luther ultimately considers Christ as the literal sense of Scripture because of the Bible's messianic unifying thread. The prologues contain multifarious insights that may be noted on occasion, but the focus of this investigation will be to illuminate the messianic dimension of Luther's perspective on how Scripture witnesses to Christ in its "letter," that is, at the textual level (literal sense).

1522

Luther's exile at the Wartburg Castle enabled him to focus on several literary projects. Chief among them was his ambition to translate the entire Bible into the German vernacular. As early as February, 1522, Luther sent a selection of his work to Wittenberg for Melanchthon's review.[30] By March, Luther departed the Wartburg with a completed translation of the NT in hand, an accomplishment achieved in only eleven weeks.[31] Commonly referred to as the *Septembertestament*, the first edition of Luther's German translation of the NT came off the Wittenberg press by September 21, 1522.[32] In the following December, a revised copy was printed, which would set the precedent for the *Deutsche Bibel*'s perpetual process of revision under Luther's oversight until his death.[33] Like the translation(s), Luther would also repeatedly revisit his prefaces to the *Deutsche Bibel* to apply various edits. In the analysis below, each preface will be examined under the heading of the year it first appeared in print. Subsequent revisions or editions will be treated concurrently as necessary to highlight any relevant developments.

Preface to the New Testament

Most likely Luther penned this preface as an introduction to either the whole NT, or at the least, to the fourfold Gospels and Acts. In an opening section that ceased to be transmitted after the first publication of the complete *Deutsche Bibel* in 1534, Luther acknowledged that despite the tradition, he would be content for the NT to proceed "without any prefaces

---

30. Kooiman, *Luther and the Bible*, 118.

31. Brecht, *Martin Luther: Shaping and Defining the Reformation*, 47.

32. Reu, *Luther's German Bible*, 162.

33. Brecht, *Martin Luther: Shaping and Defining the Reformation*, 53.

or extraneous names attached and simply have its own say under its own name."[34] Nevertheless, because so many other prefaces and interpretations erroneously instruct readers on how to distinguish law from gospel have accompanied the Bible, "Necessity demands, therefore, that there should be a notice or preface, by which the ordinary man can be rescued from his former delusions, set on the right track, and taught what he is to look for in this book, so that he may not seek laws and commandments where he ought to be seeking the gospel and promises of God."[35]

This opening comes from the 1522 edition of the *Preface to the New Testament*, and it shows the polemical purpose for which Luther adds his own prologue. This preface, as Luther explains, is a didactic device intended to teach the biblical reader "what he is to look for in this book."[36] Yet, Luther's ideal is that no such preface would be required. This sort of sentiment was reaffirmed many years later in his 1539 *Preface to the Wittenberg Edition of Luther's German Writings*, when he confesses, "I would have been quite content to see my books, one and all, remain in obscurity and go by the board."[37] Being consumed by the works of others, Luther laments, "not only is precious time lost, which could be used for studying the Scriptures, but in the end the pure knowledge of the divine Word is also lost, so that the Bible lies forgotten in the dust under the bench (as happened to the book of Deuteronomy, in the time of the kings of Judah)."[38] In fact, Luther goes on to disclose, "It was also our intention and hope, when we ourselves began to translate the Bible into German, that there should be less writing, and instead more studying and reading of the Scriptures."[39] If the circumstance requires a preface, then Luther believes that it, like any other Christian lit-

34. *LW* 35:357; WA, *DB* 6:2, "Es were wol recht und billich, das dis buch on alle vorrhede unned frembden namen außgieng, unnd nur seyn selbs eygen namen und rede furete."

35. *LW* 35:357; WA, *DB* 6:2, "[F]odert die noddurfft eyn antzeygen und vorrhede zu stellen, da mit der eynfelltige man, aus feynem allten wahn, auff die rechte ban gfuret und unterricht werde, wes er ynn disem buch gewartten sole, auff das er nicht gepott unnd gesetze suche, da er Euangeli und verheyssung Gottis suchen sollt."

36. *LW* 35:357; WA, *DB* 6:2.

37. *LW* 34:283; WA 50:657, "Bern hette ichs gesehen, das meine Bücher allesampt weren dahinden blieben und untergangen."

38. *LW* 34:283; WA 50:657, "Damit nicht allein die edle zeit und studieren in der Schrifft verseumet, sondern auch die reine erkentnis Göttliches worts endlich verloren ist, bis die Biblia (wie dem fünfften buch Mosi geschach, zur zeit der Könige Juda) unter der banck im stauge vergessen ist."

39. *LW* 34:283–84; WA 50:657, "Auch ist das unser meinung gewest, da wir die Biblia selbs zu verdeudschen anfiengen, das wir hofften, Es solt des schreibens weniger und des studirens und lesens in der Schrifft mehr warden."

erature, must "lead the way into and point toward the Scriptures, as John the Baptist did toward Christ, saying, 'He must increase, but I must decrease.'"[40]

As one can see, the role of Luther's preface is to support Scripture's self-witness rather than to supplement it. To combat the erroneous theology of which Luther accused the papacy to have erected an unscriptural "wall," excluding the rest of Christendom, a new German translation of the Bible intended for the everyday Christian necessitated aids for right interpretation.[41] For Luther, *sola Scriptura* entails that it is the supreme authority on its own interpretation; hence, his conviction that Scripture is its own interpreter.[42] On the other hand, what happens in reality, as Mark Edwards reminds, is that "in practice Scripture did not interpret itself. Human beings interpreted Scripture, and they disagreed."[43] In his study on the role of publishing in the Reformation, *Printing, Propaganda, and Martin Luther*, Edwards contends that Luther maximized the use of marginal glosses, woodcut illustrations, a theologically-predisposed translation, and prefaces for his own *Das Newe Testament Deutsche* "to assure that at least the *printed text* of Scripture interpreted itself."[44] So then, what is Luther's vision for Scripture's right interpretation?

From the start, Luther is interested in how the Old and New Testaments relate. The OT is a "book" (*buch*) that contains God's laws, commandments, and the history of the people who did or did not keep them. The NT is a "book" (*buch*) that records the gospel, the promises of God, and the history of the people who believed or did not believe them.[45] Although he locates the "gospel" in the NT, these two are not to be equivocated as if the

---

40. *LW* 34:284; WA 50:6547, "Denn auch alles ander schreiben in und zu der Schrifft, wie Johannes zu Christo, weisen sol, wie er spricht, 'Ich mus abnemen, Dieser mus zunemen.'"

41. In his treatise, *To the Christian Nobility of the German Nation Concerning the Reform of the Christian Estate* (1520), wherein he substantially articulated his doctrine of the priesthood of all believers, Luther identifies "three walls" that the Roman Catholic Church constructed between itself and the laity in need of demolishing. The "second wall" is the teaching that Rome, specifically the papacy, has the sole authoritative interpretation of Scripture. *LW* 44:133; WA 6:411.

42. The classic expression of Luther's doctrine that Scripture interprets itself appears in his defense of the clarity of Scripture in *The Bondage of the Will* (1525). See *LW* 33:24–28; WA 18:607–09.

43. Edwards, *Printing, Propaganda, and Martin Luther*, 109.

44. Ibid., 111. For further analysis of Luther and the Wittenberg Press's approach to his *German New Testament* (along with the function of the prefaces) as a publishing endeavor to increase the Reformation's progress, see all of chapter 5, "Scripture as Printed Text," 109–30.

45. *LW* 35:358; WA, DB 6:2.

OT's content was only law(s). In this preface, Luther distinguishes between the New Testament as a "book" and the "new testament" as "gospel."[46] The latter as a word of "promise" transcends both Testaments (books), and is the focal point for each division of the written Word of God. "Thus this gospel of God or New Testament," as Luther defines it, "is a good story and report, sounded forth into all the world by the apostles, telling of a true David who strove with sin, death, and the devil, and overcame them, and thereby rescued all those who were captive in sin, afflicted with death, and overpowered by the devil."[47] In some ways, it seems that Luther's definition has already eclipsed the witness of the OT except for his reference to Jesus as "a true David." This slight allusion, however, shows signs of a deeper connection within his definition of the gospel to the messianic promises in the OT.

After explaining the "testament" nuance of his gospel understanding, Luther transitions to demonstrate how "God has promised this gospel and testament in many ways, by the prophets in the Old Testament" based upon Paul's introductory words in Romans 1:1–3.[48] This position launches

---

46. "This report and encouraging tidings, or evangelical and divine news, is also called a New Testament. For it is a testament when a dying man bequeaths his property, after his death, to his legally defined heirs. And Christ, before his death, commanded and ordained that his gospel be preached after his death in all the world. Thereby he gave to all who believe, as their possession, everything that he had. This included: his life, in which he swallowed up death; his righteousness, by which he blotted out sin; and his salvation, with which he overcame everlasting damnation." *LW* 35:358–59; WA, *DB* 6:4. Shortly before penning his *Preface to the New Testament*, Luther wrote *A Treatise on the New Testament, that is, the Holy Mass* that appeared in 1520 between the publications of *To the Christian Nobility* and *The Babylonian Captivity of the Church*. Luther countered Rome's traditional view of the Mass as a perpetual sacrifice, and instead, taught how it ought to be viewed as a sign of the eternal "new testament" that Christ had already ratified through the giving of his body and blood on the cross. Christ's "testament" is the "gospel" because it promises the forgiveness of sins and eternal life as an inheritance bestowed to all who receive him by faith: "What then is this testament, or what is bequeathed to us in it by Christ? Truly a great, eternal, and unspeakable treasure, namely, the forgiveness of all sins, as the words plainly state, 'This is the cup of a new eternal testament in my blood, which is poured out for you and for many for the forgiveness of sins.'" *LW* 35:85; WA 6:358. On Luther's theology of "testament," though restricted to the "early" Luther, see Hagen, *A Theology of Testament in the Young Luther: The Lectures on Hebrews*; Hagen, "Luther, Martin," 691–92.

47. *LW* 35:358; WA, *DB* 6:4, "Also ist dis Euangelion Gottis unnd new testament, eyn gutte meher und geschren ynn alle wellt erschollen durch die Apostell, von eynem rechten David, der mit der sund, tod unnd teuffel gestritten, und uberwunden hab, unnd damit alle die, ßo ynn sunden gefangen, mit dem todt geplagt, vom teuffel uberweldiget gewesen."

48. *LW* 35:359; WA, *DB* 6:4, "Nu hat Gott solchen glauben zu stercken, dieses sein

Luther into an excursus that traces several key texts he considers as messianic predictions in the OT. To begin, Luther regards Genesis 3:15 as the "first promise" of the gospel. Of note is Luther's brief comment following the verse's quotation where he asserts, "Christ is this woman's seed [*same*], who has bruised the devil's head, that is, sin, death, hell, and all his power. For without this seed [*Samen*], no man can escape sin, death, or hell."[49] Next, Luther moves to Genesis 22:18, wherein he interprets through the intertextual link with Galatians 3 that "Christ is that descendant [*same*] of Abraham" in whom the whole world has been blessed by way of the gospel.[50] And last, Luther comes to the Davidic covenant in 2 Samuel 7:12–14, and describes it as "the kingdom of Christ, of which the gospel speaks: an everlasting kingdom, a kingdom of life, salvation, and righteousness, where all those who believe enter in from out of the prison of sin and death."[51]

In short, Luther begins the *Preface to the New Testament* promoting its proclamation of the gospel of Christ as its central purpose. The apostolic writings's testimony to Christ greatly informs the substance of "this gospel," yet so does God's promise of the Christ by his prophets. The way Luther portrays the OT's contribution to the definition of the gospel, or this "new

---

Euangelium und Testament vielfechtig im alten Testament, durch die Propheten verheyssen, Wie S. Paulus sagt Rom. 1" (1546). In the 1522 original, instead of *verheyssen* Luther wrote *versprochen*. This alteration shows little shift in thought, but does reflect in the 1546 version a more emphatic word choice since *verheyssen* would bring the connotation of "promise" as "prediction" whereas *versprochen* represents a usage of "promise" closer to that of a "pledge" or a "vow" (Wahrig, *Deutsches Wörterbuch*, s.v. "verheißen," s.v. "versprechen." Cf. "Yes even the teaching of the prophets, in those places where they speak of Christ, is nothing but the true, pure, and proper gospel— just as if Luke or Matthew had described it. *For the prophets have proclaimed the gospel and spoken of Christ*, as St. Paul here [Rom. 1:2] reports and as everyone indeed knows" (italics mine); *LW* 35:118; *WA* 10.1.1:10. Like the *Preface to the New Testament*, previously in *A Brief Instruction on What to Look for and Expect in the Gospels*, Luther grounded his view of Christ or the "gospel" as directly prophesied in the OT upon Romans 1:1–2. Similarities abound in the *Preface to the New Testament* and *A Brief Instruction*. Published in 1521 as an introduction to the *Church Postils*, it seems likely that *A Brief Instruction* was perhaps source material for Luther's later formation of the *Preface of the New Testament* in 1522. In several places, the wording, structure, and thought are nearly identical.

49. *LW* 35:359; *WA, DB* 6:4, "Christus ist der same dises weybs, der dem teuffel seyn heubt, das ist, sund, tod, helle und alle seyne krafft zurtretten hatt, Denn on disen Samen kan keyn mensch der sund, dem todt, der hellen entrynnen."

50. *LW* 35:359; *WA, DB* 6:6, "Christus ist der same Abrahe . . . ."

51. *LW* 35:359–60; *WA, DB* 6:6, "Das ist das reich Christi, dauon das Euangelion lautt, eyn ewiges reich, Eyn reich des lebens, der seligkeyt und gerechtigkeyt, dareyn komen aus dem gefengnis der sund unnd todt, alle die da glewben."

testament," is through recounting the messianic predictions in the OT text. In other words, Luther's definition of the "gospel" in the NT is expressed as the fulfillment of the messianic prophecy in the OT. The promise of the Messiah in the OT *is* the promise of the gospel of the person and work of Jesus Christ to which the NT bears witness and heralds. Moreover, Luther continues, "There are many more such promises of the gospel in the other prophets as well," and as examples, he quotes Micah 5:2[52] (Bethlehem as the birthplace of the Messiah) and Hosea 13:14[53] (ransom, cross, and resurrection).[54]

Once he has briefly tracked the messianic line laid by the prophets in the "letter" of the OT, Luther's next step is to restate his definition of the gospel: "The gospel, then, is nothing but the preaching about Christ, Son of God and of David, true God and man, who by his death and resurrection has overcome for us the sin, death, and hell of all men who believe in him."[55] As can be observed, bookending Luther's excursus on OT messianic texts are similar definitions of the gospel which assume that the NT's apostolic proclamation of the forgiveness of sins through Jesus Christ's cross and resurrection is bound up with Jesus's identity as the long-expected Messiah who would be both the Son of God and the Son of David.[56] Luther's vision

52. Micah 5:2, "But you, O Bethlehem Ephrathah, who are too little to be among the clans of Judah, from you shall come forth for me one who is to be ruler in Israel, whose origin is from of old, from ancient days."

53. Hosea 13:14, "Shall I ransom them from the power of Sheol? Shall I redeem them from Death? O Death, where are your plagues? O Sheol, where is your sting? Compassion is hidden from my eyes."

54. *LW* 35:360; WA, *DB* 6:6, "Solcher verheyssung des Euangeli sind viel mehr auch ynn den andern propheten, als . . ."

55. *LW* 35:360; WA, *DB* 6:7, "So ist nu das Euangelium nichts anders, denn eine predigt von Christo, Gottes und Davids Son, warem Gott und Mensch, der fur uns mit seinem sterben und aufferstehen, aller menschen Sünde, Tod und Helle uberwunden hat, die an in gleuben" (1546). Cf. *A Brief Instruction* (1521), "For at its briefest, the gospel is a discourse about Christ, that he is the Son of God and became man for us, that he died and was raised, that he has been established as a Lord over all things . . . The gospel is a story about Christ, God's and David's Son, who died and was raised and is established as Lord." *LW* 35:118; WA 10.1.1:9–10.

56. From a sermon on Matthew 22:34–36 for the "Eighteenth Sunday after Trinity," Luther preached on the two greatest commandments in connection with Jesus's question to the Pharisees of whose son is the Christ. Here one can also see another example of the messianic framing of Luther's gospel definitions as articulated in the *Preface to the New Testament*. In this sermon, Luther's conception of the gospel is similarly displayed in Jesus's dialogue about his own messianic identity as normed by Psalm 110. Luther explains that the blindness of the Pharisees to read this passage as a portrayal of the Messiah (Son of David) to be the Incarnate Son of God was because they had

of the gospel is charged with messianic accordance, whether pertaining to the atonement or the incarnation.[57] Thus, the reason why the NT's (book) chief task is the proclamation of the promise of the "new testament" (gospel) of Jesus Christ is because the apostolic authors are announcing that the prophets's promises of the hoped for person and work of the Messiah have been realized in this Jesus, who has come so that by faith Christ can be "your own."[58]

PREFACE TO THE EPISTLE OF ST. PAUL TO THE ROMANS

Perhaps the most recognized of Luther's prologues, his *Preface to Romans* is a controlling document for how one ought to read and to interpret the rest of the NT. Luther's first recommendation for reading this "purest gospel" (*lauterst Euangelion*) rightly is to grasp its language and become equipped with a theological knowledge of Pauline concepts such as "law," "sin," "righteousness," and "faith."[59] Before a lengthy survey of each chapter, Luther offers his own definitions for the keywords he deems as integral for faithful interpretation of Romans.[60]

---

not been taught by the Holy Spirit. Apart from the Spirit's illumination, Luther says one cannot harmonize Psalm 110 to understand the meaning "as our articles of faith teach us to believe; that Christ was both David's true natural son of his blood and flesh and also David's Lord, whom David himself must worship and hold as God." Luther, "Eighteenth Sunday after Trinity: The Law and the Gospel, Christ (Matthew 22:34–36)," 193–94.

57. Though his objective is primarily biographical, Brecht keenly recognizes, "This one gospel as a sermon about Christ *is audible in the messianic prophecies of the Old Testament*, and it is described in different ways in the New Testament writings." Brecht, *Martin Luther: Shaping and Defining the Reformation*, 51; italics mine.

58. *LW* 35:361; WA, *DB* 6:8, "Christus sey deyn eygen . . ." Cf. *A Treatise on the New Testament*, "Therefore wherever in Scripture God's testament is referred to by the prophets, in that very word the prophets are taught that God would become man and die and rise again, in order that his word, in which he promises such a testament, might be fulfilled and confirmed. For if God is to make a testament, as he promises, then he must die; and if he is to die, then he must be a man. And so that little word 'testament' is a short summary of all God's wonders and grace, fulfilled in Christ." *LW* 35:84; WA 6:357.

59. *LW* 35:363; WA, *DB* 7:2.

60. In this definitional excursus, it is clear that Luther aligns his understanding of the literal sense in biblical interpretation with the grammatical-historical approach. To put it another way, Luther believes that for one to understand the doctrine of justification as the ultimate aim of the Apostle Paul in his Letter to the Romans, the interpreter must engage the writing's rhetorical and literary textual features that coincide with their corresponding theological sense and/or meaning.

Inasmuch as Luther's prime interests in Romans are, unsurprisingly, justification by faith and the law/gospel distinction, the clearest allusion to the messianic dimension of Christ as Scripture's *sensus literalis* comes in the form of unveiling the flow of the inter-theological relationships of Christ and the gospel, Word and Spirit, and faith and love. Luther's thought traces the movement in this manner: first, love fulfills the law, but love and pleasure for the law are given only by the Holy Spirit. Yet one is not indwelt by the Holy Spirit apart from faith in Jesus Christ. And last, knowledge of Jesus Christ is revealed only by God's Word or gospel, which is requisite for the creation of saving faith.[61]

What causes this summary to contribute beyond being a simple affirmation of basic doctrinal truth from Christian orthodoxy is the nuance heard in Luther's explanation for "God's Word or gospel" (*Gottis wort oder Euangelion*).[62] The full statement unfolds as follows: "Faith, moreover, comes only through God's Word or gospel, which preaches Christ, *saying that he is God's Son and a man*, and has died and risen again for our sakes, as [Paul] says in chapters 3[:25], 4[:25], and 10[:9]."[63] The gospel, namely, that "which preaches Christ" (*das Christum prediget*), parallels the Messiah's twofold identity as the Son of God and of man already described more fully in the *Preface to the New Testament* that is linked with David and the messianic lineage. Though stated in passing, even in this instance one can assume that Luther's conception of the "gospel" is informed from the collective witness of both the OT and the NT concerning the promise of the coming person and work of Jesus Christ and its fulfillment. So, to reverse Luther's logic, the gospel of the preached-Christ contained in the Scriptures is the source where God creates true Christian faith, imparts the Holy Spirit to indwell the believer, and thereby produces a life of loving obedience and good works towards God and one's neighbor.

One additional example where Luther appears to assume the messianic underpinning to the gospel in his *Preface to Romans* is in a reference to Genesis 3:15. While defining unbelief as the root to all sin, Luther writes, "For this reason, in the Scriptures it is called the serpent's head and the head of the old dragon, which the seed [*samen*] of the woman, Christ, must tread under foot, as was promised to Adam, Genesis 3[:15]."[64] He is consis-

61. *LW* 35:368; WA, *DB* 7:6.

62. *LW* 35:368; WA, *DB* 7:6.

63. Italics mine; *LW* 35:368; WA, *DB* 7:6, "So kompt der glawbe nicht, on alleyne durch Gottis wort oder Euangelion, das Christum prediget, wie er ist Gottis son und Mensch, gestorben und afferstanden umb unsern willen, wie er am .3 .4 und .10. Capitel sagt."

64. *LW* 35:369; WA, *DB* 7:8, "unglawb, als die wurtzel, safft und heubt krafft aller

tent with his remarks from the *Preface to the New Testament* in identifying Christ as the textual referent of the promise God made to Adam and Eve. Although Luther moves on from Genesis 3:15 without further explication, this brief scriptural proof points to the grander reality of the textually determined contours of Luther's understanding of Paul's "the gospel of God" (Rom 1:1–2), which now the Apostle is to proclaim in fullness post Christ's first advent, cross, resurrection, and ascension.

Preface to the Epistle of St. Paul to the Galatians

Surprisingly, Luther's *Preface to Galatians* for the 1522 *German New Testament* is extremely brief with little theological reflection. Moreover, the 1546 edition remains basically identical to the first version. Given its length and lack of substance, this preface is not able to add much to the study beyond where some inferences could be made. The best, and probably only, example occurs as he summarizes Paul's teaching from Galatians 1 and 2 "that everyone must be justified without merit, without works, without law, through Christ alone."[65] In his next comment, he says that in Galatians 3 and 4, Paul proves this doctrine of justification by faith alone in Christ alone "with passages of Scripture, examples, and analogies. He shows that the law brings sin and a curse rather than righteousness. Righteousness is promised by God, fulfilled by Christ without the law, given to us—out of grace alone."[66]

That God "promised" (*verheyssen*) righteousness is consistent with the language Luther uses to speak of how the Christ (Messiah) and his gospel were "promised" in the OT by the prophets. Luther's reading of Scripture as a whole was set forth in the *Preface to the New Testament* and the *Preface to Romans*. The gospel is the unifying purpose of the Old and New Testaments, but this "gospel" is carefully defined as having to do with the direct prediction of the Messiah and the work he was to accomplish. The arrival and accomplishment of this "promise" from the level of the literal sense of the OT text is now what the apostolic writers, especially here in the Epistles,

---

sunde, wilchs ynn der schrifft auch darumb des schlangen kopff und allten trachen hwbt heist, den des weybs samen Christus, zutretten mus, wie Adam versprochen wart" (1522). Once again, in the 1546 copy of this preface, Luther enlists *verheissen* instead of *versprochen* to say that Christ was "promised" to Adam.

65. *LW* 35:384; WA, *DB* 7:172, "und schleust, das on verdienst, on werk, on gesetz, sondern alleyn durch Christum, yderman muß rechtfertig werden."

66. *LW* 35:384; WA, *DB* 7:172, "bewert er das alles mit schrifften, exempel und gleychnissen, und zeygt, wie das gesetz viel mehr sund und maledeyung bring den gerecktickeyt, wilch alleyn aus gnaden von Got verheyssen, durch Christon on gesetz erfullet und uns geben ist."

proclaim as the good news of Christ and his benefits. So, though Luther provides little detail in this preface, his guiding logic appears to be consistent with his exegetically produced Christ-centered biblical theology, which is an approach that he considers to be in sync with the Apostle Paul given that, as stated above, salvation in Christ alone is explicated in Galatians 1 and 2 followed by its scriptural proof (i.e., OT accordance) in Galatians 3 and 4.

Preface to the Epistle of St. Paul to the Colossians

This preface is brief, and thus, lacks the opportunity to contribute significantly to the study. On the other hand, in his description of Colossians 1, Luther does raise an angle worth pursuing. He recaps that in chapter 1, Paul "delineates what the gospel and faith are, namely, a wisdom which recognizes Christ as Lord and God, crucified for us, which has been hidden for ages but now brought into the open through his ministry."[67] Would Luther's comment about the former "hiddenness" (*verporgen*) of the gospel truth of "Christ as Lord and God, crucified for us" contradict the case for a *direct* promise of the Messiah and his gospel in the "letter" of the OT prophetic writings? Luther, of course, is simply borrowing Paul's verbiage from Colossians 1:26, but in light of the Reformer's emphatic claim that the prophets specifically promised and/or predicted the Messiah throughout the OT, how then should one understand this promise of the gospel to be "hidden"?[68] In response to this possible objection, it seems Luther has already submitted an explanation that takes into consideration its impact upon the discussion over literal and spiritual senses.

In his 1516 *Lectures on Romans*, the *scholia* for Romans 11:25[69] features a succinct reflection on whether Paul's word choice of "mystery" should cause the interpreter to be on the lookout for a "mystical sense" (*mysticus sensus*).[70] Luther rejects the argument that understands Paul to mean that a "hidden" or "mystical" sense is buried beneath the surface literary level of the text in need of discovery. The "mystery" of which Paul speaks in Romans 11:25, Luther deems a "mystery" in "the absolute sense, because it is hidden

---

67. *LW* 35:386; WA, *DB* 7:224, "und streycht aus, was das Euangelion und glawbe sey, nemlich, eyn weyßheyt die Christum eynen herrn und God erkenne, fur uns gecreutzigt, die von der welt her verporgen, und nu durch seyn ampt erfur bracht sey."

68. Col 1:26, "*the mystery* (το μυστηριον) hidden for ages and generations but now revealed to his saints."

69. Rom 11:25, "Lest you be wise in your own sight, I want you to understand *this mystery* (το μυστηριον τουτο), brothers: a partial hardening has come upon Israel, until the fullness of the Gentiles has come in."

70. *LW* 25:431; WA 56:439.

to all."[71] In the context of Romans 11:25, what is "hidden," yet disclosed to the prophets was the inclusion of the Gentiles and the hardening of Israel. In other words, although it was revealed through the prophetic writings, its full meaning had not been fully grasped by the hearers/readers of God's Word. Luther then goes on to say that Paul's use of "mystery" in "the absolute sense" occurs elsewhere in Romans 16:25[72] (the Incarnation) and in Colossians 1:26 (the Incarnation and the gospel of Christ to the Gentiles). Thus, "hiddenness" to Scripture's hearers and/or readers is not determinate of the theological substance of the Bible's *sensus literalis* at the grammatical-historical level. Lack of interpretive skill, spiritual blindness, and/or awaiting fulfillment of that which is latently prophesied all seem to be, according to Luther, contributing factors to various so-called "mysteries," but this dynamic should not grant the formation of a hermeneutic that separates the "letter" from the "Spirit" in order to locate the divine meaning revealed supposedly behind, beneath, or above the textual witness of the biblical author.

Preface to the First Epistle of St. Peter

Luther's original *Preface to the New Testament* (1522) included at the end an aside titled, "Which are the true and noblest books of the New Testament."[73] It was an attempt to rank which NT writings were the best and most important. At the top of Luther's list were the Gospel of John, Paul's corpus, and 1 Peter.[74] Therefore, it comes as a surprise that Luther does not expound upon 1 Peter at length in its preface. Much like the other prologues, besides the *Preface to Romans*, the *Preface to First Peter* follows the similar pattern of beginning with a few sentences to encapsulate the writing's main idea, and then, summarizes each chapter. The most opportune moment in this preface to connect it to this study's interest occurs when Luther comments on chapter 1 stating, "He [Peter] shows that this salvation has not been merited by us but was first proclaimed by the prophets."[75] It is likely that Luther

71. *LW* 25:431; WA 56:439, "Sed absolute Misterium est id, quod omnes latuit."

72. Romans 16:25, "Now to him who is able to strengthen you according to my gospel and the preaching of Jesus Christ, according to the revelation of *the mystery* (μυστηριου) that was kept secret for long ages." It is noteworthy that in his marginal gloss for Rom 16:25, Luther writes, "The question arises how it could be hidden and yet known to the prophets, and thus not only made manifest now but also then." *LW* 25:131; WA 56:154.

73. *LW* 35:363–64; WA, *DB* 6:10, "Wilchs die rechten und Edlisten bucher des newen testaments sind."

74. *LW* 35:363–64; WA, *DB* 6:10.

75. *LW* 35:390; WA, *DB* 7:298, "[U]nnd zeygt an, wie die selb nit von uns verdient,

is referencing 1 Peter 1:10–12, since this passage deals with how the OT prophets prophesied about the coming Christ and the gospel.[76]

From his *Sermons on the First Epistle to St. Peter* in 1522 (the same year as the dating of the preface), Luther's reflection on 1 Peter 1:10–12 unveils the depth of his understanding of the phrase, "was first proclaimed by the prophets," that is mentioned only in passing in the *Preface to First Peter*. A few excerpts will support the relationship. The first sentence that begins his interpretation of 1 Peter 1:10 is similar to that quoted above from the preface in the *Deutsche Bibel*. He writes, "Here St. Peter refers us to Holy Scripture in order that we may see there how *God keeps His promise [verheyssen] not because of any merit on our part* but out of pure grace."[77] Next, Luther contends that one must study the Scriptures to be certain of the faith on the basis of NT texts such as Romans 1:2 and 3:23, where Paul demonstrates that the gospel of God about the person of Christ and the doctrine of justification by faith alone originate in God's promises through the prophets.[78] This conviction launches Luther into an excursus on the abiding relevance of the OT for Christians because of its real witness to Christ. In a selection characteristic of Luther's full interpretation of 1 Peter 1:10–12, one can see how firmly convinced he is that the primary task of the prophets was to testify to the coming Messiah of whom the apostles announced as Jesus Christ:

> For God sent the prophets to the Jews to bear witness to the Christ who was to come. Consequently, the apostles also convicted the Jews everywhere from their own Scriptures and proved that this was the Christ. Thus the books of Moses and the prophets are also Gospel, since they proclaimed (*verkundiget*) and described (*beschrieben*) in advance what the apostles preached (*gepredigt*) or wrote later about Christ.[79]

---

sondern zuuor durch die propheten verkundigt sey."

76. It is notable that when Luther says that salvation in Christ "was first proclaimed (*verkundigt*) by the prophets," he adopts the same word for his translation of the clause in 1 Pet 1:12: "wilchs euch nu *verkundiget* ist" ("which is now proclaimed/announced to you"). The connection seems clear between the preface and the translation that both the prophets and the apostles through the Holy Spirit have "proclaimed" or "announced" (*verkündigen*) Christ and his gospel for the believer's good (i.e., salvation). WA, *DB* 7:300.

77. Italics mine; LW 30:18; WA 12:274, "Hie weyst uns S. Petrus zu ruck ynn die heylige schrifft, das wyr darynne sehen, wie uns Gott durch keynes verdiensts willen, sondern auß blosser gnad, hallte das er verheyssen hat."

78. LW 30:18; WA 12:274.

79. LW 30:19; WA 12:274–75, "Denn Gott hatt die propheten darumb zü den Juden geschickt, das sie von dem zukunfftigen Christo sollten zeugnis geben. Darumb haben die Apostel auch allenthalben die Juden uberweysst und auß yhrer eygenen schrifft,

Since Luther's sermons on 1 Peter occur in the same year as the writing of his epistle's preface for inclusion in the *German New Testament*, Luther's simple assertion, "was first proclaimed by the prophets," from the prologue can be seen as a shorthand for the position he more fully articulates in his exposition of 1 Peter 1:10–12. Thus, despite that the Reformer does not expound upon this viewpoint in the preface, he still shows signs of a deeper conviction regarding the OT's prophecy of the Messiah as fundamental to the nature of the gospel and the apostolic witness in the NT.

Preface to the Epistle to the Hebrews

The *Preface to Hebrews* marks a transition in Luther's own thinking. As aforementioned, Luther advised what NT writings were the most valuable at the end of his original 1522 *Preface to the New Testament*. Even though this addendum ceased reproduction after 1537, Luther opened his *Preface to Hebrews* in the 1546 *Deutsche Bibel* in the same manner as he did in the 1522 *German New Testament*: "Up to this point we have had [to do with] the true and certain chief books of the New Testament. The four which follow have from ancient times had a different reputation."[80] The "four" to which Luther is alluding are: Hebrews, James, Jude, and Revelation.

Even though he questions its apostolicity, Luther regards Hebrews favorably. His principal admiration for it concerns two compliments. First, Luther commends the writing's doctrine of Christ as the Great High Priest because the author develops this teaching "masterfully and profoundly on the basis of the Scriptures."[81] And second, the epistle "discloses a firm grasp of the reading of the Scriptures and of the proper way of dealing with

---

das das Christus were. Also sind die bücher Mosi und die propheten auch Evangelium, syntemal sie eben das zuvor verkundiget und beschrieben haben von Christo, das die Apostel hernach gepredigt odder geschrieben haben."

80. *LW* 35:394; WA, *DB* 7:344, "Bis her haben eyr die rechten gewissen hewbt bucher des newen testaments gehabt, Dise vier nach folgende aber, haben vor zeytten eyn ander ansehen gehabt." Luther visually emphasized this uncertainty in addition to his verbal suspicions. In the "Table of Contents" for the *German New Testament*, Luther separated these four letters from the other NT writings by a blank space, indented them several lines to the right out of sync with the other entries, and left them unnumbered. Although the 1546 contents page shows the blank space removed, Hebrews, James, Jude, and Revelation remain indented and unnumbered. WA, *DB* 6:12–13. For further discussion, see Edwards, *Printing, Propaganda, and Martin Luther*, 113; Reu, *Luther's German Bible*, 169–76.

81. *LW* 35:395; WA, *DB* 7:344, "die vom priesterthum Christi meysterlich unnd grundlich aus der schrifft redet."

them."[82] As is fitting to Hebrews's substance, it seems that Luther recognizes its dependency upon the OT for doing its Christian theology and appreciates the author's approach to handling the theological relationship of the two Testaments; however, he does not delve into the specifics of the author of Hebrews's hermeneutic.

PREFACE TO THE EPISTLES OF ST. JAMES AND ST. JUDE

If the *Preface to Romans* is the most famous of Luther's prologues, then the *Preface to James and Jude* is the most infamous. In the *Preface to the New Testament*'s appendix, "Which are the true and noblest books of the New Testament," Luther dismisses James as an "epistle of straw" (*stroern Epistel*).[83] His reason for this low estimation is because "it has nothing of the nature of the gospel about it."[84] Said differently, James only preaches the law, albeit God's law.[85]

To understand Luther's "strawy" appraisal of James, another preface can provide some context. In his *Preface to Hebrews*, Luther alludes to 1 Corinthians 3:12 and praises the author for building upon the apostolic foundation with gold, silver, and precious stones, despite lacking apostolicity. He encourages Christians to utilize the Epistle to the Hebrews for its approved teachings even if "wood, *straw*, or hay are perhaps mixed with them."[86] Thus, as Reformation historian Timothy Wengert explains:

> [Luther] used the word "straw" not as some sort of strange German insult but as an echo of Paul's picture in 1 Corinthians 3:12 about building on the foundation of Christ with either straw or gold and precious stones. James builds on the foundation all right, but he uses only straw, in contrast to the gold standard of John, Paul, and Peter.[87]

---

82. *LW* 35:395; WA, *DB* 7:344, "eyn rechten feynen gryff und mas zeygt, die schrifft zu lesen und handelln."

83. *LW* 35:362; WA, *DB* 6:10. On the history of James's interpretation during the Reformation, see George, "'A Right Strawy Epistle': Reformation Perspectives on James," 369–82; McNutt, "James, 'The Book of Straw,' in Reformation Biblical Exegesis," 157–76.

84. *LW* 35:362; WA, *DB* 6:10, "den sie doch keyn Euangelisch art an yhr hat."

85. *LW* 35:395; WA, *DB* 7:384.

86. Italics mine; *LW* 35:395; WA, *DB* 7:344, "ob villeight etwas holltz, *stro* odder hew, mit unter gemenget werde."

87. Wengert, *Reading the Bible with Martin Luther*, 3.

Additionally, in the *Preface to the Three Epistles of St. John*, Luther consistently portrays James this way as he contrasts it with John's manner of warning against works absent from faith. Luther prefers 1 John over James to issue this reminder, since the latter does so by "harping on the law" (*treyben auffs gesetz*) rather than stirring up Christians to love others as they have been loved by God.[88] Returning to the *Preface to James and Jude*, Luther criticizes it once again for "James does nothing more than drive [*treybt*] to the law and to its works."[89] In short, James is to remain in the Bible, but because of his fixation on the law to the neglect of the gospel of Christ, Luther cannot regard this letter on the same plane as other uncontested apostolic writings in the NT.

In order to evaluate James's approach towards Christian instruction, Luther submits his understanding of an apostle's office, which then leads him to make claims about the relationship of Scripture to Christ and the gospel. "[T]he office of a true apostle," Luther describes, is "to preach of the Passion and resurrection and office of Christ, and to lay the foundation for faith in him, as Christ himself says in John 15[:27], 'You shall bear witness to me.'"[90] Apostles as authors, therefore, compose scriptural writings with the supreme purpose of testifying to Jesus Christ. From this standpoint, Luther makes a holistic judgment for the biblical canon, "All the genuine sacred books agree in this, that all of them preach [*predigen*] and inculcate [*treyben*] Christ. And that is the true test by which to judge all books, when we see whether or not they inculcate [*treyben*] Christ. For all the Scriptures show us Christ."[91] From this selection comes Luther's popularly noted formula, *was Christum treibet*, that is often translated as "what drives/pushes/ inculcates Christ." For Luther, the Bible as a whole is written to drive humanity to Christ by faith to receive the promise of God's salvation in him.

88. *LW* 35:393; WA, *DB* 7:326.

89. *LW* 35:396–97; WA, *DB* 7:386, "Aber diser Jacobus thutt nicht mehr, den treybt zu dem gesetz und seynen werken." Luther's usage of the German word, *treiben*, to describe the nature of James's urging of the law is the same term he enlists to prescribe what a true apostolic writing does, that is, "drive/push Christ" (*Christum treiben*). The clear juxtaposition between James and other certain "apostolic" writings is missed in the English. See below for further discussion.

90. *LW* 35:396; WA, *DB* 7:384, "Denn das ampt eyns rechten Apostel ist, das er von Christus leyden und aufferstehen und ampt predige, unnd lege des selben glawbens grund, wie er selb sagt Johan. 18. yhr werdet von myr zeugen." In the 1546, the reference had been edited to John 15; see WA, *DB* 7:385.

91. *LW* 35:366; WA, *DB* 7:384, "Und daryn stymmen alle rechtschaffene heylige bucher uber eynes, das sie alle sampt Christum predigen und treyben, Auch ist das der rechte prufesteyn alle bucher zu taddelln, wenn man sihet, ob sie Christum treyben, odder nit, Syntemal alle schrifft Christum zeyget."

Because Luther founds this conviction upon Romans 3:21—where Paul attests to the reality that the Law and the Prophets had witnessed to the righteousness of God apart from the law—one must grant that the Reformer perceives that his interpretive position on Christ as the *sensus literalis* of Scripture finds textual endorsement. In Luther's vision, he sees Romans 3:21 as a sample case of an apostle telling Bible readers that what the NT writings proclaim about Christ and the gospel is nothing other than that which the OT prophets had long foretold. Although an allusion to it is latent in his reference to Romans 3:21, Luther's canonical-principle, *was Christum treibet*, should not be mistaken as a dogmatic conviction imposed upon the entire scope of the Bible. Clearly from all that has been treated thus far from the prefaces to the NT, in Luther's thought Christ is the center of Scripture because he is in the direct line of sight of every prophet's and apostle's pen. Unfortunately, both for Luther and for James, this epistle's voice did not bear enough resemblance to how the Reformer heard other scriptural writers testifying to God in Christ.[92]

Preface to the Revelation of St. John

The *Preface to Revelation* that accompanied the first edition of the *German New Testament* was eventually replaced in 1530 by an entirely rewritten one. In the 1522 version, Luther proffers several reasons for why he struggles to accept Revelation's apostolicity, though his conclusion rests ultimately upon the same charge he leveled against James's epistle, namely, "Christ is neither taught nor known in it. But to teach Christ, this is the thing which an apostle is bound above all else to do; as Christ says in Acts 1[:8], 'You shall be my witnesses.' Therefore I stick to the books which present Christ to me clearly and purely."[93]

By 1530, Luther had completed a total revision of the *German New Testament*. In addition to translation alterations, Luther supplanted the brief 1522 *Preface to Revelation* with an expanded introduction, and it remained virtually untouched all the way to the 1546 edition of the complete *Deutsche Bibel*.[94] Whereas Luther confesses in the 1522 preface that "I miss more

92. As for Jude, Luther believes that it must be a copy of 2 Peter. The preface is about a single paragraph in length without any substantial elaboration. *LW* 35:397; *WA, DB* 7:386.

93. *LW* 35:399; *WA, DB* 7:404, "das Christus, drynnen wider geleret noch erkandt wirt, wilchs doch zu thun fur allen dingen eyn Apostel schuldig ist, wie er sagt Act. i. yhr solt meyne zeugen seyn, Darumb bleyb ich bey den buchern, die myr Christum hell und reyn dar geben."

94. Reu, *Luther's German Bible*, 183, 229.

than one thing in this book," for the 1530 (1546) revision, he endeavors to interpret the writing in full, chapter by chapter.[95] For the purposes of this study, only an early portion of the preface is relatable.

To start the preface, Luther identifies two different kinds of prophecy; one that interprets the prophetic writings and another that makes predictions about subject matters not already present within Scripture.[96] Of the latter Luther delineates three types. The first one occurs "simply in words, without images and figures—*as Moses, David, and others of the prophets prophesy [weissagen] about Christ,* and as Christ and the apostles prophesy about Antichrist, false teachers, etc."[97] This statement is reminiscent of a phrase from Luther's 1522 *Preface to Revelation,* where he defends that prophets and apostles "speak clearly of Christ and his deeds, without images and visions."[98] What seems consistent in Luther's thought from the *Preface to Revelation* of 1522 to its 1530 (1546) edition is that Luther considers the "words" (*worten*) of Scripture as the locus of God's testimony to Christ through the prophetic and apostolic witness. Within this framework, the grammatical-historical approach to scriptural interpretation would be the means for discerning the OT's witness to Christ as its literal sense.

Other Prefaces

Many of the prefaces to the Pauline and the General Epistles undergo a similar form of commentary subsequent to the *Preface to the New Testament* and the *Preface to Romans.* Luther's treatment of these books of the Bible features the following common elements: (1) emphasis on the themes of justification by faith; (2) highlight the law and gospel distinction; and (3) summarizing the plain sense content of the individual writing (many times chapter by chapter). In this way, it becomes certain that Luther envisioned his *Preface to the New Testament* and *Preface to Romans* to function as the

---

95. *LW* 35:398; WA, *DB* 7:404, "Myr mangellt an disem buch nit eynerley."

96. *LW* 35:399–400; WA, *DB* 7:406.

97. Italics mine; *LW* 35:400; WA, *DB* 7:406, "Die erste thuts mit ausgedrucken worten, on bilde und figuren, wie Moses, David und der gleichen Propheten mehr, von Christo weissagen, Und wie Christus und die Apostel, von dem Endechrist und falschen leren etc." The second type of this prophecy uses images and supplies interpretations of them with words. Luther cites Joseph and Daniel's interpretation of dreams as examples. The third type foretells with images and figures, yet does not offer any clear interpretation in words. John's Revelation falls under this category for Luther.

98. *LW* 35:398; WA, *DB* 7:404, "klerlich und on bild odder gesicht von Christo und seynem thun zu redden."

theological and hermeneutical norms for how one should interpret the rest
of the NT.

Unless an epistle's subject matter elevates the interest such as Galatians
and Colossians reviewed above, Luther does not offer any direct reflection
on the matter of Christ in the OT or as the Bible's *sensus literalis*. This ab-
sence is not a sign of Luther's inconsistency, but rather an indication of how
he desires for the *Preface to the New Testament* and the *Preface to Romans*
to carry the bulk of this argumentation on behalf of the NT as a whole.
Moreover, despite his heightened perception of the Bible's unity, Luther still
seeks to represent faithfully an epistle's unique witness. Therefore, not every
NT writing raises the question of Christ in the OT to the same degree, if at
all, and so Luther does not force this discussion upon it. And finally, one
must not overlook that Luther's formulation of "justification by faith alone"
always rests upon "in/through Christ alone." How these two relate in support of the messianic ground of Luther's view of Christ as the literal sense
of Scripture will be further discussed below in the *Preface to the Acts of the
Apostles* (1533). For now, Luther grants that the NT writings may have di-
verse occasions and themes, but all of them are in different ways promoting
and explicating the same gospel. This unified vision is what Luther attempts
to capture in the *Preface to the New Testament*.

The prologues omitted from independent review under this criteria
are the prefaces to: 1 Corinthians, 2 Corinthians, Ephesians, Philippians, 1
Thessalonians, 2 Thessalonians, 1 Timothy, 2 Timothy, Titus, Philemon, 2
Peter, and the Johannine letters.

1523

Once the *German New Testament* was completed and printed, Luther moved
immediately into the translation of the Old Testament. This task was going
to prove more difficult compared to his speedy production of the NT. In a
letter to Nicholas von Amsdorf dated January 13, 1522, Luther pleads for
assistance recognizing his inability to succeed in this effort alone: "In the
meantime I shall translate the Bible, although I have here shouldered a burden beyond my power. Now I realize what it means to translate, and why no
one has previously undertaken it who would disclose his name. Of course
I will not be able to touch the Old Testament all by myself and without the
co-operation of all of you."[99] And indeed, the translation of the OT's Hebrew

99. *LW* 48:363; WA, *Br* 2:223, "Interim Biblia transferam, quamquam onus susce-
perim supra vires. Video nunc, quid sit interpretari, et cur hactenus a nullo sit attenta-
tum, qui profiteretur nomen suum. Vetus vero Testamentum non potero attingere, nisi

was a collaborative endeavor. Most likely assisted by Melanchthon and Matthew Aurogallus, Luther set to edit for publication his translation of the Pentateuch, which he had completed by December, 1522.[100] By mid-1523, a finalized version of Luther's German rendering of the Pentateuch appeared in print.[101] Similar to how the Reformer penned the *Preface to the New Testament* to introduce not only the fourfold Gospels, but perhaps more intentionally, the entire NT, the *Preface to the Old Testament* strives to accomplish these two aims; it casts a vision for the Christian reading of the OT, and he acquaints the reader with the individual books of the Pentateuch.

PREFACE TO THE OLD TESTAMENT

The writing of the *Preface to the Old Testament* in such close proximity to both the printing of the *German New Testament* and the *Preface to the New Testament* presents the reader with a coherent and unified vision in Luther's thought of how the two Testaments relate theologically with Christ as the entire Bible's *sensus literalis*. As recounted above, in several of his NT prefaces, Luther has already strongly argued that the apostolic witness to Christ finds its origin in God's promise to the prophets. Now, Luther is able to demonstrate this claim from its source.

In the first place, Luther makes no hesitation to mark the Old Testament as Christian Scripture. He responds to those who have "little regard for the Old Testament" because of the supposition that it is merely the sacred writings of the "Jewish people." These Christians wrongly assume "they have enough in the New Testament."[102] Moreover, those who teach that only a "spiritual sense" (*geystliche synn*) is to be sought in the OT only perpetuates this problem according to Luther.[103] Bible readers, instead, must learn

---

vobis praesentibus et cooperantibus."

100. Reu, *Luther's German Bible*, 187.

101. Brecht, *Martin Luther: Shaping and Defining the Reformation*, 55.

102. *LW* 35:235; *WA, DB* 8:10, the full quotation reads: "Das alte testament halten etlich gering, als das dem Judischen volck Alleyne gegeben und nu fort aus sey, und nur von vergangenen geschichten schreybe, meynen, sie haben gnug am newen testament zu suchen."

103. *LW* 35:235; *WA, DB* 8:10. Luther names Origen and Jerome as examples from church history who have held this position. With the knowledge of longevity and widespread influence of Jerome's *Vulgate* and its prefaces, one can see in such characteristic statements from this prologue as well as the *Preface to the New Testament* how Luther is consciously trying to set his own work apart from his predecessors to ensure a proper theological conception of the Bible, both at the macro level of biblical theology and at the micro level of exegesis and interpretation. For instance, in *A Brief Instruction on What to Look for and Expect in the Gospels* (1521), which predates the

from Jesus himself, who "says in John 5[:39], 'Search the Scriptures, for it is they that bear witness to me.'"[104] Luther continues with his corrective:

> St. Paul bids Timothy attend to the reading of *the Scriptures*, and in Romans 1[:2] he declares that the gospel was promised [*verheyssen*] by God in *the Scriptures*, while in 1 Corinthians 15 he says that in accordance with *the Scriptures* Christ came of the seed of David, died, and was raised from the dead. St. Peter, too, points us back, more than once, to *the Scriptures*.[105]

As can be observed, Luther emphatically demonstrates that any notion of the theological vacuity of the OT in its "letter" for Christians diverges from the apostolic authors of the NT. Moreover, to make his case, Luther does not resort to a sampling of miscellaneous occurrences of the NT's use of OT texts. For this Reformer, the identity of Christ and the nature of his gospel are at stake in a deficient view of the OT as Christian Scripture. Luther contends for the OT's ongoing relevance for Christians by showing how even from the apostles's point of view, the doctrine of Christ and what his cross and resurrection accomplished for humanity's sake cannot be conceived apart from the OT Scriptures.[106]

That Luther envisions its testimony to the coming person and work of the Messiah as the OT's main purpose is evident in his analogy of the OT Scriptures as Christ's "swaddling cloths." Luther uses this picture to encourage the readership of the *Preface to the Old Testament* not to be disheartened if the OT Scriptures prove difficult to understand. He challenges his audience to persevere in Bible study by upholding a high view of the written Word of

---

prefaces to the OT and NT, Luther's first lines read: "It is a common practice to number the gospels and to name them by books and say that there are four gospels. From this practice stems the fact that no one knows what St. Paul and St. Peter are saying in their epistles, and their teaching is regarded as an addition to the teaching of the gospels, *in a vein similar to that of Jerome's introduction*" (italics mine); *LW* 35:117; WA 10.1.1:8.

104. *LW* 35:235; WA, *DB* 8:10, "Aber Christus spricht Johannis. 5. forschet ynn der schrifft, denn die selbige gibt zeugnis von myr."

105. Italics mine; *LW* 35:235; WA, *DB* 8:10, "Und Paulus gepeut Timothy. er sole anhalten mit lesen der schrifft, und rhumet Ro. 1. wie das Euangelion sey von Gott ynn der schrifft verheyssen, und. 1. Cor. 15. sagt er, Christus sey nach laut der schrifft von Davids geblütte komen, gestorben und vom todt aufferstanden, So weyset uns auch S. Petrus mehr denn eyn mal enhyndern ynn die schrifft."

106. A valuable insight from Luther is to see the OT as "the ground (*grunden*) and proof (*beweysung*) of the New Testament" rather than looking to the New Testament to verify the Old. *LW* 35:236; WA, *DB* 8:10. Luther makes nearly the same statement in his exposition of 1 Peter 1:10 from his *Sermons on the First Epistle of St. Peter* (1522), "We must go back to the Old Testament and learn to prove (*grunden*) the New Testament from the Old." *LW* 30:18; WA 12:274.

God with the consolation: "Here you will find the *swaddling cloths* and the manger in which Christ lies, and to which the angel points the shepherds. Simple and lowly are these *swaddling cloths*, but dear is the treasure, Christ, who lies in them."[107] Just as the angel directed the shepherds to the babe in the manger who would be wrapped in swaddling cloths, Luther points Christians to the sign of the OT as the bearer of the Christ. The Law and the Prophets were written to house the promise of God's gospel concerning his Son, who is the Christ. They declare his future advent, whereupon in fulfillment of what was prophesied, the apostles now proclaim Jesus Christ's finished work of salvation to those who would receive him by faith.

As he transitions from the OT in general to a narrower focus on the Pentateuch, Luther continues his campaign to show Christ as the centerpiece of the OT through the presentation of the law's christological purpose. In his summary of Genesis he again envisions Christ as the direct referent of the messianic promises in Genesis 3:15 and 22:18. Because Genesis depicts such a bleak picture from the start in its account of Adam's Fall, ushering in sin and death for all, Luther says Moses moves quickly to extend God's promise of the Messiah to sustain his people and to guard them from utter despair. And so, Moses teaches that God has offered hope to overcome sin and death not by the law, "but by 'the seed [*samen*] of the woman,' Christ, promised [*verheyssen*] to Adam and Abraham, in order that throughout the Scriptures from the beginning faith may be praised above all works and laws and merits."[108] Genesis, therefore, "is an entirely evangelical book" for Luther due to its overarching aim to supply God's gospel promise of his Messiah for the elevation of faith over the law as the means for justification, righteousness, and eternal salvation.[109]

To reinforce his argument, Luther discusses how Moses's "true [authorial] intention" (*die rechte meynung Mose*) in the Pentateuch sets up the prime function of the law as that which reveals sin and brings shame upon

107. *LW* 35:236; WA, *DB* 8:12, "Hie wirstu die windeln und die krippen finden, da Christus ynnen ligt, dahyn auch der engel die hirtten weysset, Schleschte und geringe windel sin des, aber theur ist der schatz Christus, der drynnen ligt." Previously in *A Brief Instruction* (1521), Luther likewise taught "Now the gospels and epistles of the apostles were written for this very purpose. They want themselves to be our guides, to direct us to the writings of the prophets and of Moses in the Old Testament so that we might there read and see for ourselves how Christ is wrapped in *swaddling cloths* and laid in the manger, that is, how he is comprehended (*vorfassett*) in the writings of the prophets." *LW* 35:122; WA 10.1.1:12.

108. *LW* 35:237; WA, *DB* 8:12, "sondern durch des weybs samen Christum, Adam und Abraham verheyssen, auff das also der glaube von anfang der schrifft durch und durch gepreyset werde uber alle werck."

109. *LW* 35:237; WA, *DB* 8:12, "und ist fast eyn euangelisch buch."

any trust in human ability to be right before God.[110] Yet, Luther believes Moses is aware that a time is coming when his office will cease and give way to the office of grace administered through the Christ.[111] Here, Luther enlists Deuteronomy 18:15, a standard messianic text for support.[112] Of this passage, Luther says, "So Moses himself has told us that his office and teaching should endure until Christ, and then cease. . . . This is the noblest saying [Deuteronomy 18:15] in all of Moses, indeed *the very heart of it all.*"[113] As the conscience is oppressed to produce self-recognition of one's own spiritual blindness, Luther teaches that the law then compels the person "to seek something beyond the law and its own ability, namely, *the grace of God promised [verheyssen] in the Christ who was to come.*"[114] Conversely, the law does not condemn and then drive despondent people to hope in a promise that cannot be clearly found within the written text of God's Word. Luther's preface is making the case for the spirituality of the OT's "letter" because Moses intends in his composition of the Pentateuch to uplift fallen hearts underneath the weight of the law through hope in the promise of God concerning the Messiah and the saving work he will accomplish for their sakes.

Luther identifies this biblical reader as the law's third kind of "pupil" (*Schüler*).[115] They are the ones "who understand the intention of the law and how it demands impossible things. . . . These pupils fall away from all works and presumption and learn from the law nothing else except *to recognize sin* and *to yearn for Christ. This is the true office of Moses and the very nature of the law.*"[116] Again, Luther speaks of Moses's or the law's "intention"

110. *LW* 35:242; WA, *DB* 8:20.

111. Luther reflects upon 2 Cor 3:7–14 to understand the timing and relationship between the office of Moses (law) and the office of Christ (grace). *LW* 35:244–45; WA, *DB* 8:24, 26.

112. Deuteronomy 18:15, "The LORD your God will raise up for you a prophet like me from among you, from your brothers- it is to him you shall listen."

113. Italics mine; *LW* 35:246; WA, *DB* 8:26, "Also hat Mose auch selbs angezeygt, das seyn ampt und lere solt weren bis auff Christum und also denn auffhoren, . . . Dis ist der edlist spruch und freylich der kern ym gantzen Mose."

114. Italics mine; *LW* 35:244; WA, *DB* 8:24, "etwas weytters zu suchen, denn das gesetz und eygen vermugen, nemlich Gottis gnade eynn kunfftigen Christum verheyssen."

115. The first pupil is the one who hears the law only to despise it, and thus, endures life with a hardened heart devoid of the fear of the Lord. The second pupil hears the law, and in response, strives to fulfill it through sheer human will apart from grace. *LW* 35:245; WA, *DB* 8:26.

116. Italics mine; *LW* 35:245–46; WA, *DB* 8:26, "Die dritten sind, die Mosen klar on decke sehen, das sind sie, die des gesetzs meynung verstehen, wie es unmugliche ding foddere . . . Dise fallen ab von allen wercken und vermessenheyt, und lernen am

(*meynung*) to accomplish a twofold purpose: to expose sin and to drive sinners to hope for the promised Christ/Messiah by faith. This "intention" is a textual intention present and discernible in the OT's "letter."

For Luther, then, the messianic promises of the gospel of God concerning the person and work of his Son, Jesus Christ, constitute the *sensus literalis* of the Pentateuch, and by extension, the prophets, the entire OT, and the apostolic witness in the NT. Luther makes this canonical connection himself when he asks, "What, then, are the other books, the prophets and the histories? I answer: They are nothing else than what Moses is. For they all propagate [*treyben*] the office of Moses."[117] Moses is the grammar of the prophets and the rest of the OT writings, according to Luther, and he sets the christological trajectory for the full unfolding of the scriptural canon as the written revelation of God's Word. Moreover, the prophets maintain Moses's dual aim: "They hold fast to this purpose of keeping the people conscious of their own impotence through a right understanding of the law, and thus driving [*treyben*] them to Christ, as Moses does."[118] And so, Luther once again stresses, "Thus the prophets are nothing else than administrators and witnesses of Moses and his office, bringing everyone to Christ through the law."[119]

Perhaps as a test case, Luther segues into a short demonstration of how the law within the Pentateuch bears witness to Christ. Regarding the Aaronic/Levitical priesthood, Luther posits, "If you would interpret well and confidently, set Christ before you, for he is the man to whom it all applies, every bit of it."[120] He, then, presents various texts from the Epistle to the Hebrews—"which is sufficient, all by itself, to interpret all the figures of

---

gesetz nicht mehr, den Alleyne sund erkennen und nach Christum zu sufftzen, wilchs auch das engentliche ampt Mose und des gesetzs art ist."

117. *LW* 35:246; WA, *DB* 8:28, "[W]as sind aber nun die ander bucher der propheten und der geschichten? Antwort, nichts anders, denn was Mose ist, denn sie treyben alle sampt Moses ampt."

118. *LW* 35:247; WA, *DB* 8:28, "und halten fest drib, das sie durch des gesetzs rechten verstand, die leut ynn yhrer eygen untuchtickeyt behalten und auff Christum treyben, wie Mose thut."

119. *LW* 35:247; WA, *DB* 8:28, "Also das die propheten nichts anders sind, denn handhaber und zeugen Mose und seyns ampts, das sie durchs gesetz yderman zu Christo bringen." See also Luther's subsequent claim that encompasses the prophets *and* the NT: "For Moses is, indeed, a well of all wisdom and understanding, out of which has sprung all that the prophets knew and said. *Moreover even the New Testament flows out of it and is grounded in it, as we have heard*" (italics mine); *LW* 35:247; WA, *DB* 8:28.

120. *LW* 35:247; WA, *DB* 8:28, "Wenn du wilt wol und sicher deutten, So nym Christum fur dich, denn das ist der man, dem es alles und gantz und gar gilt."

Moses"—where the author interprets Christ as the literal sense of the OT's priestly office and sacrificial system.[121] On the one hand, he calls this interpretation the "spiritual meaning" (*geystliche bedeuttung*) of the Levitical priesthood, which seems to hint at the possibility that to see Christ as fulfillment of this office would not be assigned to the literal sense. On the other hand, as discussed above, Luther's grammatical-historical approach allows the literal sense to communicate the spiritual/theological meaning.[122] Thus, when he drafts the author of Hebrews as an example of this hermeneutical endeavor, Luther is endorsing how the Epistle to the Hebrews affirms what the Aaronic priesthood was in its own right historically while understanding what the entire system was intended to prefigure in the person and work of the Christ.

One final notable mention remains from the *Preface to the Old Testament*. In the editions of the prologue to accompany the complete *Deutsche Bibel* from 1534 and onwards, the last sentence read: "Let this suffice for the present as a brief suggestion for seeking Christ and the gospel in the Old Testament."[123] This closing word is certainly a fitting end to the preface insofar as it encapsulates the essence of Luther's agenda from start to finish for introducing not only the first five books of Moses, but the entire OT, as a textual and directly prophetic witness to Jesus Christ. The primary manner in which Luther sees the OT "witnessing" to Christ is God's promise of the Messiah spoken through the prophets, beginning with Moses and Genesis 3:15. However, in earlier versions, the preface continued with a brief discourse on aspects of Luther's Hebrew translation. Within this excursus, the Reformer suggests, "I think that if the Bible is to come up again, we Christians are the ones who must do the work, for we have the understanding [*verstand*] of Christ without which even the knowledge of the language is nothing."[124] In other words, mere lexical and syntactical knowledge of Hebrew will not do. Luther understands that translation always incorporates interpretive commitments; therefore, to rely upon Jewish or Rabbinic translators/commentators on the OT simply because these persons may be more capable with the Hebrew language is to surrender the OT's literal sense to those who reject the one to whom Luther believes all of Scripture as special

121. *LW* 35:247; WA, *DB* 8:28, "welche fast alleyne gnugsam ist alle figurn Mose zu deuten."

122. See the section in chapter 1, "Luther, Letter, Law, Literal."

123. *LW* 35:248; WA, *DB* 8:31, "Das sey dis mal gnug zur kurtzen anleitung, Christum und das Euangelium zu suchen im alten Testament" (1545).

124. *LW* 35:249; WA, *DB* 8:30, "Und achte, sol die Bibel erfur komen, so mussen wyrs thun, die Christen sind, als die den verstand Christi haben, on wilchen auch die kunst der sprache nichts ist."

written revelation from God is meant to witness. If the apostles's proclamation of Jesus of Nazareth as the Son of God and Son of David is meant to announce the arrival of the long-promised Messiah from the prophets, then translation that considers reference to this Jesus as alien to the OT's authors and their texts undermines the "ground" and "proof" for Luther's understanding of the New Testament's gospel of God (Rom 1:1–4).

1524

Throughout 1523 Luther worked diligently to finish the second installment of his German translation of the OT. In January, 1524, *Das Ander Teyl des alten testaments* (Joshua to Esther) rolled off of Melchior Lotther's Wittenberg press, and was funded by Lucas Cranach and Christian Döring.[125] The "Historical Books" did not receive any prefatory attention from Luther. Next, Luther proceeded immediately to translate the third and final part of the OT that included the poetic and prophetic writings. Beginning with the former, Luther found Job a significant challenge to render into German to the point that it was delaying the printing of the third part.[126] This setback resulted in a separate publication of the poetic books in late 1524.[127] The prophets would not see completion until several years later. The prefaces analyzed below accompanied the individual volume printed for the poetic writings.

Preface to the Book of Job

Luther's *Preface to the Book of Job* is a straightforward assessment of the writing's narrative and main theme that "God alone is righteous" (*das Gott alleyne gerecht ist*).[128] It is a relatively brief prologue and does not afford any opportunities to reflect upon Luther's messianic vision of the OT and Christ as the *sensus literalis* of Scripture.

Preface to the Psalter

Luther had been translating portions of the Psalms as early as 1513.[129] A favorite of Luther's, the Psalter received special attention as it appeared in

125. Gritsch, "Luther as Bible Translator," 64. See also Reu, *Luther's German Bible*, 195.

126. Reu, *Luther's German Bible*, 197.

127. Brecht, *Martin Luther: Shaping and Defining the Reformation*, 55.

128. *LW* 35:252; *WA, DB* 10.1:4.

129. Reu, *Luther's German Bible*, 199.

three separate editions: 1524, 1528, and 1531. The third underwent careful review from Luther's team of translators to achieve a rendering closer to the German idiom.[130] The preface to the 1524 edition of the Psalter reflects Luther's own struggle to supply proper theological definition to many keywords such as "favor" (*geute*), "fidelity" (*trewe*), and "mercy" (*barmhertzickeit*).[131] The Psalter, in Luther's view, was packed with a rich assortment of words and figures (*figuras*) that revealed "divine and holy things" (*göttlichen heyligen sachen*).[132] Nevertheless, Luther altogether avoids discussion of Christ in the Psalms.

In the 1528 update of the Psalter, a new preface supplanted the 1524 original. This newer prologue became the standard for all subsequent independent and *Deutsche Bibel* editions of the Psalter. In it, Luther abandons his previous course to discuss translation rationales for bringing the Hebrew into the German vernacular. Instead, the Reformer lavishes praise upon the Psalms, exposing his sentimental attitude towards this OT book. Near the preface's end, Luther closes, "In a word, if you would see the holy Christian Church painted in living color and shape, comprehended in one little picture, then take up the Psalter. There you have a fine, bright, pure mirror that will show you what Christendom is."[133]

Among the Psalter's many benefits for Christians, Luther grants preeminence to its witness to Christ. He offers this comprehensive estimation, "The Psalter ought to be a precious and beloved book, if for no other reason than this: it promises [*verheisset*] Christ's death and resurrection so clearly—and pictures his kingdom and the condition and nature of all Christendom—that it might well be called a little Bible."[134] Despite other

130. According to Bluhm, "It can be said without exaggeration that in the 1531 rendering, the Hebrew Psalter has virtually become a German hymnal, actually reading in many places like original German sacred poetry." Bluhm, "Luther's German Bible," 183.

131. For example, in the 1524 preface, Luther offers explanation on his decision to translate the Hebrew word חֶסֶד (*hesed*) into the German *guete* ("favor"). WA, *DB* 10.1:94; See also Reu, *Luther's German Bible*, 202–3, for an English translation of the *Preface to the Psalter* from 1524. The American Edition of *Luther's Works* does not include the 1524 version.

132. Reu, *Luther's German Bible*, 202; WA, *DB* 10.1:94.

133. *LW* 35:256–7; WA, *DB* 10.1:104, "Summa, wiltu die heilige Christlichen kriche gemalet sehen, mit lebendiger farbe und gestalt, ynn einem kleinen bilde gefasset, so nym den Psalter fur dich, so hastu einen feinen, hellen, reinen spiegel, der dir zeigen wird, was die Christenheit sey."

134. *LW* 35:254; WA, *DB* 10.1:99, "Und solt der Psalter allein des halben thewr und lieb sein, das er von Christus sterben und aufferstehung, so klerlich verheisset, und sein Reich und der gantzen Christenheit stand und wesen furbildet. Das es wol möcht

advantages of the Psalter for everyday Christian life, he esteems its direct promise of the Messiah, particularly his cross and resurrection, as its chief value. In this instance, however, it seems Luther takes this assertion for granted because the bulk of the preface commends the Psalms to its readers as an "enchiridion" (*Enchiridion*) or a "handbook" (*handbuch*) assembled by the Holy Spirit to provide a sufficient number of examples for all Christendom and believers of what the Christian life ought to resemble at the level of one's affections.[135] Luther does not expound upon how or where the Psalter "promises" (*verheisset*) the person, work, and kingdom of the Messiah to come; instead, he states his conviction outright, and most likely, leaves the justification for such a claim to demonstration in his translation and other writings on the Psalms.[136]

PREFACE TO THE PROVERBS OF SOLOMON

This preface as well as the following *Preface to Solomon's 'The Preacher'* were later replaced in 1534 with the *Preface to the Books of Solomon*, a single introduction to Solomon's three OT writings: Proverbs, Ecclesiastes, and Song of Songs.[137] In his original 1524 *Preface to Proverbs*, Luther teaches that Solomon's purpose is to present the wisdom of God—which is made known through his words and works—in contradistinction to the continual failure of humanity's hopes and plans when it trusts in itself.[138] Luther commends this writing to all young people for "daily use and practice" (*teglichen brauch und unbunge*), but neither here nor in his discussion on Proverbs in

---

ein kleine Biblia heissen" (1545). The 1545 is essentially the same as 1528 preface in this selection except where the 1545 directly mentions *der Psalter*, which is only implied in the 1528 version.

135. *LW* 35:254–55; WA, *DB* 10.1:98, 100.

136. Luther lectured on the Psalter on three separate occasions in his career: the *Dictata super Psalterium* (1513–15), the *Operationes* (1519–21), and a third set of lectures in the 1530s. As cited above, the work of Gerhard Ebeling, James Preus, and Scott Hendrix may be consulted for studies on the *Dictata*. Added to these should be Raeder, *Das Hebräische bei Luther: Untersucht bis zum Ende der ersten Psalmenvorlesung.* Raeder has also produced an important study on the *Operationes* in, *Grammatica Theologica: Studien zu Luthers Operationes in Psalmos*. For a comparative analysis of all three of Luther's lectures on the Psalms, see Lee-Chen A. Tsai's dissertation, "The Development of Luther's Hermeneutics in His Commentaries on the Psalms."

137. WA, *DB* 10.2:xii–xiii.

138. *LW* 35:261–62; WA, *DB* 10.2:2.

the 1534 *Preface to the Books of Solomon*, does he offer any material relatable to this study's primary interest.[139]

PREFACE TO SOLOMON'S "THE PREACHER"

Similar to his *Preface to Proverbs*, Luther's introduction to Ecclesiastes contents itself with an explanation of the book's main idea. As can be expected, Luther regards Solomon's aim as the intent to expose the futility of human plans and the illusion of human control over the future. In response, Solomon calls his readers to wait patiently and confidently in the sovereignty of God.[140] His comments on Ecclesiastes in the later *Preface to the Books of Solomon* (1534) span a mere two paragraphs. Despite sharing insights on the relevance of Solomon's wisdom for this present life, Luther's prefaces to Ecclesiastes do not contribute to this study's interest in the messianic dimension to his view of Christ as the literal sense of the Bible.[141]

1526

Upon the appearance of the poetic books in print (the first installment of the third part of the OT in German), other events and duties in Luther's

139. *LW* 35:261–62; WA, *DB* 10.2:4.

140. *LW* 35:264; WA, *DB* 10.2:104–6.

141. Luther lectured on Ecclesiastes in 1526. These lectures have two introductions: one is a formal preface and the other is additional prefatory remarks leading up to his notes on the biblical text. The contents of these two introductions overlap considerably; however, the latter includes an explicit appeal for the grammatical-historical approach to biblical interpretation. Luther concedes the difficulty of interpreting Ecclesiastes, and he suggests two reasons in particular for why past writers and theologians have left this biblical writing in obscurity. First, Luther says "they did not see the purpose [*consilium*] and aim [*scopum*] of the author [*Autoris*], which it is important to keep in mind and to follow in every kind of writing and even more important here" (*LW* 15:7; WA 20:9). And the second reason was their "ignorance of the Hebrew language [*linguae*] and the special style [*phrasin*] of this author, which often diverges from the ordinary usage of the language [*linguae usu*] and is very strange to our way of speaking [*consuetudine*]" (*LW* 15:7; WA 20:9). In short, Ecclesiastes cannot be rightly understood apart from discernment of Solomon's authorial intent and grasp of his grammar and style. These two components work in a reciprocal fashion. The author's intent aids the reader or commentator to make interpretive decisions through exposition of the text while Solomon's vocabulary and literary style is what communicates his meaning and purpose for the writing. "Therefore our first task," Luther declares, "will be to hold to the certain aim [*scopum*] of the book, what it seeks to accomplish and what it has in view. For if we do not know this, it will be impossible to understand its style [*stylum*] and way of speaking [*phrasim*]" (*LW* 15:7; WA 20:9).

life slowed his progress towards finishing a translation of the prophets.[142] Nevertheless, Luther utilized his employment as a professor of the Bible at the University of Wittenberg to orchestrate his teaching material in furtherance of his translating agenda. From 1524 to 1526, he lectured on the Minor Prophets. In particular, Luther had published a German translation and commentary on Habakkuk with an accompanying introduction in June, 1526.[143] For the most part, this introduction spoke generally towards the office of a prophet with only a short portion at the end devoted to Habakkuk. This small section was later retained as the formal preface for Habakkuk in the 1532 printing of the prophets in German, *Die Propheten alle Deutsch*. Since this study focuses on the prefaces of the *Deutsche Bibel*, priority will be given to the prologue in its 1532 form, supplemented by the fuller introduction that Luther penned for his earlier 1526 translation and commentary on Habakkuk when appropriate.

Preface to the Prophet Habakkuk

Luther's opening words to the preface provide the essence for his view on the prophet Habakkuk's office and message: "This Habakkuk is a prophet of comfort, who is to strengthen and support the people, to prevent them from despairing of the coming of Christ, however strangely things may go. This is why he uses every device and stratagem that can serve to keep strong in their hearts the faith in the promised [*verheissen*] Christ."[144] Most likely, as Luther explains, Habakkuk is prophesying during the time of Jeremiah prior to the Babylonian exile. Like Jeremiah, he is warning the people of impending destruction and his means of bringing "comfort" to Judah in spite of this Word from the Lord is by encouraging their hearts with the unrelenting promise of God's Messiah and the kingdom he will bring regardless of whatever plights the physical nation of Israel will experience.[145]

Although Habakkuk was not the only prophetic book Luther lectured upon leading up to the publication of *Die Propheten alle Deutsch* in 1532, his interaction with this OT writing does seem to have produced some paradigmatic thoughts about the office and message of all the prophets in

---

142. Reu, *Luther's German Bible*, 204–5.

143. Brecht, *Martin Luther: Shaping and Defining the Reformation*, 246.

144. *LW* 35:327; *WA, DB* 11.2:298, "Dieser Habacuc ist ein trost Prophet, der das volck sol stercken und auff halten, das sie nicht verzweiueln an Christus zukunfft, es stele sich wie seltzam es wolle. Darumb braucht er alle kunst und stücke, die dazu dienen, das der glaube fest bleibe jnn jrem hertizen, von dem verheissen Christo."

145. *LW* 35:327–28; *WA, DB* 11.2:298, 300.

general. From the 1526 lengthy introduction, Luther endeavors to equip with the theological, conceptual tools for assessing what at times sounds like the kingdom of Israel and at others the coming Christ and his kingdom.[146] In the first place, Luther instructs, "all the prophets direct their prophecies [*weyssagunge*] primarily toward Christ."[147] Luther substantiates this claim with Acts 3:24 and Galatians 3:24, which he believes teaches that the OT in its entirety "has been nothing else but a preparation for and forerunner of the New Testament."[148] But what of the historical dimension of the prophets's message? Luther answers still with hope in the future Messiah as the prophets's end goal:

> The fact that the prophets meanwhile reprove the people, that they pronounce many prophecies [*weyssagen*] that pertained only to their own time and served only their time, also that they have interspersed prophecies regarding heathen kingdoms and principalities, also the fact that they have performed miracles— *all this has been done to train the Jewish people and to prepare them for the advent of Christ.*[149]

In the second place, the prophets had to continue to stir up faith and hope in God's promise of the Messiah among the people of Israel in the midst of and even after the Lord's punishment upon them through Assyria and Babylon. Luther remarks that, to some degree, God temporarily had to make liars out of the prophets; nevertheless,

> That was a time to preach [*predigens*] and to comfort lest the Jews despair of *the advent of the Messiah and of His kingdom.* Here Jeremiah, Ezekiel, also Isaiah and many others before them, had to proclaim [*verkundigen*] that this would not prevent *the advent of the Christ,* so that, even if not all believed this, at least some would be preserved in faith and become partakers of *the coming Christ.* One of these prophets was our Habakkuk.[150]

146. *LW* 19:152; WA 19:350.

147. *LW* 19:152; WA 19:351, "Auffs erst ists gewis, das alle propheten furnemlich yhre weyssagunge richten auff Christum."

148. *LW* 19:152; WA 19:351, "Denn auch das gantze Alte testament nichts anders denn eyne zubereytunge und vorlauff gewest ist zum newen testament."

149. Italics mine; *LW* 19:153; WA 19:351, "Das nu die Propheten unter dem das volck straffen und viel weyssagen, das alleyne zu yhrer zeyt gegolten und gedienet hat, also auch, das sie königreiche und hirschafften der heyden haben mit eyngemenget, auch wunderzeychen gethan, ist alles geschehen, das Judisch volck ynn der zucht zu halten und auff Christus zukunfft zu bereyten."

150. Italics mine; *LW* 19:154; WA 19:352–53, "Da war zeyt predigens und tröstens, das die Juden nicht verzagten an der zukunfft Messia und seynes reychs. Hie muste

As can be observed, Luther understood Christ to be the focal point of the prophets's message due to their responsibility to announce and to perpetuate the messianic promise. Moreover, Luther sees this service as beyond mere prediction; the Word of the Lord concerning the future Messiah was to be a comfort for God's covenant people that enabled them to endure his discipline. Christ is the *sensus literalis* of Habakkuk, in Luther's analysis, because proclamation of the coming Messiah and his kingdom as the redemptive hope of God's people is what Habakkuk as a prophet had been tasked to do. In this way, Habakkuk is a preliminary example for how Luther will continue to introduce the prophets collectively and separately.

1528

As was the case with Habakkuk, Luther intended his lectures and translation of Isaiah to coincide. The translation was published in 1528 ahead of having lectured on the whole book, which Luther did not complete until February, 1530.[151] Also similar to his procedure with Habakkuk, the preface Luther wrote for his 1528 German translation of Isaiah was incorporated later into the *Deutsche Bibel*.

Preface to the Prophet Isaiah

Luther begins his *Preface to Isaiah* with an appeal for awareness of the historical context of Isaiah's prophecy. On one level, he suggests the need to read Isaiah against the canonical backdrop of 2 Kings and 2 Chronicles. At another, he encourages readers to familiarize themselves with Israel's surrounding peoples and lands.[152] Next, underneath the subheading given in the 1545 preface, "What the Prophet Isaiah Treats" (*Wo von der Prophet Jesaia handelt*), Luther divides Isaiah's message into three parts, in which the

---

Jeremias, Ezechiel, auch zuuor Jesaia und vie lander mehr sein, solchs verkundigen, das es nicht solte hyndern die zukunfft Christi, Und ob sie es nicht alle gleubten, doch etliche ym glauben erhalten wurden und des zukunfftigen Christus teylhafftig wurden. Der eyner ist auch dieser prophet Habacuc."

151. Brecht, *Martin Luther: Shaping and Defining the Reformation*, 249.

152. *LW* 35:273–75; WA, *DB* 11.1:16, 18. The use of subheadings is a noticeable addition to this preface as it appears in the 1545 *Deutsche Bibel*. Whereas the original 1528 version shows space gaps between certain paragraphs to indicate a self-contained subject matter, the 1545 preface utilizes headings like the one for Luther's discussion on the historical background to Isaiah, "Lender umb Jerusalem und Juda gelegen" ("Lands Surrounding Jerusalem [Israel] and Judah"). WA, *DB* 11.1:17.

first and the third contain comments related to his messianic understanding of Christ as the OT's literal sense.[153]

According to Luther, the initial part of Isaiah's message to Israel is twofold. First, he must issue threats of punishment for their idolatrous sins. And second, "he prepares and disposes them to expect the coming kingdom of Christ, of which he prophesies [*weissagt*] more clearly and in more ways than any other prophet."[154] From here, Luther evinces this claim with what he considers direct prophetic utterances about the person and work of the Messiah such as the virgin birth in Isaiah 7 and the passion, cross, and resurrection in Isaiah 53.[155] Then, Luther draws back and makes a holistic judgment about the message of all the OT prophets: "For all the prophets do the same: they teach and rebuke the people of their time, and *they proclaim [verkündigen] the coming and the kingdom of Christ*, directing and pointing the people to him as the common Savior of both those who have gone

153. *LW* 35:275; WA, *DB* 11.1:19. Luther also added a preface to his *Lectures on Isaiah* (1530). Although this preface and the one for the German translation of Isaiah differ at many points, considerable overlap still remains. Similar to the preface that was a part of *Deutsche Bibel*, Luther began the prologue to his *Lectures on Isaiah* recommending some principles of biblical interpretation. More strongly in the preface to the lectures, Luther outlines his vision for the grammatical-historical approach, granting priority to literary analysis as follows: "Two things are necessary to explain the prophet. The first is a knowledge of grammar [*Grammatica*], and this may be regarded as having the greatest weight. The second is more necessary, namely, a knowledge of the historical background, not only as an understanding of the events themselves as expressed in letters [*literis*] and syllables [*sillabis*] but as at the same time embracing rhetoric [*Rhetoricen*] and dialectic [*dialecticen*], so that the figures of speech [*scilicet figurae*] and the circumstances may be carefully heeded." *LW* 16:3; WA 31.2:1. One can hear the emphasis on literay analysis spoken of by Alastair Minnis that arose in the Late Middle Ages noted above.

154. *LW* 35:275; WA, *DB* 11.1:18, "Das ander, das er sie schicket und bereitet, auff das zukünfftige reich Christi zu warten. Von welchem er so klerlich und manchfeltiglich weissagt, als sonst kein Prophet thut." As will be seen throughout examination of the prefaces associated with the prophets below, Luther speaks of prophesies of "the Christ" and "the kingdom of Christ." For the latter, he provides a simple definition in his exposition on Isaiah 2:1 from the *Lectures to Isaiah* (1530): "Now follows the prophecy concerning the kingdom of Christ that is to come after the return from the captivity. But these words must be carefully noted, because the prophet speaks spiritually when he describes the church of Christ and skillfully depicts it, namely, that this kingdom is ruled by one scepter, which is the Gospel" (*LW* 16:27; WA 31.2:19). Essentially, the "kingdom of Christ" is the New Testament church, the people of God under the new covenant, who are spiritually organized in contradistinction to the theocratic society of Israel in the form of a temporal kingdom upon the earth.

155. *LW* 35:275; WA, *DB* 11.1:18.

before and those who are yet to come."[156] In short, Isaiah's prophetic task is the same as every OT prophet: to rebuke God's people of their sins and to exhort them to hope in God's promise of the Messiah to come.

Next, Luther explains that the second part of Isaiah's message pertains to Assyria as God's instrument to dispense punishment upon Israel. And the third division, in Luther's analysis, prophesies how Babylon will destroy Jerusalem. Once again, akin to his reflections on Habakkuk, Luther commends Isaiah at this point because in the midst of foretelling certain destruction and exile, the prophet offers comfort to the people, comfort that Cyrus will allow them to return to Jerusalem and that the Messiah's coming and kingdom have been unaffected by God's temporal judgment upon them.[157] Regarding the latter, the messianic hope is at the forefront of Isaiah's prophetic, authorial mind for Luther. He conveys this sentiment well, when he posits,

> For [Isaiah] is concerned altogether with the Christ, that his
> future coming and the promised [*verheissen*] kingdom of grace

156. Italics mine; *LW* 35:276; WA, *DB* 11.1:18, "Denn also thun alle Propheten, das sie das gegenwertige volck leren und straffen, daneben Christus zukunfft und reich verkündigen, und das volck drauff richten und weisen, als auff den gemeinen Heiland, beide der vorigen und zukünfftigen." Luther echoes this interpretation of the prophetic office also in the preface to the *Lectures on Isaiah* (1530). "The chief and leading theme (*Argumentum*) of all the prophets," in Luther's understanding, "is their aim to keep the people in eager anticipation of the coming Christ" (*LW* 16:3; WA 31.2:1). This prophetic purpose is not unique to Isaiah, though. In agreement with much that he has proffered in previous prefaces, Luther sets forth Moses as the forerunner for this messianic horizon. "Thus Moses, too," Luther reminds, "although he teaches many things that should be done, nevertheless always points to the well-known words in Deut. 18:15, where he also keeps the people in eager anticipation of Christ the Teacher, who will come with that authority with which He is endowed in His own right, yes, who will come as the chief Teacher and Disposer." *LW* 16:3; WA 31.2:1.

157. The opening words to his lectures on the second book of Isaiah (Isaiah 40–66) cohere closely with the preface to the *Deutsche Bibel* at this juncture, when Luther reviews what the prophet has treated thus far, followed by an outline for what to expect from the remainder of the book. Moreover, the messianic hope continues to be the focal point of Isaiah's prophecy. As he recaps, "We have heard the first one, in which the prophet has functioned as a historical prophet and leader of the army, because so far he has *prophesied concerning Christ* and concerning the defeat of the king of Assyria. Then he has both *comforted* and *reproved* the people. In the following book the prophet treats two matters: *Prophecies concerning Christ the King* and then concerning Cyrus, the king of Persia, and concerning the Babylonian captivity. This second book is nothing but prophecy, first external, concerning King Cyrus, and then spiritual, *concerning Christ*. And here the prophet is the most joyful of all, fairly dancing with promises. The next four chapters prophesy the most joyful things *concerning Christ* and the church in our time" (italics mine); *LW* 17:3, WA 31.2:261.

and salvation shall not be despised or be lost and in vain because of unbelief and great misfortune and impatience amongst his people. This, indeed, would be the case, unless the people expected it and believed confidently that it would come.[158]

Hence, the *Preface to Isaiah* introduces its readers to an OT writing whose primary purpose is christocentric, yet that christocentricity is determined by the prophetic word concerning the coming Messiah in whom OT saints were to hope by faith in God's saving promise.[159] Furthermore, Luther's presentation in the *Preface to Isaiah* places this prophet in unison with how he has thus far depicted Moses and the rest of the OT prophets in performance of their prophetic office for messianic ends.

1530

By 1530, Turkish invasion seemed imminent.[160] This event prompted Luther to turn next to the book of Daniel, where he perceived various prophesies identifying the Turks as well as the papacy to be, perhaps, the final pagan kingdoms who would rebel against God, Christ, and the church ushering in the end of time.[161] Luther published his German translation of Daniel early in 1530 with a dedicatory letter to John Frederick of Saxony and a preface, which was kept as the introduction to Daniel in the *Deutsche Bibel*.

---

158. *LW* 35:277; WA, *DB* 11.1:20, "Denn es ist yhm alles umb den Christum zu thun, das desselbigen zukunfft und das verheissen reich der gnaden und seligkeit, nicht odder durch unglauben und fur grossem unglück und ungedult, bey seinem volck verloren und umbsonst sein muste, wo sie des nicht wolten warten, und gewislich zukünfftig gleuben."

159. In the following pastoral quote from the preface to the *Lectures on Isaiah* (1530), Luther suggests that contemporary Bible readers experience the prophet's message in the same manner as did the original audience insofar as the "coming Christ" is the blessed hope for all who have faith in the promises of God for salvation, whether in anticipation of the Messiah's first or second advent. Failure to grasp this textual reality within the "letter" of the OT misses not only what the Holy Spirit is saying through the written Word of God, but likewise overlooks what the human author/prophet himself is intending to communicate. Thus, Luther digresses, "The prophets must be read in such a way that we prepare ourselves for the coming of Christ. But although the majority of the prophets do speak about a physical kingdom, yet they do (however tersely) lead to Christ. For this reason we must pay more attention to the designs [*studia*] and intentions [*Consilia*] of the prophets than to their words." *LW* 16:3; WA 31.2:1–2.

160. See Luther's 1529 treatise *On War against the Turk* in, *LW* 46:161–205; WA 30.2:107–48.

161. Brecht, *Martin Luther: The Preservation of the Church*, 96.

PREFACE TO THE PROPHET DANIEL

Notwithstanding the recognized interpretive difficulty of the material and genre, Luther devoted the book of Daniel to a thorough, chapter by chapter analysis most likely due to the historical backdrop of 1530 and the threat of war with the Turks. Thus, the *Preface to Daniel* is one of the longest prefaces among Luther's OT prologues. As can be expected due to the many images and visions in Daniel's prophecy, Luther's preface features explanatory content beyond restricting itself towards explicating the "Christ and Scripture" relationship. This examination will focus only on Luther's comments concerning how Daniel speaks about the Messiah.

In his survey of Daniel 1–6, Luther attends to the straightforward historical and theological interpretation of the text. Not until chapter 7 does Luther see Daniel's prophetic gaze turn to the Messiah. As he sketches, "In the seventh chapter begin the visions and prophecies [*weissagungen*] of the future kingdoms, especially of the kingdom of Christ, for whose sake all these visions came to pass."[162] This "kingdom of Christ," filled with the saints, will experience persecution from the Roman empire (the "Fourth Beast," Dan 7:7) and the Turks (the "little horn," Dan 7:8), who "will fight the saints and blaspheme Christ, something that we are all experiencing and seeing before our very eyes."[163]

In chapter 8, Luther interprets Daniel's vision of the ram and goat from a historicist position, narrowing its scope from the world to the Jews. Luther's assessment is that it is a description of a how the Jews would live underneath the rule of Alexander the Great prior to "the coming of the Christ" (*Christus komen*).[164] Here he attributes to Daniel the same "comforting" role that he has previously ascribed to other prophets like Habakkuk and Isaiah: "Once again the purpose is to console the Jews, that they may not despair amid the wretchedness that is to engulf them, as if Christ would leave them again and not come."[165] In other words, Daniel's vision was to reinforce the

---

162. *LW* 35:299; WA, *DB* 11.2:10, "Im Siebenden gehen an die gesichte und weissagungen, von den zukunfftigen Rönigreichen, und sonderlich von dem Reich Christi, umb welchs willen alle diese gesichte geschehen."

163. *LW* 35:300; WA, *DB* 11.2:12, "Und das selbige kleine horn, sol die Heiligen bestreiten, und Christum lectern, Welchs wire alles erfarene, und fur unsern augen sehen."

164. *LW* 35:300; WA, *DB* 11.2:12.

165. *LW* 35:300; WA, *DB* 11.2:12, "[A]uff das sie aber mal getöst warden, und nicht verzagen ynn dem iamer, der uber sie komen würde, als wolt Christus aber mal sie lassen, und nicht komen."

certainty of the messianic hope in order to sustain the Jews in the midst of a future time when they would inevitably feel abandoned by God.

However, Luther's estimation of Daniel's unique contribution as a prophet amongst his other OT co-laborers is that God had appointed Daniel to disclose a "special prophecy" (*sonderliche weissagunge*).[166] According to Luther, the OT prophets all shared the same ultimate purpose of bearing witness to Christ, but as for Daniel, "he not only prophesies [*weissaget*] of Christ, like the others, but also reckons, determines, and fixes with certainty the times and years."[167] For instance, Luther understood the seventy weeks in Daniel 9 as the precise revelation of "the number of years until Christ should come and begin his eternal kingdom."[168] Luther explains that these "seventy weeks" are to be seen as year-weeks rather than day-weeks, and thus, "seventy weeks of years total four hundred and ninety years. This is how long men were still supposed to wait for Christ, and then his kingdom was to begin."[169] Additionally, as he attempts to unpack the full theological import of the "seventy weeks," Luther discovers chronological markers for events such as Jesus's baptism, the beginning of his ministry, the crucifixion, and the destruction of Jerusalem by the Romans in AD 70.[170]

At the close of his *Preface to Daniel*, Luther returns to the overarching centrality of the promise of the coming Messiah and his kingdom to understand the OT prophets aright. Even in Daniel's case, the reader must know above all, "For this reason we see that here too Daniel always ends all his visions and dreams, however terrible, with joy, namely, *with Christ's kingdom and advent. It is on account of this advent, the last and most important thing, that these visions and dreams were given, interpreted, and written.*"[171]

---

166. *LW* 35:314; WA, *DB* 11.2:124.

167. *LW* 35:314; WA, *DB* 11.2:124, 126, "das er nicht allein von Christo, wie die andern, weissaget, sondern auch die zeit und iar zelet, stimmet und gewis setzet." Luther moves toward greater specificity when he asserts, "For Daniel freely prophesies and plainly declares that the coming of Christ and the beginning of his kingdom (that is, Christ's baptism and preaching ministry) is to happen five hundred and ten years after King Cyrus (Daniel 9),—when the empire of the Persians and of the Greeks is at an end, and the Roman Empire in force (Daniel 7 and 9)." *LW* 35:314; WA, *DB* 11.2:126.

168. *LW* 35:303; WA, *DB* 11.2:18, "das Christus kome, und sein ewiges Reich anfahe."

169. *LW* 35:303; WA, *DB* 11.2:18, "So machen nu diese siebentzig mochen .ccccxc. iar, So lange solt man auff Christus noch harren, und als denn solt er sein Reich anfahen."

170. *LW* 35:304–5; WA, *DB* 11.2:20, 24. For a critical assessment of Luther's biblical chronology that also examines the significance of Daniel for his framework, see Barr, "Luther and Biblical Chronology," 51–67.

171. *LW* 35:316; WA, *DB* 11.2:130, "Darumb sehen wir auch hie, das Daniel alle

The various "visions" and "dreams" need to receive faithful interpretation, which does not always necessitate a futurist explanation or some "hidden/ spiritual" sense; nevertheless, Luther does not consider the implementation of the grammatical-historical approach as undermining his conviction that all Scripture points to Christ. On the contrary, whether directly or indirectly, the written Word of God is meant to serve the same, unifying purpose of driving a person's heart towards God's Son, who is Lord and Savior, the long-promised Messiah.[172]

1532

Eight years after publication of the poetic books—the first installment of the third and final part of the German OT—Luther finally saw the prophets printed in full as a single volume in March, 1532. Luther titled the translation *Die Propheten alle Deutsch*; each book received its own preface, and in February, 1532, Luther drafted a new prologue to introduce the prophetic literature as a whole.[173] Since this study seeks to examine the prefaces in their chronological order, those prefaces which were published prior to *Die Propheten alle Deutsch* will not be revisited. Including the *Preface to the Prophets*, the prologues analyzed below will be those whose first appearance in print occurred with the publication of *Die Propheten alle Deutsch* in 1532.

Preface to the Prophets

Luther's reflection upon the prophetic office antedates the *Preface to the Prophets* as has been discussed above in the prior prefaces to Habakkuk,

---

gesichte und trewme, wie grewlich sie sind, ymerdar mit freuden endet, nemlich mit Christus Reich und zukunfft, umb welchs zukunfft willen, als umb das furnemest, endlich heubtstück, solche gesichte und trewme gebildet, gedeutet und geschrieben sind."

172. In his final remarks for the *Preface to Daniel*, Luther issues a similar call to Daniel's readers as he did previously in the *Preface to Isaiah*. Contemporary readers should, likewise, seek to have their own hearts driven to and comforted by the promise of the coming Christ, the only difference is that the anticipation is for his Second Advent rather than the first: "Whoever would read them [Daniel's prophecies] with profit must not depend entirely on the histories or stick exclusively to history, but rather refresh and comfort his heart with the promised and certain advent of our Savior Jesus Christ, who is the blessed and joyful redemption from this vale of misery and wretchedness. To this may he help us, our dear Lord and Savior, to whom with the Father and the Holy Spirit be praise for ever and ever. Amen." *LW* 35:316; WA, *DB* 11.2:130.

173. Brecht, *Martin Luther: The Preservation of the Church*, 97–98; Reu, *Luther's German Bible*, 208–11.

Isaiah, and Daniel. Here, Luther is able to reiterate much of the same position with further elaboration. In short, Luther teaches that an OT prophet's ministry is twofold. First, "the prophets proclaim [*verkündigen*] and bear witness to the kingdom of Christ in which we now live, and in which all believers in Christ have heretofore lived, and will live until the end of the world."[174] The "kingdom of Christ" is the spiritual reality of the church of the "new testament," which the Messiah established through his own suffering, cross, and resurrection. This message is what Luther says the prophets were charged to prophesy, and contrary to those who see no lasting value in them, Luther enlists Apostle Peter to counter this short-sighted perspective based upon 1 Peter 1:11–12.[175]

Luther believes 1 Peter 1:11–12 reveals that the prophets were consciously seeking to bear witness to the coming Christ and his kingdom in service of future believers. Moreover, the prophets also announced that for the Messiah's kingdom to begin, he must first greatly suffer for the sake of all who would enter this kingdom by faith. Therefore, Christ's subjects learn from the prophets two things:

> [F]irst, that the great glory of Christ's kingdom is surely ours, and will come hereafter; and, second, that it is nevertheless preceded by crosses, shame, misery, contempt, and all kinds of suffering for the sake of Christ. The purpose is that we shall not grow discouraged through impatience or unbelief, or despair of that future glory, which is to be so great that even the angels desire to see it.[176]

Entrance into the "kingdom of Christ," whether spiritual or physical (at the end of time), will always be preceded by some form of personal suffering, humility, and/or persecution. One wonders here if embedded in Luther's logic is Christ's teaching on how the world will hate his disciples, for "A disciple is not above his teacher, nor a servant above his master" (Matthew 10:24). The prophets proclaim this dynamic historically to the Jews who await the advent of the Messiah, enduring many hardships and

---

174. *LW* 35:265; *WA*, *DB* 11.1:2, "Denn erstlich verkündigen und bezeugen sie Christus Königreich, darinn wir itzt leben und all Christgleubigen, bisher gelebt haben, und leben warden, bis an der welt ende."

175. *LW* 35:265; *WA*, *DB* 11.1:2.

176. *LW* 35:266; *WA*, *DB* 11.1:2, 4, "das die grosse herrligkeit des reichs Christi, gewislich unser sey, und hernach komen werde, doch das zuuor her gehen, Creutz, schmach, elend, verachtung, und allerley leiden umb Christus willen, auff das wir durch ungedult odder unglauben nicht verzagt warden, noch verzweiueln an der künfftigen Herrligkeit, die so gros sein wird, das sie auch die Engel begeren zu sehen."

trials; and they preach the same "comforting" message to Christians whose existence encompasses two realms, temporal and spiritual, of which the former is the locus of Christian suffering until the Second Advent and Jesus Christ's appearing.[177]

Second, "the prophets show us many great examples and experiences which illustrate the first commandment."[178] Heretofore, Luther has not emphasized the first commandment as a significant component of the prophets's message, though its importance is certainly not foreign to his other writings.[179] For the prophets to uphold the first commandment is to wield Moses over God's people; it is the preaching of the law meant to condemn and to unveil any form of idolatrous sin while summoning repentance. Conversely, Luther perceives an element of comfort within the first commandment because of God's promise to love those who fear him.[180]

The remainder of the *Preface to the Prophets* is Luther expounding upon the second function of the prophets. In some sense, the general tone of the preface echoes the plea he made at the outset of the *Preface to the Old Testament* in 1523, namely, that the OT, and the prophetic writings in this case, have ongoing theological and spiritual significance in their "letter" for "new testament" Christians. Thus, rather than unpacking the various prophecies of Christ and his kingdom—which he will do in the individual prologues themselves—Luther utilizes the rest of the *Preface to the Prophets* to convey the relevancy of the prophets's administration of the first commandment both for the Jews as the original audience and for contemporary Christians.[181] Nonetheless, it must not be overlooked that Luther places in

177. For a brief account of how Christians inhabit two realms in Luther's thought, see Steinmetz, "Luther and the Two Kingdoms," 112–25.

178. *LW* 35:266; WA, *DB* 11.1:4, "Zeigen sie uns viel und grosse exempel und erfarunge an, des ersten gebottes."

179. See Luther's discussion on the essence of faith and good works in relation to the first commandment in *A Treatise on Good Works* (1520), *LW* 44:23–39; WA 6:204–16.

180. *LW* 35:266; WA, *DB* 11.1:4. Since Luther follows the tradition that combines the commandments "to have no other gods" (Exod 20:3) and "not to make idols" (Exod 20:4) to form the first commandment, it seems likely that he has in mind God's promise of curse and blessing that bookends these two, setting them apart from the rest of Decalogue. As God declares, "[F]or I the LORD your God am a jealous God, visiting the iniquity of the fathers on the children to the third and the fourth generation of those who hate me, but showing steadfast love to thousands of those who love me and keep my commandments" (Exod 20:5b–6).

181. By the 1545 edition of the *Preface to the Prophets*, subheadings had been inserted to highlight these two addresses. The first was "Abgötterey bey den Jüden" ("Idolatry among the Jews"), and the second was "Abgöttische bey den Christen"

first order the prophets's proclamation of the person and work of the coming Messiah.

PREFACE TO THE PROPHET JEREMIAH

"The most important thing in Jeremiah," according to Luther, is that "he gives comfort and promises [*verheisset*] that at a definite time, after the punishment is over, [the Jews] shall be released and shall return to their land and to Jerusalem, etc."[182] These "comforts" and "promises" are what prevent the Israelites from despair as they experience God's punishment through his instrument Babylon, resulting in exile. One level of God's "comforting promise" through Jeremiah is the prophecy that after seventy years in Babylonian captivity, they will return to the land.

Yet, Jeremiah's task to stir up faith and hope in God's promises is to extend beyond the announcement of physical deliverance once seventy years have passed. The messianic promise is to be the Jews's ultimate hope. Thus, the pinnacle of Jeremiah's prophetic message is that "like the other prophets, [he] too prophesies [*weissagt*] of Christ and his kingdom, especially in the twenty-third and thirty-first chapters. There he clearly prophesies [*weissagt*] of the person of Christ, of his kingdom, of the new testament, and of the end of the old testament."[183] Punishment from God's wrath is unavoidable due to the severity of the people's sinful idolatry. Through destruction and exile, Luther expects them to feel God-forsaken. The "seventy year" prophecy of return, therefore, appears to be in Luther's thought more of a prefiguring or foretaste of the coming Messiah and his kingdom as well as a reinforcement of the surety that God will not abandon his promise to send the Christ.[184] In short, Luther's portrayal of Jeremiah in this preface coheres with other

---

("Idolatry among Christians"). The 1532 preface did not use subheadings; instead, it included extra spacings between paragraphs to set apart these sections. LW 35:268–73; WA, DB 11.1:6–15.

182. LW 35:279; WA, DB 11.1:190, "Und doch daneben tröstet und verheisset auff gewisse bestimpte zeit, nach ergangener solcher strafe, die erlösung und heimfart wider jns land und gen Jerusalem etc. Und dis stuck ist das furnemest jnn Jeremia."

183. LW 35:280; WA, DB 11.1:192, "wie ander Propheten, und weissagt von Chrsto und seinem Reich, sonderlich im .23. und .31. Capitel, da er gar klerlich von der person Christi, von seinem Reich, vom Newen testament, und vom ende des alten testaments weissagt."

184. Without these "comforts" and "promises," Luther says, "For they would not have been able to think otherwise than that it was all over with them, that they were utterly cast off by God, and *that no Christ would ever come*, but that God, in great anger, had taken back his promises because of the people's sin" (italics mine); LW 35:280; WA, DB 11.1:190.

depictions of the prophets from prior prefatory material, whose primary purpose is to prophesy directly about the Messiah. This aim predominates Luther's presentation of Christ as the literal sense of Scripture in the OT, especially in the prophets.

PREFACE TO THE PROPHET EZEKIEL

The *Preface to Ezekiel* included in the 1532 *Die Propheten alle Deutsch* was later supplemented by the longer and more substantial, *A New Preface to the Prophet Ezekiel* created for the 1541 revision of the complete *Deutsche Bibel*.[185] Both will be examined in this section.

Luther's approach in the 1532 *Preface to Ezekiel* is brief, and concentrates on the prophet's main objective "to encourage the captives and to prophesy [*weissagen*] against the false prophets at Jerusalem, as well as to substantiate the word of Jeremiah."[186] Similar to his assertion in the *Preface to Jeremiah*, Luther ascribes the status of "the most important thing" (*das furnemest stück*) to Ezekiel's promise that the captives will eventually return to Judah.[187] This part of the prophecy lasts until Ezekiel 25 in Luther's outline. He, then, follows with a condensed account of Ezekiel 34–48 that highlights the prophet's testimony concerning the giving of the Holy Spirit, the coming kingdom of Christ, Gog and Magog as the final tyrants over Christ's kingdom, and the New Jerusalem.[188] Ezekiel's prophetic disclosure of messianic/christological features is merely listed without elaboration. However, he deals with Ezekiel as a witness to Christ more explicitly in *A New Preface to the Prophet Ezekiel*.

When Luther wrote *A New Preface to the Prophet Ezekiel*, he was purposefully countering the interest that had arisen among Christian interpreters in rabbinic translation and commentary on the OT.[189] This new prologue exudes a polemical attitude rather than the concise survey of the original 1532 preface. It seems that since the first *Preface to Ezekiel* had been printed, circumstances in Luther's life proved that he could not take for granted the confessional commitment to the OT as Christian Scripture. Therefore, whatever he assumed or left latent in his *Preface to Ezekiel* (1532),

---

185. Brecht, *Martin Luther: The Preservation of the Church*, 105–6.

186. *LW* 35:283; WA, *DB* 11.1:392, "die gefangen zu trösten, und wider die falschen Propheten zu Jerusalem zu weissagen, und Jeremias wort zu bestetigen."

187. *LW* 35:283; WA, *DB* 11.1:392.

188. *LW* 35:283; WA, *DB* 11.1:392.

189. Brecht, *Martin Luther: The Preservation of the Church*, 105.

he now brings to the fore to reaffirm Ezekiel's direct prophetic witness to the Messiah as Jesus Christ.

Luther begins with the vision of the four living creatures in Ezekiel 1:4–28. He interprets it as "nothing else than a revelation of the kingdom of Christ in faith here upon earth, in all four corners of the whole world as said in Psalm 19[:4]: *In omnem terram.*"[190] Throughout this preface, Luther uses his interpretation of Ezekiel's first vision as the interpretive norm for perceiving the main theme of Ezekiel's prophetic message. Essentially, Luther suggests that this vision prophesies two events: one is that Israel and Judah will reclaim the land after a time of captivity, and the other is "the best thing in this prophecy—that which the Jews will neither see nor heed—is that God promises to create something new in the land, to make a new covenant unlike the old covenant of Moses that they dream about."[191] Introduction of the "new covenant" sets Luther's course for the remainder of this prologue to Ezekiel.

Following his announcement of the "best" part of Ezekiel's prophecy, Luther cites Jeremiah 31 for biblical support and explains, "No longer are there to be two kingdoms but one kingdom, under their [the Jews] *King David who is to come*; and his shall be an everlasting kingdom, even in that same physical land."[192] At Christ's coming, he fulfilled this prophecy by establishing the new covenant through his cross and resurrection. Moreover, he instituted it in the same, physical land of "promise" and the holy city, Jerusalem. From this central location, Luther says the new, "everlasting" (*ewiger*) covenant "has broken forth from there into all the four corners of the world, and remains to the present day, both at Jerusalem and everywhere. For the place, Jerusalem, is still there, and Christ is Lord and King there as he is in all the world."[193]

---

190. *LW* 35:284; WA, *DB* 11.1:394, "ist nichts anders, meins verstands (Ein ander mache es besser) denn eine Offenbarung, des Reichs Christi, im glauben hie auff Erden, in allen vier Orten der gantzen Welt. Psal. xviii. In omnem terram."

191. *LW* 35:287; WA, *DB* 11.1:398, "und aller bestes die Jüden nicht sehen noch achten wöllen) in der selbigen Weissagung ist, Das Gott verheisst, Er wölle ein Newes schaffen im Lande und einen newen Bund machen, Nicht wie der alte Bund Mosi (da sie von treumen)."

192. Italics mine; *LW* 35:287; WA, *DB* 11.1:398, "Das sie nicht mehr zwey Königreich, sondern ein Königreich sein sollen, unter jrem künfftigen Könige David, und sol ein ewig Königreich sein, auch in dem selben leiblichen Lande."

193. *LW* 35:287; WA, *DB* 11.1:398, 400, "Sondern auch von dannen ausgebrochen in alle vier Ort der Welt, Und bleibt auch heutiges tages, beide zu Jerusalem und allenthalben. Denn die stet Jerusalem ist noch da, Und ist Christus Herr und König da selbs, wie in aller Welt."

The universal scope of Christ's kingdom in the "new covenant" challenges what it means to call oneself a true Israelite, according to Luther. On the one hand, Jews alone have the right to the title "Israel," Luther admits, "so far as the first part of the prophecy and the old covenant of Moses are concerned, though this has long since been fulfilled."[194] On the other hand, in the new covenant, "Israelites" are those who have accepted the Christ and have entered his kingdom, which expands membership to Gentiles, not only ethnic Jews. In a creative analogy, Luther uses himself as an illustration:

> For according to the old covenant I am no Israelite, or Jew. But I claim now that I am the son of St. Paul, and an Israelite or Benjamite. For Paul is my father, not the old Paul but the new Paul. He is still the old Paul, but out of the old Paul there has arisen a new Paul in Christ; and he has begotten me in Christ by the gospel, so that I am in his likeness according to the new covenant.[195]

Furthermore, Luther claims that all Gentiles who are Christians are "true Israelites" (*rechten Israeliten*) because they are "born of Christ, the noblest Jew" (*aus Christo dem edlesten Jüden geborn*).[196] To grasp the real intention of Ezekiel's prophecy, the biblical reader must recognize how "Everything, therefore, depends upon the new covenant, *which the Messiah was to found*, making all things new, as he has done."[197]

Luther's discourse on the new covenant relates to his conception of Christ as the Bible's *sensus literalis* because he is arguing that Ezekiel's prophetic announcement of this coming reality is exactly what the prophet is striving to convey to his audience. To help hear Ezekiel rightly, Luther prescribes this interpretive rule: "when the prophets say of Israel that it is to return or to be gathered in its entirety, as in Micah 2[:12], Ezekiel 20[:40], etc., *they are certainly speaking of the new covenant*, and of the new Israel from which no one will be excluded, the everlasting kingdom of Christ."[198]

194. *LW* 35:287; WA, *DB* 11.1:400, "nach dem ersten stuck, und nach dem alten Bund Mosi, der nu longest erfüllet ist."

195. *LW* 35:288; WA, *DB* 11.1:400, "Denn nach dem alten Bunde bin ich kein Israel noch Jüde, Uber nu rhüme ich mich, das ich S. Paulus son bin, und ein Israel oder BenJamin, Denn er ist mein Vater, Nicht der alle Paulus, sondern der new Paulus, der doch der selbe alte Paulus ist, Uber aus dem alten Paulo ein newer Paulus worden in Christo, und hat mich zeuget in Christo durchs Euangelium, das ich jm ehnlich bin nach dem newen Bund."

196. *LW* 35:288; WA, *DB* 11.1:400.

197. Italices mine; *LW* 35:288; WA, *DB* 11.1:400, "Darumb ligts alles an dem newen Bund, den der Messias stifften, und alles new machen solt, wie er gethan hat."

198. Italics mine; *LW* 35:288; WA, *DB* 11.1:400, "Denn wo die Propheten redden

In other words, the promise of the coming Messiah, who will institute the new covenant and establish his own kingdom, is not a spiritual, hidden meaning deposited beneath the "letter" of the text by the divine author to the ignorance of the human author. Instead, Ezekiel as an OT prophet/author is directly speaking about Christ, laboring to set the people's faith and hope firmly within God's promises to sustain them as they endure temporal hardships and punishments.

Not to see or to hear this message from the plain sense of the writing through the grammatical-historical approach is to show signs of interpretive blindness. This "blindness" is Luther's diagnosis for the Jews who rejected their own Messiah as well as his contemporaries who were inclined to "Judaizing" (*Jüdentzen*) the OT.[199] At the beginning of *A New Preface to the Prophet Ezekiel*, he cites Isaiah 29:11–12 as a prophecy "that the entire Holy Scriptures are sealed and closed to the unbelieving Jews."[200] And from the NT, Luther finds further support from the Apostle Paul in 2 Corinthians 3:14–16, wherein the Reformer deduces "that the veil of Moses remains over the Scriptures, *so long as they do not believe in Christ*."[201] In sum, a Christian reading of Ezekiel, for Luther, is one that finds Christ present in this OT writing at the grammatical-historical level through Ezekiel's intention to prophesy ultimately about the person and work of the coming Messiah. To "Christianize" (spiritual, hidden sense) or to "Judaize" (historical sense) Ezekiel is to miss entirely how the OT bears witness to Christ as Christian Scripture.

Preface to the Prophet Hosea

What one can notice up to this point is how Luther remains fairly consistent in his analysis of the prophets individually in agreement with his definition of the prophetic office from prior prefaces, especially the *Preface to the Prophets*. Aside from the more polemical *A New Preface to the Prophet Ezekiel*, Luther's review of each prophet attempts to illumine two prime characteristics: (1) where the prophet prophesies about the coming Christ and his kingdom in addition to the historical prophetic pronouncements

---

von Israel, das er gantz sole widerkomen oder versamlet werden, Als Miche. Eze. xx. und der gleichen, Das ist gewislich vom newen Bunde und vom newen Israel geredt, da nicht einer wird aussen bleiben, vom ewigen Reich Christi."

199. *LW* 35:284; WA, *DB* 11.1:394.

200. *LW* 35:284; WA, *DB* 11.1:394, "Das die gantze heilige Schrifft den ungleubigen Jüden verstegelt und verschlossen sey."

201. Italics mine; *LW* 35:284; WA, *DB* 11.1:394, "Das die decke Mosi, uber der schrifft bleibe, so lange sie nicht an Christum gleuben."

pertaining to national Israel and its land; and (2) rebuking God's people for idolatry and calling them to repentance. As will be seen for the remaining Minor Prophets, Luther continues to follow this pattern.

The *Preface to Hosea* is a short survey that does not provide detailed exposition. Luther's basic assessment is that the prophet executed the "two offices" (*zwey ampt*) well.[202] In the first place, Hosea "preached vigorously against the idolatry of his time and bravely rebuked the people, together with the king and his princes and priests."[203] This part of Hosea's message is the proclamation of the first commandment condemning the Jews's idolatrous sins. And in the second place, Hosea "also prophesied [*geweissagt*] powerfully and most comfortingly about Christ and his kingdom, as is shown particularly in chapters 2, 13, and 14."[204]

The *Preface to Hosea* concludes with a brief reflection on the matter of Hosea and Gomer's marriage. Although Luther avoids further commentary on the nature of Hosea's prophetic witness to the coming Messiah and his kingdom in chapters 2, 13, and 14, enough evidence is presented to support the claim that Luther sees Christ in this OT writing due to his conviction that Hosea is consciously speaking of Jesus Christ in the context of his first advent.

Preface to the Prophet Joel

Luther introduces Joel as one who is "highly praised in the New Testament."[205] That Peter (Acts 2:17–21) and Paul (Rom 10:13) both drew upon Joel 2 to show the person and work of Jesus Christ as in accordance with the OT prophetic witness is what justifies Luther's impression.[206] From here, Luther transitions to depict Joel in the typical twofold model.

---

202. *LW* 35:317; *WA, DB* 11.2:182. Luther most likely is referring to his description of the dual responsibility of the prophetic office in his *Preface to the Prophets*. See the discussion above on the *Preface to the Prophets* for further explanation.

203. *LW* 35:317; *WA, DB* 11.2:182, "Erstlich, das er wider die abgötterey zu seiner zeit hart gepredigt, und das volck frisch gestrafft hat, sampt dem Könige und seinen Fürsten, und Priestern."

204. *LW* 35:317; *WA, DB* 11.2:182, "Zum andern, hat er von Christo und seinem reich auch gewaltiglich und fast tröstlich geweissagt, wie denn sonderlich das .ii. .xiii. und .xiiii. Capitel anzeigen."

205. *LW* 35:319; *WA, DB* 11.2:212, "Doch ist er im Newen testament hoch berümbt."

206. *LW* 35:319; *WA, DB* 11.2:212.

In chapter 1, Luther reports that Joel first prophesies about God's punishment upon Israel at the hands of the Assyrians.[207] Leaving this word of judgment, Luther summarizes that "at the end of the second chapter and from that point on [Joel] prophesies [*weissagt*] of the kingdom of Christ, and of the Holy Spirit, and speaks of the everlasting Jerusalem."[208] Although Luther is a man of few words in the *Preface to Joel*, the introductory portion to his *Lectures on Joel* offer increased reflection upon Joel's prophetic office.[209]

Prior to his comments on the biblical text, Luther begins his *Lectures on Joel* with a comprehensive statement on what all the prophets, including Joel, proclaim. Luther declares, "All the prophets have one and the same message, for this is their one aim: *they are all looking toward the coming of Christ or to the coming kingdom of Christ.*"[210] In this framework, Luther still allows for aspects of the prophets's historical setting to be the referent; however, "Although they may mix in various accounts of things present or of things to come, yet all things pertain to this point, *that they are declaring the coming kingdom of Christ.*"[211] So, in chapter 1 and the first part of chapter 2, Luther observes Joel speaking about Israel and Judah's destruction in general ways. Because he places Joel at an early date possibly before Isaiah, Amos, and Hosea, Luther suggests that in the first chapter, Joel is recounting the Assyrian conflict, and in the second chapter, he is prophesying about the future Babylonian invasion.[212] Yet, at Joel 2:28—the passage Peter quotes in his Acts 2 sermon at Pentecost—Luther asserts, "Here the real prophecy begins" (*Hic incipit recta prophetia*).[213] This juncture marks the moment where Joel makes the transition Luther alluded to above, and goes on to reiterate once more:

207. *LW* 35:319; WA, *DB* 11.2:212.

208. *LW* 35:319; WA, *DB* 11.2:212, "Zum andern, weissagt er am ende des andern Capitels, und fort an hinaus, vom reich Christi und dem Heiligen geist, und saget von dem ewigen Jerusalem."

209. At Wittenberg, Luther lectured on the Minor Prophets from 1524 to 1526. For a helpful account, see Brecht, *Martin Luther: Shaping and Defining the Reformation*, 245–47.

210. Italics mine; *LW* 18:79; WA 13:88, "Ominum prophetarum una est sententia: hic enim unus est scopus, ut in futurum Christum seu in futurum regnum Christi respiciant."

211. Italics mine; *LW* 18:79; WA 13:88, "[Q]uanquam varias intermisceant historias sive rerum praesentium sive futurarum, tamen eo omnia pertinent, ut regnum Christi futurum declarent."

212. *LW* 18:79–80; WA 13:88–89. In the *Preface to Joel* for the *Die Propheten alle Deutsch*, Luther modestly proposes that Joel might have prophesied at the same time as Amos and Hosea. *LW* 35:319; WA, *DB* 11.2:212.

213. *LW* 18:105; WA 13:108.

> You see, it is the custom of the prophets that when they have declared that prophecy for which they had been sent, they put aside what has taken place after the revelation of their prophecy and *immediately go on to prophesy about Christ.* Although all the prophets were sent to announce some temporal punishment, *yet they would always connect something about Christ to it too.* Here the prophet Joel did the same thing. He quickly passes across from the Jews to the future people of Christ, and he meanwhile skips everything that took place after the declaration of the prophecy about the destruction of all Israel. So he clearly is beginning a new prophecy here.[214]

From the combination of Luther's thoughts in his *Lectures on Joel* and his succinct overview in the *Preface to Joel* for the *Die Propheten alle Deutsch* in 1532, one can see Luther's strong resolve to listen to the prophet bear witness to the Messiah and to prepare the people's hearts for his coming. Thus, the key for finding Christ in this OT writing is to discern how Joel performs his prophetic office to predict and to picture Christ and his kingdom through grammatical-historical interpretation of the prophecy's "letter." Luther demonstrates this approach in the *Lectures on Joel* by working from a guiding definition of what a prophet of the Lord does while aiding the reader to employ literary analysis such as his insight on how Joel 2:28 clearly signals a textual shift from the material that preceded it.

PREFACE TO THE PROPHET AMOS

In Amos's attack on Israel's "vices and idolatry, or false sanctity" (*laster und abgötterey, oder falsche heiligen*), Luther notes, "No prophet, I think, has so little in the way of promises and so much in the way of denunciations and threats."[215] Due to the general tone of the book, Luther seems relieved when

214. Italics mine; *LW* 18:105–6; *WA* 13:108, "Hic enim est mos prophetis, cum prophetiam suam, ad quam erant missi, nunciaverunt, dimittunt hoc quod interim post revelatam prophetiam factum est et statim de Christo pergunt prophetare. Licet enim omnes prophetae ad temporalem aliquam poenam nunciandam missi sunt, tamen semper etiam de Christo annectebant. Idem hic egit propheta Iohel, qui mox transit a populo Iudaeorum ad futurum populum Christi omissis interim omnibus iis, qua gesta sunt post annunciatam prophetiam de devastando universo Israhele. Itaque plane incipit hic novam prophetiam et sic."

215. *LW* 35:230; *WA, DB* 11.2:226, "Das mich kein Prophet dunckt so wenig verheissung, und so gar durch eitel schelten und drewen, haben." Even in the prologue to his *Lecutres on Amos*, Luther's assessment of Amos's prophecy captures the prophet's main message of warning and judgment. In a formula that normally contains Luther's disclosure of an OT prophet's witness to Christ, to capture Amos's distinct message he

he can say that the final chapter's end is "where he prophesies [*weissagt*] of Christ and his kingdom and closes his book with that."[216]

The *Preface to Amos* is brief and offers a general overview of the book. Luther foregoes further explication of the nature of Amos's prophetic word concerning Christ in the writing's last chapter. Once again, one may return to his lectures on the Minor Prophets that preceded the 1532 publication of *Die Propheten alle Deutsch* to shed light on Luther's comments in the translation's preface. As one may expect, when Luther states that Amos does not prophesy of Christ until "the end of the last chapter" (*aus ende des letzen Capitels*), it is Amos 9:11–15 to which the Reformer alludes. The closing words to his exposition of Amos 9:10 anticipate this textual shift: "Now follows a beautiful passage about the kingdom of Christ, who is going to restore the despised kingdom of David and lead Israel back into an eternal security, namely, in a spiritual way by the preaching of the Gospel of faith."[217]

On Amos 9:11, regarding the time when God will "raise up the tent of David," Luther points out the intertexual link with Acts 15:16–18 in support of the interpretation that understands Amos prophesying about the universal scope of the coming messianic kingdom and the inclusion of the Gentiles; therefore, the NT's usage of this passage in Acts 15:16–18 corroborates his claim that "we must properly take this to mean the kingdom of Christ."[218] To add, Luther interprets this verse in light of Isaiah 11:1 to affirm that both prophets through similar Davidic imagery are making the same announcement, namely, "This is the kingdom of David, from which the Messiah was to rule."[219] In Amos 9:12, concerning the "remnant of Edom," he teaches that it refers to "the remnants of Edom and of all nations who are going to

---

proposes instead, "The sum (*Summa*) and scope (*scopus*) of the prophet Amos, then, is this: He rebukes and admonishes Israel to come to its senses and repent of its wickedness." *LW* 18:128; *WA* 13:159.

216. The full quotation gives a clearer picture of Luther's impression: "He is violent too, and denounces the people of Israel throughout almost the entire book until the end of the last chapter, where he prophesies of Christ and his kingdom and closes his book with that." *LW* 35:320; *WA, DB* 11.2:226, "Er ist aber auch hefftig, und schilt das volck Israel fast durchs gantze buch aus, bis aus ende des letzen Capitels, da er von Christo und seinem Reich weissagt, und seind buch damit beschleusst."

217. *LW* 18:188; *WA* 13:204, "Iam sequitur locus elegans de regno Christi, qui sit restituturus regnum contemptum Davidis et reducturus Israhelem in aeternam securitatem nempe spiritualiter praedicando euangelium fidei etc."

218. *LW* 18:189; *WA* 13:204, "Hic locus proprie, ut dixi, de regno Christi est intelligendus."

219. *LW* 18:189; *WA* 13:204–05, "i. e. regnum David, de quo regnare debuit Messias."

believe the Gospel."[220] And last, for Amos 9:14, "And I will turn back the captivity of My people," Luther reads the prophet as saying, "He is speaking about a spiritual leading and turning back . . . All were brought back with this leading back—as many as believed the Gospel when Christ came and were brought into that tent of David by faith."[221]

Though it appears a degree of tension exists between Luther and Amos because of how relentlessly Amos preaches the law and rebukes sin in his writing, it is commendable that the Reformer does not dismiss the surface literalness of the biblical text by forcing a christological interpretation upon it to make this Minor Prophet more amenable for NT Christian readers. His approach lets Amos *be* Amos while striving to discern where the prophet fulfills the task that primarily constitutes his identity as an OT prophet of the Lord. Luther waits to find at the end of the book a passage where it seems evident that Amos is articulating a prophetic word concerning the messianic hope. And with, perhaps, a hint of subtlety, Luther remarks, "and [he] closes his book with *that.*"[222]

Preface to the Prophet Obadiah

Luther's *Preface to Obadiah* features a general survey of Obadiah's prophecy against Edom. As is common with Luther's analysis of the Minor Prophets, he does not often observe them prophesying about Christ until the end of their writings. Obadiah, likewise, follows suit as Luther notes, "At the end he prophesies [*weissagt*] of Christ's kingdom, that it shall not be at Jerusalem only, but everywhere."[223] Luther believes that Obadiah anticipates how the messianic kingdom is not to be reserved for Israel or Judah alone; instead, Obadiah "mixes all the nations together, Ephraim, Benjamin, Gilead, the Philistines, the Canaanites, Zarephath. This cannot be understood to refer

---

220. *LW* 18:189; WA 13:205, "Hoc est, non solum Iudaei erunt in hoc tabernaculo sed etiam reliquiae Edom et omnium gentium, quae euangelio sunt crediturae."

221. *LW* 18:190; WA 13:205, "De spirituali reductione et conversione loquitur, . . . Hac reductione reducti sunt omnes, quotquot Christo veniente euangelio crediderunt et in tabernaculum illud Davidis per fidem sunt translate."

222. Italics mine; *LW* 35:320; WA, *DB* 11.2:226, "und seind buch damit beschleusst."

223. *LW* 35:322; WA, *DB* 11.2:250, "Am ende weissagt er von Christus Reich, das sole nicht allein zu Jersusalem, sondern allenthalben sein." Luther proposes the same synopsis in the introduction to his *Lectures on Obadiah*, "Then, from the destruction of those nations which by the judgment of God had destroyed the kingdom of Judah, *he goes over to the kingdom of Christ, which is going to come through the Gospel and in which the remnants of Ephraim, Israel, and others were to flourish*" (italics mine); *LW* 18:194; WA 13:216.

to the temporal kingdom of Israel, for according to the law of Moses these tribes and people had to remain separate and distinct in the land."[224]

The *Lectures on Obadiah* reveal a fuller picture of Luther's interpretation. The *Preface to Obadiah* tells that the prophet begins his prophecy about the "kingdom of Christ" at the end of the book. In his prior lectures, Luther identifies this transition at Obadiah 1:17.[225] Luther understands Obadiah to be foretelling the end of the physical kingdom of the Jews while imparting hope that a new kingdom will be recovered at Mount Zion. As Luther explains, "Now that the Jews have been carried off into captivity and the Edomites who mocked the Jews have in turn been destroyed, he promises another kingdom, which we can understand in no other way than as the spiritual kingdom of Christ spread among all nations through the Gospel."[226] Moreover, Luther assigns "Mount Zion" in Obadiah 1:17 to Jerusalem, the city where the Messiah will begin his "new kingdom" and from where the gospel of this kingdom will be carried out to bring in subjects from all nations.[227] In his exposition of the remaining verses from Obadiah 1:18–21, Luther continues the theme of how Obadiah discloses the messianic hope and its "newness" beyond the demise of the physical, temporal kingdom of the Jews operative only under the old covenant.

PREFACE TO THE PROPHET JONAH

Luther allots the bulk of the *Preface to Jonah* to determining Jonah's identity. Contrary to Jerome and others who claim that Jonah was the son of the Zarephath widow from 1 Kings 17:8–24, Luther contends that Jonah was the son of Amittai, and lived under the rule of King Jeroboam based upon 2 Kings 14:25.[228] In Luther's estimation, Jonah's major contribution as an OT prophet is how God used him to prefigure the spread of the gospel to

---

224. *LW* 35:322; *WA, DB* 11.2:250, "Denn er menget alle völcker jnn einander, als Ephraim, BenJamin, Gallaad, Philister, Cananiter, Zarpath, welchs nicht kan vom zeitlichen reich Israel verstanden warden, da solche stemme und volck im lande unterscheiden sein müsten, nach dem gestze Mosi."

225. Luther's first words for Obadiah 1:17 are: "Here begins the latter section of this prophecy." *LW* 18:200; *WA* 13:220.

226. *LW* 18:200; *WA* 13:220, "[I]n qua abductis in captivitatem Iudaeis et vastatis rursum Idumaeis, qui Iudaeis insultaverant, promittit aliud regnum quod non potest aliud intelligi nisi regnum spirituale Christi per euangelium propalatum in omnes gentes."

227. *LW* 18:201; *WA* 13:221.

228. *LW* 35:323–24; *WA, DB* 11.2:258.

the Gentiles.[229] Outside of this observation, Luther is silent in the *Preface to Jonah* regarding more direct or explicit ways Jonah may have prophesied of the coming Christ.[230]

PREFACE TO THE PROPHET MICAH

Whereas Luther's *Preface to Jonah* is lacking in content associated with how the prophet is a witness to Christ, the *Preface to Micah* abounds with such material in only a few short paragraphs. From the start, Luther says that Micah and Isaiah were contemporaries who "preached almost the very same word concerning Christ."[231] Also, in contrast to his impression of other prophets like Amos and Obadiah whose words of judgment predominate their prophecies, Luther describes Micah as "one of the fine prophets who rebukes the people severely for their idolatry and *constantly refers to the coming Christ and to his kingdom*."[232] So, Micah intersperses prophetic utterances of the coming Messiah in the midst of his task to uphold the first commandment rather than saving them until the end.

More specifically, Luther identifies Micah 5:2 as a messianic text that grants the prophet a unique assignment to disclose the city of Bethlehem as the Messiah's birthplace. Here, Luther finds endorsement from Matthew

229. *LW* 35:324; WA, *DB* 11.2:258, 260. Cf. Luther's statement from the preface to his *Lectures on Jonah*: "The role of this prophet was to be the prophet to the Gentiles, and this was his special duty alone." *LW* 19:4; WA 13:241.

230. Luther's *Lectures on Jonah* (Latin text) contains various attempts to interpret the book in reference to Christ, primarily in a figural sense. For instance, commenting upon Jonah 1:11, Luther calls Jonah a "figure of Christ" (*figura Christi*) (*LW* 19:14; WA 13:248). At the end of his lectures, Luther closes with the following summation to illustrate how Jonah's narrative prefigures Christ's person and work: "Christ came into 'the sea,' that is, into the world. And when He had come into the world, 'the sea' was disturbed because of Him, since the Son of God was received by some but not by others. He was devoured by 'a large fish,' that is, by Satan, the ruler of this world. For Satan and hell and death 'swallowed' Christ when He was hanging on the cross, as if they would destroy Him, but He could not be held by them, for that was impossible, as Peter says, Acts 2:24. And so it was necessary for Him 'to be vomited up.' He came back to life, and this became an opportunity for life, which before had been an opportunity for death. In this way death has become the door to life for us; disgrace has become the elevation to glory; condemnation and hell, the door to salvation. And this has happened through Christ, who was sinless, etc." *LW* 19:31; WA 13:258.

231. *LW* 35:324; WA, *DB* 11.2:270, "von Christo schier cinerley wort gepredigt haben."

232. Italics mine; *LW* 35:324; WA, *DB* 11.2:270, "Es ist aber der feinen Propheten einer, der das volck umb jrer abgötterrey willen hefftiglich strafft, und den künfftigen Christum, und sein reich, jmer dar anzeucht."

2:5–6. The pinpointing of the Messiah's origin is just another factor from the prophets to increase certainty in the Jews's hope that God would, indeed, make good on his promises to send the Christ despite their own experiences of divine punishment. The prophets collectively provide both general and specific characteristics of the coming Messiah and his kingdom in order to serve the people's faith. Luther's assertion in his exposition of Micah 5:2 from the *Lectures on Micah* displays this conviction:

> You see, that faith might be made certain, a definite person, place, and time had to be designated for the newborn church. So here the prophet is describing the definite place, just as other prophets described the time when this King was going to come, namely, after the Babylonian captivity. The person, then, is Christ; the place, Bethlehem; the time, after the Babylonian captivity.[233]

To return to the *Preface to Micah* for *Die Propheten alle Deutsch*, Luther condenses his view of Micah's writing into an illustrative statement of how he perceives Christ as the literal sense of Scripture in the prophets: "In short he denounces, he prophesies [*weissaget*], he preaches [*prediget*], etc. *Ultimately,* however, his *meaning* [*meinung*] is that even though Israel and Judah have to go to pieces, *Christ will yet come and make all things good.*"[234] A similar synopsis was made previously in his preface to the *Lectures on Micah*. Instead of Isaiah, Luther regards Micah and Hosea as sharing in the same prophecy for "[t]hey both saw so many prophets and such a complete expression of the Word sent in vain, they saw so many prophets despised and, in fact, killed that they foretold that both kingdoms would be destroyed. *Yet there was the clear promise of God that the kingdom of David would be an external kingdom, that no leader would be taken away from the throne of David until the Messiah would come.*"[235] Such pronouncements show the

---

233. *LW* 18:247; WA 13:324, "Oportuit enim certam personam, certum locum et certum tempus pro nascentis ecclesiae exordio designari, ut fides certificaretur. Ideo hic certum locum describit propheta sicut et alii prophetae tempus quo venturus erat hic rex nempe post captivitatem Babylonicam. Persona ergo Christus est, locus est Bethelehem, tempus est post captivitatem Babylonicam."

234. Italics mine; *LW* 35:325; WA, *DB* 11.2:270, "Summa, Er schillt, er weissaget, prediget, etc. Aber endlich ist das seine meinung, Wenn es gleich alles mus zu drümmern gehen, Israel und Juda, so wird doch der Christus komen, ders alles gut machen wird."

235. *LW* 18:208; WA 13:300, "Viderunt frustra mitti tam multos prophetas, tam copiosum verbum, viderunt prophetas contemni, immo occidi, ideo utrumque regnum praedicebant devastandum, quod tamen promissionem deit habebat apertam, nempe externum fore regnum David, non auferendum ducem de solio David, donec

import of the messianic hope for Luther's vision of Christ in the OT. The aim of the prophets like Micah, in Luther's portrayal, could be summed up as the progressive revelation of the coming Messiah, his salvation, and his kingdom as a message of promise for the people's faith and of comfort for their hope.

Preface to the Prophet Nahum

For the overall theme of Nahum, Luther says that the prophet is "[t]rue to his name," which the Reformer takes to mean, "*consolator,* or comforter."[236] Nahum's prophecy mainly "comforts God's people, telling them that their enemies, the Assyrians, shall in turn be destroyed."[237] Yet, beyond this temporal promise, Luther regards Nahum 1:15 as the christological horizon where lasting hope is given to the prophet's audience.[238] Although he concedes that a historical referent could be in this passage's view, Luther replies, "nevertheless, this is a general prophecy [*weissagung*] referring also to Christ. It declares that the good news and the joyous worship of God, taught and confirmed by God's word, shall remain in Judah."[239] In his comments on Nahum 1:15 from his *Lectures on Nahum,* Luther offers further explanation of how this text is "a general prophecy referring to Christ."

Of Nahum 1:15, Luther claims, "There is no other passage in this prophet which we can take as related to Christ except this one."[240] It is at this juncture in Nahum's prophecy that Luther can digress, "In this way are we all convinced that *there is not any one prophet* who did not blend

---

veniert Messias: sic enim aperte habet promissio."

236. *LW* 35:326; WA, *DB* 11.2:288, "Also tröstet er nach seinem namen (Denn Nahum heisst Consolator, auff Deudsch, Ein tröster), . . ." Cf. "The Preface and Hypothesis for the Prophet Nahum" to his *Lectures on Nahum:* "Even the name of the prophet fits the prophecy. You see, Nahum means 'comforter,' or 'comforted,' to the Jews. He does justice to his name in every respect through his prophecy, for there is nothing else in it than comfort for the remnant of the people of Judah, which had been preserved from the destruction of Israel." *LW* 18:281; WA 13:371.

237. *LW* 35:236; WA, *DB* 11.2:288, "das volck Gottes, wie jre feinde die Affyreer, sollen widderumb verstöret werden."

238. Nah 1:15, "Behold, upon the mountains, the feet of him who brings good news, who publishes peace! Keep your feasts, O Judah; fulfill your vows, for never again shall the worthless pass through you; he is utterly cut off."

239. *LW* 35:326; WA, *DB* 11.2:288, "Doc ists ein gemeine weissagung, auch auff Christum, das jnn Juda bleiben solt die gute botschafft, und der fröliche Gottes dienst, durch Gottes wort, geleret und bekrefftiget."

240. *LW* 18:295; WA 13:380–81, "alioqui nullus est alius in hoc propheta locus, qui de Christo intelligi posset praeter hunc."

something of his prophecy with the coming of Christ and the grace to be revealed through Christ."[241] This "blending" requires careful interpretive discernment, which leads Luther to consider how Nahum 1:15 could have an expansive meaning, where the prophet has both temporal and spiritual promises in mind. So, Luther posits,

> I believe that we must not only take this passage to refer to the Gospel of grace promised and revealed to us through Christ, by which believers become the sons of God and coheirs with Christ, but I think we must also understand it to apply to temporal promises such as to a vanquished and routed enemy, to the spoils gathered, to a hallowed peace, etc. I really think that he makes this as a general statement about temporal victory to which he still connects in a general way the grace of Christ and the Gospel.[242]

It seems Luther senses the tension to do justice to this text within its historical setting while not dismissing its Christian-theological purview. Even though he allows for scant evidence of prophecies about the coming Christ in Nahum, when Luther does highlight its presence, he interprets the prophetic account within the context of the future Messiah's person and work conjoined with its implications for the faith and hope of God's people awaiting the first advent.

Preface to the Prophet Zephaniah

In this preface, Luther introduces Zephaniah as a peer to Jeremiah and that both men prophesied God's punishment upon Judah and Jerusalem culminating with the Babylonian exile.[243] Not until his summation of chapter 3 does Luther acknowledge that Zephaniah "prophesies [*weissagt*] gloriously and clearly of the happy and blessed kingdom of Christ, which shall be spread abroad in all the world."[244] Moreover, Luther credits Zephaniah

241. *LW* 18:295; WA 13:380, "Sic nobis omnibus persuasum est non esse unum aliquem prophetarum, qui non immiscuerit aliquid suae prophetiae de venturo Christo et de revelanda per Christum gratia."

242. *LW* 18:295; WA 13:381, "Ita etiam in hoc nostro propheta Nahum non solum de euangelio gratiae per Christum nobis promissae et exhibitae, qua credentes fiunt filii dei et cohaeredes Christi, sed etiam de temporalibus promissionibus puto hunc locum esse intelligendum ut de victo et fuso hoste, de collecta praeda, de sancita pace etc. Proinde generali sentential dictum puto de Victoria temporali, cui tamen gratia Christi et euangelium generaliter sit insertum."

243. *LW* 35:328; WA, *DB* 11.2:310.

244. *LW* 35:329; WA, *DB* 11.2:310, "Im dritten Capitel, weissagt era us der massen

with abundantly bearing witness to Christ in short space, for "Although he is a minor prophet, he speaks more about Christ than many other major prophets, almost more than Jeremiah even."[245] It is almost as if Luther sees Zephaniah working from the premise that the "comfort" must be in proportion to the sorrow. A remedy to guard the Jews from utter despair due to their Babylonian captivity, Zephaniah offers much prophetic proclamation of the messianic hope so that the people could "be sure that after this punishment they would receive grace again and *get the promised* [*verheissen*] *Savior, Christ, with his glorious kingdom.*"[246]

Luther's perception of Zephaniah's prophecy of Christ is primarily within the context of Jesus's messianic identity and work. The Jews had from God a clear messianic promise of a particular Christ with revealed characteristics of his person and ministry for ushering in a new, spiritual kingdom whose breadth would encompass all nations. The hope of God's people in Zephaniah, therefore, is not merely in the promise of their return to the land; it is that God's divine discipline and punishment against their sinful idolatry will not interfere with the certain, future reality that they will one day "get [their] promised Savior, Christ, with his glorious kingdom."[247] For this prophetic word to be an actual "comfort" to the Jews, the proclamation of Christ in this manner must be at the surface literalness of the OT text.

Preface to the Prophet Haggai

To begin the *Preface to Haggai*, Luther informs the reader of the new historical setting Haggai represents compared to most of the prophets already reviewed, for he "is the first prophet given to the people after the Babylonian captivity, and by his prophecy the temple and the worship of God were set up again."[248] As a post-exilic prophet, Haggai had to proclaim afresh the

---

herrlich und klerlich, von dem frölichen und seligen reich Christi, das jnn aller welt ausgebreitet solt werden." Cf. with a similar assessment from the introduction to his *Lectures on Zephaniah*, "Among the minor prophets, he makes the clearest prophecies about the kingdom of Christ." *LW* 18:319; WA 13:480.

245. *LW* 35:329; WA, *DB* 11.2:310, "Und wie wol er klein Prophet ist, So redet er doch mehr von Christo, denn viel andere grossen Propheten, auch schier uber Jeremiam."

246. *LW* 35:329; WA, *DB* 11.2:310, "Sondern gewis weren, das sie nach solcher strafe, wider zu gnaden komen, und den verheissen Heiland Christum mit seinem herrlichen Königreich kriegen solten."

247. *LW* 35:329; WA, *DB* 11.2:310.

248. *LW* 35:329; WA, *DB* 11.2:320, "Haggai ist der erst Prophet, so nach dem gefengnis Babel dem volck gegeben ist, durch welch weissagung, der Tempel und Gottes

Word of God to the people who "had fallen into great doubt whether the temple would ever be rebuilt."[249] Still, Haggai's exhortation and "comforting" prophetic word is not limited to temporal, physical concerns for the Jews. In the final chapter, Luther observes that Haggai "prophesies [*weissagt*] also of Christ in chapter 2, that he shall soon come as a 'comfort of all nations,' by which he indicates in a mystery that the kingdom and the laws of the Jews shall have an end, and the kingdoms of all the world shall be destroyed and become subject to Christ."[250]

To offer an example of Luther's understanding concerning how Haggai bears witness to Christ, his thoughts on Haggai 2:6 from the *Lectures on Haggai* are emblematic.[251] When Haggai reports that God will once again "shake" all of creation, Luther reads it as a reference to the Lord's toleration of the wicked until the time of Christ. Meanwhile, God continues to work through the physical kingdom of the Jews to rebuild the temple despite their

---

dienst wider angerichtet ward."

249. *LW* 35:329; WA, *DB* 11.2:320, "Denn das volck war fast jnn zweiuel gefallen, ob der temple solt widderumb gebawet werden." Cf. Luther's similar account in the preface to his *Lectures on Haggai*, "The Word of God has this character that it is made known and comes when man is most desperate over everything, when he thinks that nothing is less likely to happen than what the Word of God says most certainly will happen . . . For the violence of the neighboring peoples was such that the Jews were forced to build with one hand and to fight with the other to ward off the hostile nations. Yet, against all these fierce and powerful foes this one weak prophet here dares to rise up and prophesy about rebuilding the temple. So he orders this handful of people, who had just recently been snatched from a most burdensome captivity, to stand up against a mad and inflated king who didn't want them to rebuild the temple." *LW* 18:369; WA 13:533.

250. *LW* 35:330; WA, *DB* 11.2:320, "Er weissagt auch von Christo, im andern Capitel, das er schier komen solt, ein Trost aller Heiden, damit er heimlich anzeigt, das der Jüden reich und gesetz solt ein ende haben, und aller welt Königreiche zerstöret, und Christo unterthan werden." When Luther encounters Haggai 2:1 in his prior *Lectures on Haggai*, he communicates the same interpretation. On Haggai 2:1, he comments, "Here the new chapter and a new discourse begin . . . With this passage the prophet begins a third discourse, in which he comforts the people as he describes the kingdom of Christ which was coming and which was, in fact, imminent and had to be declared immediately. Here, you see, the prophet is describing the kingdom of Christ in such a way that it appears as if it were standing at the door (as we commonly say). He declares it as so near that there is hardly another of the prophets who achieves the same thing. He gives himself completely over to a description of the kingdom of Christ so that the people most certainly should believe the truth of His promises." *LW* 18:379; WA, *DB* 11.2:539.

251. Hag 2:6, "For thus says the LORD of hosts: Yet once more, in a little while, I will shake the heavens and the earth and the sea and the dry land."

continual unbelief because he had promised their "fathers" that through them the Messiah would come.[252] So, Luther asserts,

> He looks only at the coming kingdom of Christ. Because of Him—that is, Christ the King—he tolerates all men alike, since indeed Christ was going to be born of one of them. This passage very clearly and very obviously convinces all the Jews so that they are unable to contradict it. You see, it clearly indicates that this first people (that is, the Jews) would endure in the flesh up to the coming of Christ. It could not perish before Christ's birth. Because of Christ the external people were being preserved, and God was calling them His people, separate and select from all the nations of the earth.[253]

For the remainder of his exposition of Haggai 2, Luther unfolds the various facets of Haggai's prophecy of the coming Messiah and his kingdom and how this forthcoming reality strengthens the hopes of the Jews whose faith in the certainty of God's eschatological promises is continually under the threat of unbelief. In this way, the *Lectures on Haggai* reveal what Luther sketches in his *Preface to Haggai* for the *Die Propheten alle Deutsch* about chapter 2 of this OT prophet's writing. Once again, the messianic portrait, exemplified here by the prophet Haggai, serves as the essence of Luther's view of Christ as the central subject matter (i.e., the literal sense) of the OT.

PREFACE TO THE PROPHET ZECHARIAH

Luther's *Preface to Zechariah* starts by placing Zechariah alongside Haggai, who together summoned the Jews to rebuild Jerusalem and to reestablish themselves as an ordered society following the Babylonian exile. Zechariah, in Luther's characterization, "is truly one of the most comforting of the prophets."[254] In execution of this aspect of his prophetic office, Luther says that Zechariah offers "many lovely and reassuring visions, and gives many

---

252. *LW* 18:381; WA 13:540.

253. *LW* 18:381; WA 13:540, "Non respicit in merita aut demerita sed tantum in futurum regnum Christi. Propter illum scil. regem Christum tolerat omnes iuxta, siquidem ex ipsorum erat nasciturus Christus. Hic autem locus apertissime et evidentissime convincit Iudaeos omnes, ut non possint contradicere, nam aperte indicat primum illum populum (hoc est Iudaeos) carnalem mansurum ad adventum Christi. neque potuit perire ante natum Christum, propter quem servabatur populus externus, quem separatum et selectum ab omnibus nationibus terrae vocabat deus suum populum."

254. *LW* 35:330; WA, *DB* 11.2:328, "Und ist fur war der aller tröstlichsten Propheten einer."

sweet and kindly words" for the Jews's encouragement to press forward in
pursuit of national recovery in the face of resistance and hardships. This
aim sums up what concerns Zechariah's prophecy until chapter 5 in Luther's
outline.[255]

At this moment in the preface, Luther proceeds to highlight key chapters that include explicit predictions of the coming Christ and his kingdom.
To start, Luther posits that Zechariah 5 speaks of "the false teachers who
are later to come among the Jewish people, and who will deny Christ."[256] In
chapter 6, Luther reports that Zechariah "prophesies [*weissagt*] of the gospel
of Christ and the spiritual temple to be built in all the world, because the
Jews denied him and would not have him."[257] That "the whole world shall be
opened to the coming gospel of Christ" as a result of Alexander the Great's
empire and "the King Christ [will come] into Jerusalem on an ass" are direct
prophecies Luther attributes to Zechariah 9 and 10.[258] The eleventh chapter
features the climax of this prophet's witness to the coming Messiah and the
new kingdom he will establish. Luther summarizes:

> [H]e prophesies [*weissagt*] that Christ shall be sold by the Jews
> for thirty pieces of silver, for which cause Christ will leave
> them, so that Jerusalem will be destroyed and the Jews will be
> hardened in their error and dispersed. Thus the gospel and the
> kingdom of Christ will come to the Gentiles, after the sufferings
> of Christ, in which he, as the Shepherd, shall first be beaten, and
> the apostles, as the sheep, be scattered. For Christ had to suffer
> first and thus enter into his glory.[259]

255. *LW* 35:330–31; WA, *DB* 11.2:328, "Denn er viel lieblicher und tröstlicher gesichte fur bringt, und viel süsser und freundlicher wort gibt, . . ."

256. *LW* 35:331; WA, *DB* 11.2:328, "Im funfften, weissagt er unter einem gesicht
des brieues und scheffels von den falschen lerern, die hernach komen solten, im Jü-
dischen volck, die Christum verleugnen würden."

257. *LW* 35:331; WA, *DB* 11.2:328, "Im Sechsten, weissagt er von dem Euangelio
Christi, und dem geistlichen temple jnn aller welt zu bawen, weil jn die Jüden verleug-
ten und nicht haben wolten."

258. *LW* 35:331; WA, *DB* 11.2:328, "Im neunden, gehet er jnn die zukünfftigen zeit,
und weissagt erstlich, cap. ix. wie der grosse Alexander solte Tirum, Zidon und die
Philister gewinnen, damit die gantze welt geöffenet würde dem zukünfftigen Euangelio Christi, und füret den König Christum zu Jerusalem ein, auff einem esel etc."

259. *LW* 35:331; WA, *DB* 11.2:328, "Aber im .xi. weissagt er, das Christus von
den Jüden verkaufft solt werden umb dreissig silberlinge, Darumb er sie auch verlas-
sen würde, das Jerusalem endlich zerstöret, und die Jüden im jrthum verstockt und
zerstrewet solten werden, Und also das Euangelion und das reich Christi unter die
Heiden komen, nach dem leiden Christi, damit er vorhin also der Hirtegeschlagen,
und die Apostel als die schafe zerstrewet solten werden, Denn er muste vorhin leiden,

As with most of the Minor Prophets, Luther's lectures from 1524 to 1526 provide further illumination on his interpretive and theological presentation in their respective prefaces for *Die Propheten alle Deutsch* in 1532. Luther's exegesis of Zechariah is no exception, and contains a tremendous amount of textual exposition in reference to the coming Christ and his kingdom. From a broader perspective, understanding how Zechariah falls into line with Luther's general definition of an OT prophet shows continuity with previous iterations while displaying what the Reformer considers the essence of his prophecy's purpose. The prefatory writings to the *Lectures on Zechariah* supply such material.

From the Latin manuscript of these lectures, Luther's introductory thoughts feature a general assessment of the post-exilic prophet's task. The primary responsibility of prophets such as Haggai and Zechariah, in Luther's estimation, could be singularly summed up as: "to comfort the remnant of a dispersed people wretchedly afflicted by captivity and to encourage them not to despair."[260] But as has been shown thus far in the investigation of Luther's vision of an OT prophet, this "comforting" role foremost consists of the proclamation of the Messiah. And so, Luther says that Zechariah's prophetic word of consolation ensures that, "*They should not lose confidence that the divine promises made to them about their coming King would be fulfilled:* that Christ their King would finally come in spite of their totally desperate situation, in spite of their devastated land, in spite of a dispersed people facing a miserable death."[261]

In addition to the original *Lectures on Zechariah* in Latin, Luther subsequently reworked the material to appear in German for publication as a single volume in 1527.[262] Following the formal preface to the German edition, Luther includes further introductory comments before engaging the biblical text. His first words recall what Habakkuk himself has already

---

und also jnn seine herrligkeit komen."

260. *LW* 20:3; *WA* 13:546, [N]empe hoc unum maxime agere, ut confortentur et animentur reliquiae populi dispersi per captivitatem misereque afflicti, ne desperent, . . ."

261. Italics mine; *LW* 20:3; *WA* 13:546, "ne diffident promissionibus divinis de futuro rege sibi promissis, fore ut impleantur, venturum tandem regem Christum, utut res in summa sit desperatione, utut terra vastata, populus dispersus sit et misere perierit."

262. The Latin lectures are translated from the Alternburg text (*WA* 13) published posthumously from student manuscripts. The German text (*WA* 23) represents Luther's second lectures on Zechariah that he had published himself in December, 1527. The manuscript evidence for Luther's lectures on the Minor Prophets is complex, and has a long history. For a concise account, see the editor's "Introduction" to *LW* 18:ix–xii.

taught, namely, "that the office and the preaching of the old prophets were twofold. *First, they were to educate the people and prepare them for the coming kingdom of the Messiah.*"[263] The second office, according to Luther, pertains to admonishing the Jews to submit to the custodial function of the Law until the first advent of the Christ.[264] In the meantime, Zechariah must continue to comfort the Jews with the messianic hope "so that these people might not despair of this kingdom, even though it might appear to them that the kingdom would never come, because they were so greatly tormented, oppressed, taken captive, and led away by the Gentiles."[265]

In short, Luther reckons Zechariah to be a "model" (*stücken*) prophet who ably fulfills his office through general and specific prophecies of the coming Christ and his kingdom.[266] While doing so, Zechariah faithfully wields the double-edged sword of preaching the law followed by the "comforting" word of hope in God's sure messianic promise.

PREFACE TO THE PROPHET MALACHI

Luther opens the preface, telling that Malachi was the last OT prophet prior to Christ's birth. "He is a fine prophet," Luther goes on to say, "and his book contains beautiful sayings about Christ and the gospel."[267] Luther keeps the *Preface to Malachi* brief, so he does not move forward to uncover these instances of christological prophecies. He does, however, allot space to indicate how Malachi predicts the ministry of John the Baptist. He presents this prophecy through the lens of the NT's use of the OT, when he reflects, "Again he prophesies [*weissagt*] of the coming of John the Baptist, as Christ himself in Matthew 11 interprets that of which Malachi writes, calling John

---

263. Italics mine; *LW* 20:158; WA 23:501, "Im Propheten Habacuc wir gehöret, wie der allten Propheten ampt und predigt sey gewesen von den zweyen stücken: Das erst, das sie das volck ynn zucht hielten und bereitten auff das zukünfftig reich Messie."

264. In this passage, Luther cites Gal 3:24 for support, where the Apostle Paul explains, "So then, the law was our guardian until Christ came, in order that we might be justified by faith." Here, Luther paraphrases, "The Law was our custodian until Christ came." *LW* 20:158: WA 23:501, "Das gesetze ist unser schulmeister gewesen auff den zukünfftigen Christum."

265. *LW* 20:158; WA 23:501, "und auch trösten, das sie nicht dran verzweifeln sollen, obs sich gleich lest ansehen, als wolts nicht komen, weil sie so wurden geplagt, untergedruckt, gefangen und weggefurt von den heiden."

266. *LW* 20:159; WA 23:502.

267. *LW* 35:332; WA, *DB* 11.2:362, "Und ist ein feiner Prophet, ders schöne sprüche hat, von Christo und dem Euangelio."

his messenger and Elijah."[268] Hereafter, Luther recounts Malachi's denunciations against God's people from their failure to tithe properly to their propensity to divorce.[269]

Luther's statement about Malachi's prophetic testimony to Christ is upfront, though in passing in the *Preface to Malachi*. A few notable examples of these prophecies about the coming Christ can be found in his *Lectures on Malachi*. In his exposition of Malachi 3:1, Luther identifies Christ as the "messenger of the covenant" (*angelus testamenti*) who is "the Lord whom you seek" (*Dominator, quem vos desideratis*).[270] Because the Messiah appears to be anticipated in this verse, Luther asserts, "The covenant [*testamentum*] is the promises of God, which all point to Christ, even the temporal promises."[271] This all-encompassing statement reinforces the messianic nature of his view that Christ is the *sensus literalis* of Scripture. All promises from God, both temporal and eternal, are meant to direct the Jews's hearts to hope for the long-promised Messiah, through whose life, ministry, death, and resurrection, the gospel of this "new testament" for the forgiveness of sins would be offered to all nations, where faith is the only requirement to become an heir of such an inestimable inheritance.

To introduce Malachi 4 concerning the "day" that is coming (Mal 4:1), Luther immediately declares: "All this is being said about Christ."[272] A few lines later, he clarifies that this "day" is "the day of Christ's kingdom."[273] Malachi 4:2, and the prophecy of the future "Sun of Righteousness," of course, affords Luther ample opportunity to wax eloquently on how Christ and his

---

268. *LW* 35:332; WA, *DB* 11.2:362, "Item, er weissagt von der zukunfft Johannis des Teuffers, wie es Christus selbs, Matthei .xi. deutet, und Johannem, seinen Engel und Eliam nennet, dauon Maleachi schreibt."

269. *LW* 35:332–33; WA, *DB* 11.2:362, 364.

270. *LW* 18:409; WA 13:693.

271. *LW* 18:409; WA 13:693, "Testamentum promissiones dei sunt, quae omnes tendunt in Christum, etiam temporales." Richard Dinda, translator for the *Lectures on Malachi* for vol. 18 of the American edition of *Luther's Works*, rendered "testamentum" as "covenant" in this selection. Given Luther's subsequent comments on how this "testamentum" requires someone's death, transliterating the word into the English "testament" probably fits best within the context of Luther's theology of testament, which stands in contrast to the notion of a biblical covenant as a bilateral agreement. "Testamentum" in Luther is soley a one-way promise from God that requires death; a covenant does not; this thought appears to be what the Reformer is clearly expressing at this point. For a brief and insightful comparison between "testament" and "covenant" in Luther's theology, see Hagen, "Luther, Martin," 691–92.

272. *LW* 18:417; WA 13:700, "Haec omnia de Christo dicuntur . . ."

273. *LW* 18:417; WA 13:701, "'Veniet dies' scil. regni Christi."

gospel fulfill this prophecy.[274] And last, Luther's closing reflection on Malachi 4:4, wherein the prophet exhorts the people of God to "remember" the Law of Moses, provides a fitting summation of his interpretation of Malachi's prophetic witness to Christ:

> Malachi has now prophesied about the kingdom of Christ, but it has not yet come. He says: "In the meantime, be included under the Law until that Sun shines. The Law will last until the time of Him who will not come without first sending ahead His messenger, who will say that He is there. Therefore neither neglect Moses nor put him aside. He bears witness to you about Christ; he holds you back from evil. When the time comes for Me to free you, I will send you My messenger in the spirit and courage of Elijah, etc." This passage, then, is the closing of Holy Scripture, the end of the Old Testament. Here the prophet stops and waits for the messenger Elijah, who is John the Baptist, . . .The time of the Gospel is the day. All the rest is night and darkness, You see, Christ Himself is the Sun.[275]

In short, an apt characterization of Luther's portrayal of the OT prophet's office and message could take the form of Malachi's (Malachi 3:1) and Isaiah's (Isaiah 40:3) prophecy of John the Baptist's (Matthew 3:3) ministry: "Prepare the way of the Lord," the appearing of the promised Messiah, the Sun of Righteousness.

1533

From 1529 to 1530 with the help of others, Luther worked to complete an exhaustive revision of his *German New Testament*. During his seclusion at the Coburg fortress awaiting the commencement of the Ausburg Diet, Luther labored over these revisions and also made plans to write a treatise solely devoted to the doctrine of justification.[276] It is within this setting that

---

274. *LW* 18:417; WA 13:701.

275. *LW* 18:419; WA 13:702–3, "Malachias prophetavit nunc de regno Christi sed nondum adest. Interim, inquit, concludamini in lege, donec ille sol elucescat. Lex duret ad illum, qui non veniet nisi praemisso nuncio, qui dicet eum adesse. Nolite ergo negligere et seponere Mosen, qui testificatur vobis de Christo et cohercet vos a malo. Et quando tempus aderit, ut liberem vos, mittam vobis nuncium in spiritu et virtute Heliae etc. Hic ergo textus est clausula scripturae sanctae, finis veteris testamenti. Hic cessat prophetia et expecatur nuntius Helias, qui est Ioannes Baptista, . . . Tempus eaungelii dies est, reliqua Omnia nox et Tenebrae. Ipse enim Christus est sol."

276. Reu, *Luther's German Bible*, 183. For Luther's projected sketch of this work that was never completed, see WA 30.2:657–76.

Luther edited both his translation of the Old and New Testaments and the prefaces. Probably the most significant outcome for the prefaces due to this sustained meditation upon justification was the creation of a brand new prologue to introduce the book of Acts. It appeared in print for the first time with the 1533 *German New Testament,* and thereafter, was incorporated into the complete editions of the *Deutsche Bibel* beginning in 1534.[277]

PREFACE TO THE ACTS OF THE APOSTLES

The intrigue of Luther's *Preface to Acts* resides in his fresh appraisal of Luke's main objective. Luther's opening lines establish the contrastive backdrop, when he submits that, "Contrary to what has sometimes been the practice, this book should not be read or regarded as though St. Luke had written about the personal work or history of the apostles simply as an example of good works or good life."[278] To counter such an approach to Acts, Luther proposes, "Rather it should be noted that by this book St. Luke teaches the whole of Christendom, even to the end of the world, that *the true and chief article of Christian doctrine is this: We must all be justified alone by faith in Jesus Christ,* without any contribution from the law or help from our works."[279] What Luther seeks to persuade biblical readers of is that Luke's narrative purpose involves primarily a theological aim, not a mere historical one. Thus, he concludes, "This doctrine is the chief intention [*meinung*] of the book and the author's principal reason for writing it."[280]

Although the *Preface to Acts* does not offer explicit instruction on how to read Christ as the literal sense of Scripture, Luther's doctrinal formula of

277. Ibid., 227–29; Brecht, *Martin Luther: The Preservation of the Church,* 103.

278. *LW* 35:363; WA, *DB* 6:414, "Dis Buch sol man lesen und ansehen, nicht, wie wir etwan gethan haben, als hette Sanct Lucas darinn allein die eigen personliche werck odder geschichte der Aposteln geschrieben, zum exempel guter werke, odder gutes lebens."

279. Italics mine; *LW* 35:363; WA, *DB* 6:414, "Sondern darauff sol man mercken, das Sanct Lucas mit disesem buch, die gantze Christenheit leret, bis an der welt ende, das rechte heubstück Christlicher lere, Nemlich, wie wir alle müssen gerecht werden, allein durch den glauben an Jhesu Christo, on alles zuthun des Gesetzes, odder hülffe unser werck."

280. *LW* 35:363; WA, *DB* 6:414, "Solch stuck ist seine furnemeste meinung und ursache dieses buchs zu schreiben." In his notes from his edition of the 1530 *German New Testament,* Luther reveals what he wishes to convey in a preface for Acts, when it appears in print again with the rest of the *Deutsche Bibel.* Under a heading that says, "Acta Apostolorum. in fronte Libri," he writes, "Actus Apostolorum liber est proprie pertinens ad probandum, iustificationem contingere sine operibus et sola fide." WA, *DB* 4:457.

"justification by faith alone *in Jesus Christ*" assumes it. Now that the long-promised Messiah and his kingdom have come, the gospel of that "kingdom" is to be proclaimed in fullness to the ends of the earth. Therefore, in his analysis of Acts, Luther places the apostolic preaching of Peter, Paul, Stephen, and Philip in first order. These are the most important elements of the book of Acts in Luther's view for understanding Luke's authorial purpose. Moreover, Luther considers Luke's Acts to contain example after example of what it means to preach *and* to receive the gospel of Jesus Christ for both Jews and Gentiles. At every instance, "You will find that it all adds up to one thing: we must come into grace and be justified only through faith in Christ, without law and works."[281] Luther even goes so far as to suggest, "this book might well be called a commentary on the epistles of St. Paul."[282]

In the end, the ability to be justified by faith presupposes the person and work of Jesus Christ. So from this vantage point, the doctrine of justification ought not to be viewed as a competing subject with "Christ" for Luther's conception of the *sensus literalis* of Scripture; rather, the one is made possible by the other.

1534

The publication of Luther's German translation of the prophets in 1532 marked a milestone in his goal to offer the entire Bible in the vernacular. With Scripture printed in multiple parts since the *Septembertestament* of 1522, the task now for Luther and his translation committee was to submit everything to revision for a first edition of the complete Bible. In August, 1534, Luther's dream came to fruition under the title, *Biblia, das ist, die gantze Heilige Schrifft Deudsch. Mart. Luth. Wittemberg.*[283] As early as 1539, the committee had reconvened to consider a major revision of the complete *Deutsche Bibel.*[284] The fruit of these labors appeared with the edition of 1541

281. *LW* 35:364; WA, *DB* 6:416, "So wirstu finden, das es alles dahin gehet, das wire allein durch den glauben Christi, on Gesetz und werck müssen zur gnaden komen, und gerecht werden."

282. *LW* 35:364; WA, *DB* 6:414, "Darumb dis buch, wol möcht heissen eine glose uber die Episteln Sanct Pauli."

283. WA, *DB* 6:1. Reu writes, "At all events, everything that Luther and his friends had possessed from the beginning, particularly after 1522, of wisdom and ability, of conscientiousness and fidelity, of labor, and of prayer and supplication and spiritual experience in the preparation of a German Bible was poured into the preparation of the first complete Bible in 1534." Reu, *Luther's German Bible*, 223.

284. Reu, *Luther's German Bible*, 233–36; Kooiman, *Luther and the Bible*, 178. For the manuscript of Rörer's *Protocol* and Luther's notes beginning in 1539 that chart

followed by subsequent revisions for reprinting in 1543 and 1545, the latter being the final edition of the *Deutsche Bibel* updated and published under Luther's supervision before his death.[285] Luther's last activity on his German translation of the Bible consisted of more edits to the New Testament, most likely only of Romans and 1 and 2 Corinthians.[286] These alterations made it into the posthumously published *Deutsche Bibel* of 1546 under the care of Rörer to whom Luther entrusted oversight of the Bible's revision.[287]

---

the course for the planned edits that became the 1541 *Deutsche Bibel*, see WA, *DB* 3:167–577; WA, *DB* 4:1–278.

285. Reu *Luther's German Bible*, 248.

286. For Luther's 1544 notes on proposed reworkings of Roman–2 Corinthians, see WA, *DB* 4:313–85; Reu, *Luther's German Bible*, 251–52.

287. That Luther's final efforts of editing were focused on the NT explains why the 1545 version of the OT prefaces are treated as their final form whereas the NT prefaces reach their last stage in the 1546 edition of the *Deutsche Bibel*.

3

Hermeneutical Implications of the Prefaces for Christ as the *Sensus Literalis* of Scripture

THE OT HAS PROPHESIED OF THE COMING MESSIAH, AND THE NT HAS PRO-
claimed Jesus of Nazareth to be that promised Christ, the Son of God
and Son of David. The Bible's textual *telos* is to make Christ known, each
Testament and biblical author doing so with their own voice, though all are
in christological harmony. Luther's approach to Scripture on display in the
prefaces is a theological conviction persuaded by exegetical and interpretive engagement with the biblical text, where Scripture has determined its
own referential centrality. Luther accepts what he considers to be Scripture's
clear presentation of its prime subject matter, and thus, as an interpreter he
searches the pages of the Bible to see this unity unfold in isolated texts as
"Scripture interprets Scripture" in fulfillment of its purpose to disclose God
in Jesus Christ. This view, therefore, is not foremost a dogmatic principle for
Luther, though to think of biblical exegesis dislocated from the *regula fidei*
would create the very interpretive problem he zealously desires to overturn
at several points in the Bible-prefaces. Rather, the presupposition of Christ
as the literal sense of Scripture is, as Gary Simpson has helpfully termed, "an
intrascriptural warrant" in Luther's method.[1]

Luther's messianic reading of the OT is the determining factor for his
comprehensive vision of the Bible's christocentricity. Yet, how one characterizes Luther's approach will have reciprocal effects for understanding the
OT as *Christian Scripture* in general. As previously discussed, Christine
Helmer's essay, "Luther's Trinitarian Hermeneutic and the Old Testament,"
recognizes the biblical interpreter's dilemma. This age's reception of the historical-critical method has placed claims of the OT's referentiality to Christ

---

1. Simpson, "'You shall bear witness to me': Thinking with Luther about Christ and
the Scriptures," 383.

or to the Trinity in its "letter" outside the bounds of exegetical legitimacy.[2] Given this setting, she reflects, "With the retreat of theological claims to accommodate the results of historical criticism, the question of how the Old Testament can inform Christian theology continues to be posed."[3] Among various attempts to revitalize the OT's contributive role in Christian doctrine such as Wilhelm Vischer's, *Das Christuszeugnis des Alten Testaments,* Helmer highlights James Preus and Heinrich Bornkamm's renewed interest in Luther's promulgation of Christ as Scripture's *sensus literalis.*[4]

As was noted in chapter 1, Helmer's evaluation of Preus is slight, since the "early" Luther is the subject of his study.[5] Bornkamm, on the other hand, represents in Helmer's estimation an interpretation of Luther's approach to the OT normed by modern commitments. Although Bornkamm acknowledges the significance of Luther's search for prophetic references to Christ in the OT, Helmer considers Bornkamm's portrayal deficient insofar as he characterizes Luther's understanding of the OT's witness to Christ as proclamation, not prediction.[6] If theological interpretation of the OT takes "Christian" shape only because it is being adopted into a supposed alien

2. Helmer, "Luther's Trinitarian Hermeneutic and the Old Testament," 49.

3. Ibid., 50.

4. Ibid. Vischer sounded the alarm against the historical-critical method's dominance over OT studies and theology early in the twentieth century. He published a two-volume work, *Das Christuszeugnis des Alten Testaments* (*The Witness of the Old Testament to Christ*), in which he strove to demonstrate the reality of Jesus Christ as the primary referent of the OT's theological witness. His project, expectedly, was greatly contested, and was often dismissed as allegorical. For an introduction to Vischer's life and works, see Felber, "Vischer, Wilhelm," 1011–16. It is worth noting Luther's influence on Vischer's program. One can easily see how Luther's vision for Christ as the OT's literal sense permeated Vischer's own approach to the OT. In the introduction to the first volume of *The Witness of the Old Testament to Christ,* akin to Luther, Vischer quotes John 5:39 as a heading for the chapter (and, most likely, for his entire proposal) followed by this opening paragraph: "The Bible testifies beyond doubt, with the attestation of the Holy Spirit, that Jesus of Nazareth is the Christ. This is what makes it the Holy Scripture of the Christian Church. For the Christian Church is the company of all those who, on the basis of the biblical testimony, recognize and believe that Jesus is the Christ, i.e., the Messiah of Israel, the Son of the living God, the Saviour of the world." From here, Vischer draws upon and quotes Luther profusely from many of the same prefaces and writings reviewed in this study. Despite the accusations of his recourse to allegory, Vischer's introduction exhibits an extremely similar theology of the Christian Bible to Luther's that identifies Christ as its literal sense on the basis of the biblical text's ultimate purpose to testify to the messianic hope, promised and fulfilled. Vischer, *The Witness of the Old Testament to Christ,* 7.

5. Helmer, "Luther's Trinitarian Hermeneutic and the Old Testament," 66–67n12. She has in mind Preus, *From Shadow to Promise.*

6. Ibid., 66n12.

"gospel" framework or a confessional Christian theological system that is only the product of the NT and church tradition, then the OT text itself has no material contribution. Helmer goes on to present an alternative proposal that affirms the OT's independent contribution to the Christian doctrine of the Trinity by way of Luther's defense in *On the Last Words of David* (1543) of the OT's trinitarian substance (*res*) communicated through the semantic equivalence of the prophets with the Holy Spirit's divine authorship. Similar to Helmer's purpose, this study's goal in its focus upon the messianic dimension of Luther's hermeneutic is to argue for the textual basis of Luther's belief that Christ is the *sensus literalis* of Scripture.

The Messiah in the OT: Luther's Main Rationale for Christ as the *Sensus Literalis* of Scripture

The prefaces form a composite account of many aspects of Luther's outlook on Scripture. Undoubtedly, Christ shines forth in his presentation both as its central subject matter and the focal point that drives its narrative. Luther's wisdom in generating prefaces to each Testament as a whole recognizes the necessity for biblical interpretation to engage the sacred books and inspired authors within the full scope of Scripture's divine testimony. In these prefaces, one encounters Luther's biblical theology on display, and to regard its nature as merely a "gospel-centrism" misses not only the textual orientation of Luther's carefully articulated definition of the "gospel," but also the distinct way he depicts the Bible's referential witness to Christ subsequently in his introductions to its individual books.

Moreover, Luther's commitment to Christ as the literal sense of the Bible is conjoined with his struggle to persuade others of the OT's abiding theological relevance in its "letter." What is found, then, in the prefaces that manifests the textual determination of Jesus Christ as Scripture's *sensus literalis* is the OT's promise of the Messiah proclaimed as fulfilled in the NT. The prefaces unveil Luther's conviction that Christ is the Bible's ultimate meaning in its grammatical-historical sense. The aim at this point, therefore, is not to evaluate the validity of Luther's designation of certain passages as messianic; therefore, isolating individual texts to observe the Reformer's exegesis will be overpassed. Instead, a biblical-theological pattern of messianic texts from both the OT and NT will be highlighted, which provide a window into the textual fabric of Luther's approach to Scripture that finds its end in Christ. The goal is to show that despite the likelihood that other doctrinal sensibilities contribute to his christocentric vision of the Bible, it is Scripture's textual witness to the messianic portrait of Jesus that is preeminently responsible for pressuring the interpreter to concede Christ as its literal sense.[7]

Luther is prone to enlist a select group of biblical passages to ground the theological portrayal of Holy Scripture as a book foremost about Christ. The OT texts trace the promise of the Messiah through its narrative while the NT texts tend to be passages that are looking backwards at the OT, making pronouncements about the nature of its prophetic word in relation to Jesus.[8] For instance, Genesis 3:15 and Romans 1:1–2 will quickly be seen as perhaps the most substantial pillars for upholding his messianic understanding of the Bible's witness to Christ. Though a pattern is discernible and some consistency in sequencing does appear at times, this practice is in no way a fixed strategy. To begin, the *Preface to the New Testament* (1522) showcases this biblical-theological hermeneutic explicitly.

Preface to the New Testament (1522)

As noted in chapter 2, the content of Luther's definition of the gospel that opens the *Preface to the New Testament* is structured by his messianic reading of the OT's prophetic word complimented by the NT's apostolic task now to proclaim Jesus Christ's message of the "new testament" to the ends of the earth.[9] Luther's objective for the prologue to the New Testament as a "book" is to clarify its central message as the "gospel" of the "new testament." Luther, however, does not permit this "gospel of the new testament" to be thought of as a formulation solely constructed by the New Testament writings. Rather, he supplies a series of OT passages to unearth the roots of what the apostles now announce as in full bloom. The main text Luther

---

7. On the concept of biblical "pressure" in the theological interpretation of Scripture, see Yeago, "The New Testament and the Nicene Dogma," 152–64; Rowe, "Biblical Pressure and Trinitarian Hermeneutics," 295–312.

8. Key OT texts are: Genesis 3:15, 22:18; Deuteronomy 18:15–18; and 2 Samuel 7:12–14. Key NT texts are: Luke 24; John 5:39, 46; Acts 3:21–36 (as fulfillment of Deuteronomy 18:15–18); Acts 17:11; Romans 1:1–4, 3:21; and 1 Peter 1:10–12. These are the most frequently cited passages as well as the ones upon which Luther rests the greatest weight for his argument. Siggins appears to recogonize this phenomenon in Luther's argumentation for Christ in the OT. As this study has observed, Siggins also pays special attention to the repetitive use of certain OT messianic predictions as well as NT warrants for applying the OT to Christ. See Siggins, *Martin Luther's Doctrine of Christ*, 20–27.

9. *LW* 35:358; WA, DB 6:4.

offers as scriptural proof that grants him permission to proceed in this interpretive manner is Romans 1:1–3.[10]

The Apostle Paul's own prefatory words to his Epistle to the Romans provide the license for Luther to read the OT as a direct witness to Jesus. Thus, before he introduces his OT messianic narrative framework, Luther writes, "God has promised this gospel and testament in many ways, by the prophets in the Old Testament, as St. Paul says in Romans 1[:1–3], 'I am set apart to preach the gospel of God which he promised beforehand through his prophets in the holy scriptures, concerning his Son, who was descended from David,' etc."[11] Romans 1:1–3, then, become a gateway to perceiving where and in what way God promised the gospel concerning his Son through the prophets written down as Holy Scripture. The first messianic promise appears in Genesis 3:15 with the prophecy that the woman's "seed" (*same*) will come to conquer "sin, death, hell, and all [the devil's] power."[12] This same prophecy of a future "seed" is continued in Genesis 22:18, when "God promised Abraham, 'Through your descendant [*Samen*] shall all the nations of the earth be blessed.' Christ is that descendant [*same*] of Abra-

10. Luther's approach in his argument for Christ in the OT often consists of citing or alluding to various biblical texts as "scriptural proofs" of his case. Many of these texts, as will be shown, are a part of a standard biblical-theoloigcal framework that reflects prior scriptural interpretation, yet are applied in the continual hermeneutical circle of "Scripture as its own interpreter." In today's usage, the term "proof-text" emits a negative connotation, usually reserved for the wrong use of biblical passages out of their context to support whatever teaching or position being advocated. However, "scriptural proof" within the church's interpretation of the Scriptures was prominent and utilized as a form of exegetical method. Oskar Skarsaune succinctly argues that in the history of biblical interpretation "exegesis" and "scriptural proof" were often treated as equivalent in his essay, "Schriftbeweis und Christologisches Kerygma in Der Ältesten Kirchlichen Schriftauslegung," 45. Skarsaune takes Justin Martyr's *Dialogue with Trypho* for his test case, and interestingly, he notes that one of the prime uses of "scriptural proof" as an "exegetical method" is as a means for legitimizing the NT's gospel of Jesus Christ as that which is in accord and in direct fulfillment of the OT's prophecy of Israel's Messiah. Skarsaune, "Schriftbeweis und Christologisches Kerygma in Der Ältesten Kirchlichen Schriftauslegung," 46. See also Young, "Exegetical Method and Scriptural Proof: The Bible in Doctrinal Debate," 291–304. For a brief historical overview and critical thoughts on the prospect of "scriptural proof" in theological interpretation, one may consult Treier, "Proof Text," 622–24.

11. *LW* 35:358; WA, *DB* 6:4, "Nu hat Gott solchen glauben zu stercken, dieses sein Euangelium und Testament vielfechtig im alten Testament, durch die Propheten verheyssen, Wie S. Paulus sagt Rom. 1. Ich bin ausgesondert zu predigen das Euangelium Gottes welchs er zuuor verheissen hat durch seine Propheten, in der heiligen Schrifft, von seinem Son, der im geboren ist von dem samen David etc." (1546).

12. *LW* 35:359; WA, *DB* 6:6, "Christus ist der same dises weybs, der dem teuffel seyn heubt, das ist, sund, tod, helle und alle seyne krafft zurtretten hatt."

ham, says St. Paul in Galatians 3[:16]; he has blessed all the world, through the gospel."[13] Still following what he considers to be the messianic lineage, Luther moves from Abraham to David: "Again God made this promise to David in 2 Samuel 7[:12–14] when he said, 'I will raise up your son [*Samen*] after you, who shall build a house for my name, and I will establish the throne of his kingdom forever. I will be his father, and he shall be my son [*Son*]; etc."[14]

The material content of Luther's definition of the "gospel" is the OT prophecy of the messianic hope. The NT endorsement for this method-ological construction is Paul's statement in Romans 1:1–3. In this mani-festation of his holistic biblical-theological framework that sees Scripture's gaze squarely fixed upon Christ, a messianic retelling takes place utilizing Genesis 3:15; 22:18; and 2 Samuel 7:12–14. As highlighted above in chapter 2, Luther gives the impression that these texts are just the tip of the iceberg, so to speak, because along with Micah 5:2 and Hosea 13:14 (both are pas-sages that Luther considers direct prophecies of the Messiah), "There are many more such promises of the gospel in the other prophets as well."[15] To end this brief excursus into the OT, Luther closes this initial section of the *Preface to the New Testament* with a restatement of the "gospel" that parallels the one he submitted from the start.

Luther reveals key elements in his explanation of the "gospel" before and after his account of God's promise of it to the prophets. Those essential attributes are: (1) Jesus Christ is the Son of God and Son of David; (2) he is truly God and truly man; (3) his death and resurrection have instituted the promise of a "new testament"; (4) his death and resurrection have overcome sin, death, and hell; and (5) he offers righteousness and eternal life to all who believe in him.[16] That Luther chooses to offer messianic predictions

13. *LW* 35:359; WA, *DB* 6:7, "Item, Gen. xxii. verhies ers Abraham, Durch deinen Samen, sollen alle Völcker auff Erden gesegnet werden. Christus ist der same Abrahe, spricht S. Paulus Gal. iii. Der hat alle Welt gesegnet, durchs Euangelium" (1546). The 1522 preface used *versprach* instead of *verhies*.

14. *LW* 35:359; WA, *DB* 6:7, "Item, So verhies ers David ii. Sam. vii da er saget, Ich wil erwecken deinen Samen nach dir, Der sol meinem Name nein Haus bawen. Und Ich wil den Stuel seines Königreichs bestetigen ewiglich. Ich wil sein Vater sein, und er sol mein Son sein etc." Again, the 1522 preface used *versprach* instead of *verhies*. On another note, why the English translator decided to render *Samen* as "son" is uncertain, since this rendering entirely misses the emphasis of Luther's German in his quotations of Genesis 3:15, 22:18, and 2 Samuel 7:12–14. In each of them, he is tracing the "seed" or "offspring" theme in the biblical narrative as a streamlined messianic promise.

15. *LW* 35:360; WA, *DB* 6:6, "Solcher verheyssung des Euangeli sind viel mehr auch ynn den andern propheten, als . . ."

16. See chapter 2 where both definitions of the "gospel" are given. *LW* 35:358–60;

between his two "gospel" declarations for textual support is an indication that he considers these aspects of Jesus Christ's person and work as characteristics of the prophets's prophecies of the coming Messiah; therefore, the "gospel" as a whole is attuned to a messianic orientation.

The pattern typified in the *Preface to the New Testament* is not its first occurrence. Previous writings reveal themselves as the breeding grounds for development of this biblical-theological framework, which progressively becomes a formative principle in the Reformer's hermeneutic. One of the earliest instances can be witnessed two years prior in *A Treatise on the New Testament, that is, the Holy Mass* (1520). Here, as in the *Preface to the New Testament* (1522), Luther first moves from a conception of the gospel as "testament" to a demonstration of how it was promised by the prophets in the OT.

Showing signs of the *Preface to the New Testament*'s structural dependence upon his thought in this 1520 treatise on the Lord's Supper, Luther says that this word of promise (i.e., the gospel as a "new testament") had been anticipated since the Fall. So, just as his practice would be later in the *Preface to the New Testament* (1522), Luther highlights a series of "gospel/ testament promises" from the OT directly related to the messianic hope. Beginning with Genesis 3:15, he traces the "seed" (*samen*) theme through: Gen 9:9–11 (promise to Noah and his sons); Gen 12:1–3, 15:6, 18:10–14, 22:18 (Abrahamic promises, including Christ as the "seed"); allusion to David's and other OT prophets's authorial roles in making the messianic promise continually "renewed and made more definite" (*immer baß und baß vornewet und vorkleret ist*); and last, Moses, "who declared the same promise under many forms in the law."[17] This list culminates in Christ's own words in the New Testament (book), when he "made a promise or solemn vow, which we are to believe and thereby come to righteousness and salvation. This promise is the words just cited, where Christ says, 'This is the cup of the New Testament.'"[18] In short, both treatises offer a nuanced definition of the gospel as a "new testament" grounded upon God's promise of the Messiah in the OT Scriptures.

In the following year of 1521, Luther penned *A Brief Instruction on What to Look for and Expect in the Gospels* as a preface to the publication of his *Church Postils*. Many features from this prologue can be matched with

---

WA, *DB* 6:4, 6.

17. *LW* 35:82–83; WA 6:356–57, "Darnach ist Moses kummen, der die selb zusagung mit vielen figuren des gesetzs betzeychnet hatt."

18. *LW* 35:84; WA 6:357, "Also auch ym newen testament hat Christus ein zusagen oder gelubd than, an wilche wir glauben sollen und da durch frum und selig werden, das sein die vorgesagte wort, da Christus sagt 'das ist der kilch des newen testaments.'"

content in both the *Preface to the New Testament* (1522) and the *Preface to the Old Testament* (1523), yet for now, only those places where they parallel in the display of Luther's biblical-theological hermeneutic under review will be highlighted.

The order of Luther's procedure in the *Preface to the New Testament* is: (1) statement of the gospel; (2) dual use of Romans 1:1–3 for definitional support and defense of this gospel promised in the OT; (3) list of OT messianic predictions/promises; and (4) restatement of the gospel.[19] Similarly, *A Brief Instruction*'s sequence is: (1) statement of the gospel; (2) dual use of Romans 1:1–4 for definitional support and defense of this gospel promised in the OT; and (4) restatement of the gospel. Absent from this pattern in contrast to its occurrence in the *Preface to the New Testament* is the list of key messianic texts immediately subsequent to citation of Romans 1:1–4. Luther shows how the OT promises the Messiah as Jesus Christ in other ways in *A Brief Instruction* that still cohere with his general scriptural logic on this matter and will be treated below.

Luther opens *A Brief Instruction* by defining the "gospel" in a few variations. Directly prior to his usage of Romans 1:1–4, Luther offers this description: "For at its briefest, the gospel is a discourse about Christ, that he is the Son of God and became man for us, that he died and was raised, that he has been established as a Lord over all things."[20] He, then, quotes Romans 1:1–4 as an example of this "gospel" testified to in full, and as a summary of the fourfold Gospel's message about Jesus Christ. After the complete quotation from Romans 1:1–4, Luther right away restates the "gospel" with the declaration, "There you have it. The gospel is a story about Christ, God's and David's Son, who died and was raised and is established as Lord. This is the gospel in a nutshell."[21]

As aforementioned, missing from this sequence is the series of key OT messianic texts prior to the restatement of the gospel. Luther, nevertheless, does not eclipse this part of his method. Reflecting upon his condensed

---

19. Luther's order in *A Treatise on the New Testament* is: (1) statement of the gospel as a "new testament"; (3) list of OT messianic predictions/promises; and (4) restatement of the gospel as a "new testament." What's missing from the pattern as it appears in the *Preface to the New Testment* is the double use of Rom 1:1–3 prior to the citation of key OT messianic prophecies.

20. *LW* 35:118; WA 10.1.1:9, "Denn auffs kurtzlichst ist das Euangelium eyn rede von Christo, das er gottis ßon und mensch sey fur unß worden, gestorben unnd aufferstanden, eyn herr ubir alle ding gesetzt."

21. *LW* 35:118; WA 10.1.1:10, "Da sihestu, das das Euangelium eyn historia ist von Christo, Gottis und Davids ßon, gestorben und aufferstanden unnd tzum herrnn gesetzt, wilchs da ist summa summarum des Euangeli."

definition of the "gospel," Luther remarks that Paul and Peter "teach nothing but Christ, in the way we have just described, so their epistles can be nothing but the gospel."[22] So too, "even the teaching of the prophets, in those places where they speak of Christ, is nothing but the true, pure, and proper gospel—just as if Luke or Matthew had described it. For the prophets have proclaimed the gospel and spoken of Christ, as St. Paul here [Rom. 1:2] reports and as everyone indeed knows."[23] The allusion to Romans 1:1–2 is implicit, and harkens back to his previous quotation of Romans 1:1–4. Once again, it serves as a heading into the OT's messianic witness to Christ. As an example of the biblical phenomenon Paul is identifying, Luther offers Isaiah 53 as a direct prophecy of the death of Christ, and thus, maintains that Isaiah "has written the pure gospel."[24]

Later in *A Brief Instruction*, Luther returns to this topic to build upon the premise of the NT's proclamation of the gospel of Jesus Christ as nothing other than what the OT has already promised. The OT is where "people like us should read and study, drill ourselves, and see what Christ is, for what purpose he has been given, how he was promised, and how all Scripture tends toward him."[25] This time Luther first quotes from John 5:46 and 39 for textual support: "For he [Jesus] himself says in John 5[:46], 'If you believed Moses, you would also believe me, for he wrote of me.' Again [John 5:39], 'Search and look up the Scriptures, for it is they that bear witness to me.'"[26] Then, for further corroboration, Luther once again enlists a portion from Paul's own prologue to his Epistle to the Romans, saying,

> This is what St. Paul means in Romans 1[:1–2], where in the beginning he says in his greeting, "The gospel was promised by God through the prophets in the Holy Scriptures." This is why the evangelists and apostles always direct us to the Scriptures

22. *LW* 35:118; WA 10.1.1:10, "Weil auch Paulus und Petrus nichts anders denn Christum leren auff vorgesagte weyße, ßo mügen yhre Epistell nichts anders denn das Euangelium seyn."

23. *LW* 35:118; WA 10.1.1:10, "Ja auch die propheten, die weyl sie das Euangelium vorkundigt und von Christo gesagt haben, alß hie. S. Paulus meldet und yderman wol weyß, ßo ist yhr lere an dem selben ortt, da sie von Christo redden, nichts anders denn das ware lautter recht Euangelium, alß hetts Lucas oder Mattheus beschrieben."

24. *LW* 35:118; WA 10.1.1:10, "hatt er das lautter Euangelium geschrieben."

25. *LW* 35:122; WA 10.1.1:15, "Da sollt unßer studirn und leßen sich uben und sehen, was Christus sey, wo tzu er geben sey, wie er vorsprochen sey, und wie sich alle schrifft auff yhn tziehe, . . ."

26. *LW* 35:122; WA 10.1.1:15, "als er selb sagt Johan. 5: Wenn yhr Mosi glewbetet, tzo glewbetet yhr auch myr, denn von myr hatt er geschrieben. Item: forschet und suchet die schrifft, den die selbige ists, die von myr getzeugniß gibt."

and say, "Thus it is written," and again, "This has taken place in order that the writing of the prophets might be fulfilled," and so forth.[27]

From here, Luther follows with a complete quotation of 1 Peter 1:10–12, another important NT text that greatly informs the hermeneutic that leads him to the conclusion that Christ is the *sensus literalis* of Scripture at the level of its "letter." "What else does St. Peter here desire," Luther asks, "than to lead us into the Scriptures? It is as if he should be saying, 'We preach and open the Scriptures to you through the Holy Spirit, so that you yourselves may read and see what is in them and know of the time about which the prophets were writing.'"[28] Luther's next statement is a brief allusion to Luke 24:45, which "says that Christ opened the minds of the apostles to understand the Scripture."[29]

To summarize, *A Brief Instruction*'s sequence of (1) a "gospel" definition followed by (2) a quotation from Romans 1:1–4 with (4) a final restatement of the gospel anticipates the pattern Luther will emulate in the *Preface to the New Testament*. Additionally, Luther utilizes Paul's introduction to Romans to set the parameters of a complete summation of the "gospel" and to defend the notion that God has explicitly predicted these key components to Jesus Christ's person and work manifest in the messianic hope prophesied by the prophets in the OT. This practice of scriptural proof is also employed in the *Preface to the New Testament*.

Between *A Treatise on the New Testament* (1520), *A Brief Instruction* (1521), and the *Preface to the New Testament* (1522), Luther's portrayal of "how all Scripture tends toward him [Christ]" comes in the form of a "gospel" declaration that incorporates essential characteristics that God has long-promised through the prophets in the OT Scriptures about the coming person and work of the Messiah.[30] Because Luther is a theologian of the whole Christian Bible, he trusts the apostolic testimony of passages such as

27. *LW* 35:122; WA 10.1.1:15, "Das meynet sanct Paulus Ro. 1., da er ynn forn an ym gruß spricht, Das Euangeli sey von got vorsprochen durch die propheten ynn der heyligen schrifft. Daher geschichts, das die Euangelisten unnd Apostel ymer da runs ynn die schrifft weyßen unnd sprechen: Alßo ists geschrieben. Item: das ist geschehen, das die schrifft der propheten erfullet wurden a."

28. *LW* 35:123–24; WA 10.1.1:16, "Was will hie mit S. Petrus, denn uns ynn die schrifft furen? als solt er sagen: wyr predigen und offenen euch die schrifft, durch den heyligen geyst, das yhr selbs mugt leßen unnd sehen, was drynnen ist, unnd von wilcher tzeytt die propheten geschrieben habenn."

29. *LW* 35:123; WA 10.1.1:16, "das Christus hab den Aposteln den vorstand auffthan, das sie die schrifft vorstunden."

30. *LW* 35:122; WA 10.1.1:15, "und wie sich alle schrifft auff yhn tziehe."

Romans 1:1–4, Luke 24 and John 5:39–46 (Christ's own instruction), and 1 Peter 1:10–12 as authoritative pronouncements about the literal sense of the OT's textual referentiality.

Preface to the Old Testament (1523)

Both *A Brief Instruction* and the *Preface to the New Testament* include strong appeals for Christ in the OT, so it is fitting that Luther would revisit this campaign with equal to greater force in the *Preface to the Old Testament*. Undeniably, the overwhelming concern in this preface can be summed up with the prologue's final sentence, "Let this suffice for the present as a brief suggestion for seeking Christ and the gospel in the Old Testament."[31] This last word forms an inclusio with Luther's starting point from the preface's onset to make the case for the OT's perduring voice beyond its original historical audience all the way to its sixteenth-century one, and so on. From this beginning, semblances of Luther's messianic, biblical-theological framework appear immediately.

The first manifestation occurs in Luther's utilization of NT texts that look backwards upon the OT, explaining how the antecedent witness is to be understood as Christian Scripture. Luther sees two related problems for Christian approaches to the OT. One is that the OT has no contemporary value because its identity is restricted to Israel's "religious writings," causing it to be "out of date, containing stories of past times."[32] The other problem is the practice of some interpreters who assume the first premise, and then believe that the OT Scriptures can only be recovered for NT Christians through pursuit of a "spiritual sense" (*geystliche synn*) behind its "letter."[33] To counter both misguided positions, Luther argues for Christ as the *sensus literalis* of all Scripture because he is the OT's literal sense.[34]

In the *Preface to the New Testament* (1522), Romans 1:1–3 was the normative NT passage for illuminating the OT's true meaning. Luther draws upon Romans 1 again in the *Preface to the Old Testament*, but also

---

31. *LW* 35:248; WA, *DB* 8:31, "Das sey dis mal gnug zur kurtzen anleitung, Christum und das Euangelium zu suchen im alten Testament" (1545). This was the last sentence in editions beginning with the first complete *Deutsche Bibel* in 1534 and thereafter.

32. *LW* 35:235; WA, *DB* 8:10, "und nu fort aus sey, und nur von vergangenen geschichten schreybe."

33. *LW* 35:235; WA, *DB* 8:10.

34. For a contemporary defense of the enduring literal sense witness of the OT as Christian Scripture, see Seitz, "The Old Testament as Abiding Theological Witness: Inscripting a Theological Curriculum," 3–12.

incorporates multiple texts from his bank of NT apostolic advisements on the nature of the OT's scriptural witness. At this point, the *Preface to the Old Testament* (1523) exhibits close parallels to *A Brief Instruction* (1521), revealing another facet of the textual schematic from which he draws when contending for Christ as the OT's literal sense, and by extension, all of Scripture's. In a section recounted above from *A Brief Instruction*, where Luther advocates for the OT's "letter" as a witness to Christ, he stands upon these texts in sequence: Jn 5:46, 36; Rom 1:1–2; Acts 17:11; and 1 Pet 1:10–12.[35] These passages all indicate, for Luther, that the main function of the OT as Christian Scripture is to promise and to prophesy about the Messiah. When attacking bankrupt approaches to the OT that empty its literal sense of Christ, Luther repeats this procedure in near identical form in the *Preface to the Old Testament*.

For those who would constrict themselves to discovery of a "hidden/spiritual" sense in the OT biblical text, Luther levies the following list of NT evidence to the contrary: John 5:39; 1 Timothy 4:13 (implied); Romans 1:2; 1 Corinthians 15:3–4; 1 Peter 1:10–12 (implied); and Acts 17:11.[36] That these passages orient the manner of the OT's witness to Christ beyond general prefigurings or types, Luther qualifies his usage of John 5:39 and Romans 1:2 with 1 Corinthians 15:3–4, wherein Paul affirms "that in accordance with the Scriptures Christ came of the seed of David, died, and was raised from the dead."[37] In other words, what Jesus teaches in John 5:39, Paul in Romans 1:2, and Peter, who likewise, "points us back, more than once, to the Scriptures," is that the OT is no "dead letter" because at a literary level, Moses and the prophets are all divinely inspired authors unveiling the person and work of the coming Messiah.[38]

Second, Luther's messianic-mindedness regarding Christ as the OT's *sensus literalis* narrows to Moses's office and teaching. The figurehead passage in Luther's biblical-theological pattern is Genesis 3:15. Although it does not appear amidst the NT passages cited above, Luther allows this text to dominate his survey of Genesis as he introduces the individual books of the Pentateuch. In his single paragraph synopsis of Genesis, Luther does not mention Isaac, Jacob, or even Joseph. He contents himself to a description of

35. *LW* 35:122; *WA* 10.1.1:15.

36. *LW* 35:235–36; *WA*, *DB* 8:10.

37. *LW* 35:235; *WA*, *DB* 8:10, "und 1. Cor. 15. sagt er, Christus sey nach laut der schrifft von Davids geblütte komen, gestorben und vom todt aufferstanden."

38. *LW* 35:235; *WA*, *DB* 8:10, "So weyset uns auch S. Petrus mehr denn eyn mal enhyndern ynn die schrifft." Based upon previous invokings of Peter in this context, it is most likely that 1 Pet 1:10–12 is the place in the Petrine writings to which Luther is referring.

humanity's plight due to the Fall. To provide hope for future salvation from sin and death, God promises through Moses (as author of Genesis) that this redemption will come "by 'the seed [*samen*] of the woman,' Christ, promised to Adam and Abraham, in order that throughout the Scriptures from the beginning faith may be praised above all works and laws and merits."[39] This presentation, then, sets the general trajectory for the unfolding of the rest of the biblical narrative.[40] Genesis is predominantly about faith in God's promise of the coming "seed," the Messiah who will defeat sin, death, and the devil; hence, Luther can regard it as "an exceedingly evangelical book" (*fast eyn euangelisch buch*).[41]

Thus far, though out of the more consistent order exemplified in comparison between *A Treatise on the New Testament* (1520), *A Brief Instruction* (1521), and the *Preface to the New Testament* (1522), elements of Luther's biblical-theological hermeneutic have occurred in the *Preface to the Old Testament* (1523) through utilization of NT texts such as Romans 1:1–2 and John 5:39 to argue for Christ in the OT at the level of its literal sense in addition to elaboration upon Genesis 3:15 as the messianic catalyst for the entire scope of Scripture. The next significant component that appears in the *Preface to the Old Testament* is his messianic interpretation of Deuteronomy 18:15–19. Although this passage is not included in the three writings mentioned above, Luther repeatedly invokes this text in other writings with the same intent of illumining the messianic contours of the OT's witness to Christ.[42]

39. *LW* 35:237; WA, *DB* 8:12, "durch des weybs samen Christum, Adam und Abraham verheyssen, auff das also der glaube von anfang der schrifft durch und durch gepreyset werde uber alle werck."

40. At its core, the Bible is a "tale of two seeds" in Luther's biblical-theological scheme. For instance, in his 1539 treatise, *On the Jews and Their Lies*, he contends that the entire scope of Scripture is meant to tell of these "two seeds [*Samen*], the serpent's and the woman's" (*LW* 47:217; WA 53:482). On the relationship of the messianic promise in Genesis 3:15 to the NT, in a 1534 sermon from the *House Postils* for "Easter Monday, Luke 24:13–35," he asserts, "The whole New Testament flows out of this promise concerning Christ." Luther, "Easter Monday (Luke 24:13–35)," 25.

41. *LW* 35:237; WA, *DB* 8:12.

42. Luther preached a sermon on John 5:39–40 in 1545 for his friend Justus Jonas, who had been called to Halle as the pastor. This entire sermon is a fascinating example of the connection between the messianic hope and Christ as the center of Scripture in Luther's biblical-theological hermeneutic. In particular, he spends the bulk of the sermon linking Jesus's teaching in John 5:39–40 with Moses's messianic prophecy in Deuteronomy 18:15–19. In the following, Luther attempts to parapharase what Moses is saying in this text: "O dear people of Israel, behold, you have me here as a prophet and teacher. I teach you the Law and the Ten Commandments, from which you learn to know your sin and, likewise, what you ought to do and not to do. That is my office.

Already enmeshed in a discussion on the Mosaic Law's christological purpose, Luther declares that "Moses himself has told us that his office and teaching should endure until Christ, and then cease, when he says in Deuteronomy 18[:15–19], 'The Lord your God will raise up for you a prophet like me from among your brethren—him shall you heed,' etc."[43] Luther interprets Moses to be prophesying of a new Prophet who will bring a new word:

> For since God here promises [*verheyst*] another Moses whom they are to hear, it follows of necessity that this other one would teach something different from Moses; and Moses gives up his power and yields to him, so that men will listen to him. This prophet cannot, then, teach the law, for Moses has done that to perfection; for the law's sake there would be no need to raise up another prophet. *Therefore this word was surely spoken concerning Christ and the teaching of grace.*[44]

For Christ's messianic portrait, Genesis 3:15 supplies the imagery of the "seed" who will remove sin's curse, and Deuteronomy 18:15–18 adds that this Messiah will also have a new and better prophetic office and message to supersede Moses. Moreover, Luther proffers Moses's attempt at self-deflection as "the noblest saying in all of Moses, indeed the very heart of it all."[45] In short, the Law not only by implication drives sinful humans to

---

When I shall cease preaching, however, and die, God will give you another Preacher and Teacher, one born of your own flesh and blood, just like me. Now, when God gives you that Teacher, Him you shall hear, and take His words and preaching to heart and believe them. I, however, am not that Prophet of whom I speak and write. *I testify concerning Him and am giving and leaving you this Book, in order that you may study and learn from it to find Him and to recognize Him in it. When He comes in His time and begins to preach, then I will hand over my mastership to Him.* So open your ears and eyes and read what I write or have written, and listen diligently to Him. Receive His preaching and believe in Him, for He will give you eternal life" (italics mine); *LW* 58:251; WA 51:5.

43. *LW* 35:246; WA, *DB* 8:26, "Also hat Moses auch selbs angezeygt, das seyn ampt und lere solt weren bis auff Christum und als denn auffhoren, da er spricht Deutro. 18. Eynen propheten wirt dyr der HERR deyn Gott erwecken aus deynen brudern wie mich, den soltu horen etce."

44. Italics mine; *LW* 35:246; WA, *DB* 8:26, "Denn weyl Gott hie eyn andern Mose verheyst, den sie horen sollen, zwinget sichs, das er etwas anders lereen wurde denn Mose, und Mose seyn macht yhm ubirgibt und weicht, das man ihenen horen sole, So kan yhe der selb prophet nicht gesetz leren, denn das hat Mose auffs aller hohist aus gericht, und keyn nott umbs gesetzs willen eynen andern propheten zu erwecken, drumb ists gewiss von der gnaden lere und Christo gesagt."

45. *LW* 35:246; WA, *DB* 8:26, "Dis ist der edlist spruch und freylich der kern ym

Christ because it shows their spiritual desperation for grace, but even built into the office of the Law's supreme prophet, Moses, is the direct promise of a coming Prophet who will preach the "new" word of the gospel and institute the "new testament," making the old one under Moses automatically obsolete.[46]

Other features of the *Preface to the Old Testament* could contribute to the messianic basis for Luther's construal of Christ as Scripture's literal sense, and some of these have been alluded to in chapter 2 and/or will be examined later in this chapter. For now, the aim has been directed towards identifying key characteristics of Luther's biblical-theological hermeneutic that is formed by interpretation of multiple biblical texts, which together constitute a collective and coherent framework for a messianic reading of Scripture. This pattern, or pieces of it, also appears in various other writings, thus, showing signs of a developed paradigm in Luther's thought.

Another such writing similar in content and usage to the *Preface to the Old Testament* is *How Christians Should Regard Moses*. Originally, what became *How Christians Should Regard Moses* was a sermon Luther preached in 1525 during his series on Exodus that lasted from 1524 to 1527.[47] In 1526, the sermon was extracted for publication as a separate pamphlet. *How Christians Should Regard Moses* also experienced prefatory usage when in 1527 it was added as an introduction to a volume of Luther's sermons on Genesis that he had preached previously in little over a year's time from 1523 to 1524.[48] The multipurpose use of *How Christians Should Regard Moses* saw it later included with a printing of his exposition of the Ten Commandments, which were also sermons taken from the same Exodus series.[49]

---

gantzen Mose." Cf. the same impression given as the first words to his comments on Deuteronomy 18:15 in *The Deuteronomy of Moses with Notes* (1525): "This is the chief passage in this whole book and a clearly expressed prophecy of Christ as the new Teacher." *LW* 9:176; WA 14:675.

46. Cf. Luther on Deuteronomy 18:15 in *The Deuteronomy of Moses with Notes* (1525): "But there cannot be another word beyond the word of Moses, unless it is the Gospel, since everything that belongs to the teaching of the Law has been transmitted most perfectly and amply by Moses, so that nothing further can be added." *LW* 9:176; WA 14:675. In addition, the next discussion in the *Preface to the Old Testament* to his reflections upon Deuteronomy 18:15–19 is an application of his theology of "testament" to a comparision between the "old testament" under Moses's office and the "new testament" to be established by Jesus Christ, the Prophet promised in Deuteronomy 18:15–19. *LW* 35:246; WA, *DB* 8:28.

47. Brecht, *Martin Luther: Shaping and Defining the Reformation*, 285.

48. *LW* 35:159.

49. Brecht, *Martin Luther: Shaping and Defining the Reformation*, 285.

Luther's priority in *How Christians Should Regard Moses* is to offer instruction for the right distinction of law and gospel when interpreting the OT Law, specifically the Decalogue. He fears that if this theological discernment is not learned, the tragic result will be to turn Christ into Moses.[50] Ultimately, Luther claims that the Mosaic Law does not pertain to Christians; nevertheless, Moses still has ongoing value for believers in three ways. The first benefit to be gained is Moses's authoritative account of natural law.[51] The third is the "beautiful examples of faith, of love, and of the cross" depicted throughout the Pentateuch.[52] The second, however, "is the best thing," namely, "the promises [*verheyssungen*] and pledges of God about Christ."[53]

Underneath Luther's second and "best thing" to note in Moses is where portions of his biblical-theological hermeneutic come to the fore. Furthermore, it is fitting to the context since as has been shown above, Luther follows a loose pattern of textual argument when approaching the subject of Christ in the OT. On this side of the cross, the Reformer says he does "not sweep him under the rug" (*nicht unter den banck stecken*) because "in Moses there are the promises of God which sustain faith."[54] He, then, recounts "the promises and pledges of God about Christ" with these texts: Genesis 3:15; 22:18; and Deuteronomy 18:15–16, and closes by telling, "Many are these texts in the Old Testament, which the holy apostles quoted and drew upon."[55] Finally, Luther concludes his discourse on the second benefit of Moses for Christians with the recap, "Summing up this second part, we read Moses for the sake of the promises about Christ, who belongs not only to the Jews

50. If Moses is allowed to reign over "new testament" Christians, Luther vividly vows, "We would rather not preach again for the rest of our life than to let Moses return and to let Christ be torn out of our hearts. We will not have Moses as ruler or lawgiver any longer." *LW* 35:164; WA 16:372. (Unless otherwise noted, all citations for *How Christians Should Regard Moses* will refer to text "U.") Luther shares this concern also in *A Brief Instruction* (1521): "Be sure, moreover, that you do not make Christ into a Moses, . . ." *LW* 35:119; WA 10.1.1:9.

51. *LW* 35:166; WA 16:376.

52. *LW* 35:173; WA 16:391, "Zum dritten lesen wyr Mosen von wegen der schonen exempel des glawbens, liebe und des creutzes ynn den Vettern Adam, Abel, Noe, Abraham, Isaac, Jacob, Mose und also durch und durch."

53. *LW* 35:168; WA 16:381, "Zum andern find ich ynn Mose, das ich aus der natur nicht hab, das sind verheyssungen und zufagungen Gotes von Christo. Das ist das best."

54. *LW* 35:169; WA 16:382, "Zum andern sind darynn die zusagung Gottes, damit der glaub erhalten wird."

55. *LW* 35:169; WA 16:382–83, "Der sprüche sind viel ym alten Testament, Die haben die heyligen Apostel gefurt und anzogen."

but also to the Gentiles; for through Christ all the Gentiles should have the blessing, as was promised to Abraham."[56]

Once again, when Luther has the opportunity to contend for Christ in the OT, he resorts to a presentation of direct messianic prophecies beginning with the first promise in Genesis 3:15 of a "seed" (*samen*) carried through to Abraham (Gen 22:18; allusion).[57] Next, as in the *Preface to the Old Testament*, Luther appropriately inserts Deuteronomy 18:15 from his guiding framework insofar as Moses's prophecy of a coming new Prophet who will deliver a new word contributes another layer to the Messiah's OT portrait. Although Luther does not incorporate any of his paradigmatic NT texts such as Romans 1:1–2 or John 5:39, one can sense that they are lurking closely behind his statement, "Many are these texts in the Old Testament, *which the holy apostles quoted and drew upon*."[58]

Prefaces to the Individual and Groups of Books of the Bible

But what of the rest of the prefaces? Does Luther faithfully carry out this vision for reading Christ as the *sensus literalis* of Scripture because of its messianic focal point as he introduces the individual parts of the Bible rather than the whole? A brief review of how other prefaces cohere with the theological and interpretive approach that Luther set forth in the *Preface to the New Testament* and the *Preface to the Old Testament* will now be presented. The following discussion will presume familiarity with the data covered in chapter 2.

New Testament

Certainly Luther desired the *Preface to the New Testament* and the *Preface to the Epistle of St. Paul to the Romans* to function normatively over the way the rest of the NT was to be understood in terms of its prime subject matter. The *Preface to the New Testament* undoubtedly conveys that Christ is its

---

56. *LW* 35:173; *WA* 16:390, "Zum andern, wie ytzund gesagt ist, lesen wyr Mosen umb der verheyssung willen, die von Christo lauten, der nicht alleyn denn Juden, sondern auch den Heyden zugehort. Denn durch yhn solten alle Heyden den segen haben, wie Abraham verheyssen war."

57. Luther links Gen 3:15 and 22:18 with the promise of a "seed" (*samen*). As is customary, the English translator renders *samen* as "seed" in the context of Gen 3:15, but changes it to "descendants" in reference to Gen 22:18. Despite working within *samen*'s semantic range, the English misses the deliberate verbal connection between these two texts represented in Luther's German. *LW* 35:169; *WA* 16:382.

58. Italics mine; *LW* 35:169; *WA* 16:383.

center. For the most part, this preface exudes the air of a definitional treatise on the "gospel," and as has been previously argued, that "gospel" definition is essentially the apostolic announcement of the full-orbed messianic hope promised by the prophets.

When one encounters Luther's *Preface to the Romans*, he or she will not find a rehashed *Preface to the New Testament*. Instead, the *Preface to the Romans* represents for Luther the definitive account of the apostolic preaching of the gospel, which is how Luther characterizes the overall nature of the NT.[59] If the *Preface to the New Testament* is meant to clarify the content of the "gospel" and the identity of Jesus Christ in relation to the OT, then the *Preface to Romans* is intended to epitomize the nature of the apostolic preaching that the other NT writings will practice each in their own way. Now that the Christ has come and his work is finished, the NT writings explicate and herald this "gospel" and its benefits, summoning everyone to faith that "comes only through God's Word or gospel, which preaches Christ, saying that he is God's Son and a man, and has died and risen again for our sakes."[60] As discussed in chapter 2, the description of "God's Word or gospel" succinctly mirrors the thicker account in the *Preface to the New Testament*.

Concerning Luther's biblical-theological hermeneutic, only Genesis 3:15 explicitly appears, and when it does, it is treated as the starting point for humanity's hope that the power of sin would be severed at its root of unbelief through "the seed [*same*] of the woman," that is, "Christ, [who] must tread [it] under foot, as was promised to Adam, Genesis 3[:15]."[61] Here, as in other writings, the first messianic prediction forms the bedrock for the rest of Scripture's witness to Jesus Christ, which places the Bible's Christology primarily within the context of the messianic hope.

---

59. Earlier in *A Brief Instruction* (1521), Luther categorized the OT as truly "Scripture" whereas the "new testament" as "gospel" is not primarily a message to be written down, but rather is "good news" meant for proclamation. As Luther explains, "Yet [the OT] alone bears the name of Holy Scripture. And the gospel should really not be something written, but a spoken word which brought forth the Scriptures, as Christ and the apostles have done. This is why Christ himself did not write anything but only spoke. He called his teaching not Scripture but gospel, meaning good news or a proclamation that is spread not by pen but by word of mouth." *LW* 35:123; WA 10.1.1:17. This topic will be discussed further in a later section.

60. *LW* 35:368; WA, *DB* 7:6, "So kompt der glawbe nicht, on alleyne durch Gottis wort oder Euangelion, das Christum prediget, wie er ist Gottis son und Mensch, gestorben und afferstanden umb unsern willen."

61. *LW* 35:369; WA, *DB* 7:9, "den des Weibes same Christus zutretten mus, wie Adam verheissen ward, Gen. am iii."

Another slight instance of his biblical-theological hermeneutic upon which he perceives Paul to ground the gospel's message of justification by faith, forgiveness of sins, and the gift of Christ's righteousness is an implicit allusion to Romans 3:21–22.[62] Near the end of his brief survey of Romans 3, Luther writes, "God forgives all former sins to demonstrate that we are helped only by his righteousness, which he grants in faith, and which was revealed at that time through the gospel and *was witnessed to beforehand by the law and the prophets.*"[63] Romans 3:21–22 is a text to be added among other likeminded NT passages such as Romans 1:1–2, Luke 24, or John 5:39 in Luther's collection of verses from which he contends for Christ and the details of the gospel present in the OT's literal sense. Moreover, he will enlist Romans 3:21 again in a similar theological context in the *Preface to the Epistles of St. James and St. Jude.*[64]

Luther's prologues to the rest of the Pauline epistles are brief overviews of the letters's occasions, chapters, and main themes. Because Luther has labored to unpack his NT theology in the first two prefaces, he now highlights the coherence between the epistles with the task of the gospel's proclamation epitomized by Paul in Romans. So, for instance, in the *Preface to the First Epistle of St. Paul to the Corinthians*, the church has forgotten "the main thing . . . that *Christ is our* salvation, righteousness, and redemption."[65] Or, in the *Preface to the Epistle of St. Paul to the Galatians*, Paul's initial success in escorting the Galatians to the "true Christian faith, from the law to the gospel" now has to be re-taught to remind them "that everyone must be justified without merit, without works, without law, *through Christ alone.*"[66] In the *Preface to the Epistle of St. Paul to the Ephesians*, Paul teaches that the gospel of how sinners become righteous, godly, saved, and freed people from law, sin, and death, God predestined in eternity to be "earned and sent

62. Rom 3:21–22a, "But now the righteousness of God has been manifested apart from the law, although *the Law and the Prophets bear witness to it*—the righteousness of God through faith in Jesus Christ for all who believe" (italics mine).

63. Italics mine; LW 35:373; WA, DB 7:14, "der uns alle vorige sund vergibt, da mit er beweyse, das seyne gerechtigkeyt, die er gibt ym glauben, alleyne uns helffe, die zu der zeyt durchs Euangelion offinbart und zuuor durchs gesetz und propheten betzeuget ist."

64. See discussion below.

65. Italics mine; LW 35:381; WA, DB 7:84, "das heubtstück . . . Das Christus unser Heil, gerechtigkeit, erlösung ist."

66. Italics mine; LW 35:384; WA, DB 7:172, "Die Galater waren durch sanct Paulus zu dem rechten Christen glawben und uns Euangelion von dem gesetz bracht . . . , das on verdienst, on werk, on gesetz, sondern alleyn durch Christum, yderman muß rechtfertig werden."

forth *through Christ.*"[67] And perhaps with echoes of the *Preface to New Testament*, in the *Preface to the Epistle of St. Paul to the Colossians*, Luther pares down Paul's teaching in chapter 1 into a delineation of "what the gospel and faith are, namely, a wisdom that recognizes *Christ as Lord and God, crucified for us.*"[68]

The General Epistles exhibit similar consistencies, especially the prefaces to the Petrine and Johannine letters. Despite his suspicion of the remaining four, some positive contributions are present. As was noted in chapter 2, Luther appreciates Hebrews because its author develops a Christology of Jesus as the Great High Priest in accordance with the OT, thereby embodying the right interpretation of the OT as Christian Scripture.[69] To put it another way, Luther sees the author of Hebrews as an example of one who correctly hears the literal sense witness of the OT.[70] The *Preface to James and Jude* is almost entirely devoted to a general excursus on the office of an apostle, and thus, does not see the respective writings as significant contributions to the apostolic preaching of the gospel.[71] Next, the revised *Preface to the Revelation of St. John* from 1530 includes an allusion to Luther's biblical-theological hermeneutic in the first part of his description of predictive prophecy: "The first [type] expresses itself simply in words, without images and figures—as Moses, David, and others of the prophets prophesy about Christ."[72] This statement is revealing in several ways: (1) the OT contains direct prophecies of Christ; (2) those prophecies are ascribed to the prophetic and authorial roles of Moses, David, and others; and (3) their prophetic utterances are communicated in simple "words" (*worten*), which hints at the grammatical-historical sense.

67. Italics mine; *LW* 35:385; WA, *DB* 7:190, "und durch Christum verdienet und außgangen ist."

68. Italics mine; *LW* 35:386; WA, *DB* 7:224, "was das Euangelion und glawbe sey, nemlich, eyn weyßheyt die Christum eynen herrn und God erkenne, fur uns gecreutzigt."

69. *LW* 35:395; WA, *DB* 7:344.

70. Concerning the author of Hebrews, Luther observes, "Thus it is plain that this is the work of an able and learned man; as a disciple of the apostles he had learned much from them and was greatly experienced in faith and practiced in the Scriptures." *LW* 35:395; WA, *DB* 7:344.

71. Luther's discussion on the indicator of a "sacred book" as that which "inculcates/drives Christ" will be treated below in a later section.

72. *LW* 35:400; WA, *DB* 7:406, "Die erste thuts mit ausgedrucken worten, on bilde und figuren, wie Moses, David und der gleichen Propheten mehr, von Christo weissagen."

Lastly, Luther's reflections on the nature of Acts well encapsulates his vision for what the NT writings subsequent to the fourfold Gospels are doing. His reappraisal in the *Preface to the Acts of the Apostles* from 1533 suggests that this NT book is no mere historical narrative. It is best perceived as an account of true apostolic preaching and right reception of the gospel of God concerning his Son. From Luther's vantage point, Luke's prime interest is to sound forth the charge to all Christendom that "the true and chief article of Christian doctrine is this: We must all be justified alone by faith *in Jesus Christ*, without any contribution from the law or help from our works."[73] Given this reading, the most important features in Acts are the apostolic sermons. To overlook these would be to bypass the author's main intention for crafting such a work as well as what constitutes it as Christian Scripture.

In sum, even if the apostolic preaching of the gospel places justification by faith and the forgiveness of sins at its forefront, the basis for these truths is always *solus Christus*; therefore, although the remainder of the NT prefaces may emphasize the benefits of the Messiah's person and work realized in Jesus Christ, this material focus does not shift the foundation for Christ as the literal sense of Scripture away from its messianic cornerstone towards a vague "gospel-centrism;" instead, it works from its messianic grounding while constantly pointing back to it.

Old Testament

The *Preface to the Old Testament* covers the Pentateuch, so "What, then, are the other books, the prophets and the histories?"[74] Or what of the wisdom and poetry writings? How do they continue the witness to Christ launched by Moses? As with the *Preface to the New Testament* (1522) and the *Preface to Romans* (1522), one ought to drape the *Preface to the Old Testament* (1523) over the canvas of the prologues for the individual OT books. Whatever is said or not said in these prefaces must be held against the backdrop of the *Preface to the Old Testament*. Luther affirms a tightly unified witness between Moses and the rest of the OT, for the latter derives its purpose from the former; therefore, if preeminent among Moses's tasks is to prophesy of

73. Italics mine; *LW* 35:363; WA, *DB* 6:414, "das rechte heubstück Christlicher lere, Nemlich, wie wir alle müssen gerecht werden, allein durch den glauben an Jhesu Christo, on alles zuthun des Gesetzes, odder hülffe unser werck."

74. *LW* 35:246; WA, *DB* 8:28, "[W]as sind aber nun die ander bucher der propheten und der geschichten?"

the coming Messiah, it will be so for all others inspired by God to produce writings that are Holy Scripture.[75]

The "historical" books from Joshua to Esther were translated for the *Deutsche Bibel*, but did not receive prefaces. The wisdom and poetic books that followed in print did, however. These included prologues to the Psalter and Solomon's writings: Proverbs, Ecclesiastes, and Song of Songs. The *Preface to the Psalter* (1528) tells that Psalms has much to offer its contemporary readers, as Luther affirms, but the greatest purpose of this book is that "it promises Christ's death and resurrection so clearly—and pictures his kingdom and the condition and nature of all Christendom—that it might well be called a little Bible."[76] The Psalter's supreme function, on the other hand, does not prohibit diversity in its content or use, which Luther then proceeds to discuss. Moreover, this diversified witness within the OT canon manifests itself in Luther's assessment of Solomon's three writings. Instead of slipping back into allegory, Luther tries to preserve the discrete voice of these books, summarizing them as the revealed wisdom of God for an obedient life within the spiritual and temporal realms.[77]

With prefaces missing for the "historical" books and the *Preface to the Psalter* as the anchor among the poetic writings for messianic referentiality, the prophets are left to carry the weight of Christ as the *sensus literalis* of the OT forecasted in the *Preface to the Old Testament*. And with these prefaces, Luther does not disappoint.

Luther's account of the separate testimonies to Christ in the OT prophetic writings can be condensed into his own twofold formula explicated in the *Preface to the Prophets* (1532). As expounded upon in chapter 2,

75. On the derivation of the full scope of the OT's prophetic word from Moses's office, Luther answers the question he begged above, "I answer: They are nothing else than what Moses is. For they all propagate [*treyben*] the office of Moses." *LW* 35:246; WA, *DB* 8:28.

76. *LW* 35:254; WA, *DB* 10.1:99, "das er von Christus sterben und aufferstehung, so klerlich verheisset, und sein Reich und der gantzen Christenheit stand und wesen furbildet. Das es wol möcht ein kleine Biblia heissen" (1545).

77. Upon a full reading of the *Preface to the Books of Solomon* (1534), Luther's interpretation of Proverbs fits with his depiction also of Ecclesiastes and Song of Songs: "It may properly be called a book of good works, for in it he teaches *how to lead a good life before God and the world*" (italics mine); *LW* 35:258; WA, *DB* 10.2:6. His prologues to Solomon do not force upon the texts a so-called "Christianized" reading to find an explicit christological referent; rather, Luther appears committed to do justice to their subject matter. Interestingly, in contrast to his complaint against James's epistle, which allegedly does not "drive/push" (*treiben*) Christ as a true apostle should, but instead preaches the law, Luther does not seem to find the same problematic in Solomon's works or call their canonical status into question, even though his description of them centers on wisdom, not *was Christum treibet*.

Luther says in the *Preface to the Prophets* that a prophet has the dual role (1) of prophesying about the coming Christ and his kingdom and (2) of preaching the law, calling God's people away from sinful idolatry and unbelief.[78] A notable moment is when Luther invokes 1 Peter 1:10–12, a key NT text from his biblical-theological hermeneutic, to support the prophet's primary function to bear witness to the Messiah. In this way, Christ and his future salvation are directly promised in the prophets, thus making their writings perpetually relevant for the Christian church because "as St. Peter boasts in 1 Peter 1[:11–12] that the prophets were not serving themselves in the things which were revealed to them, but us. It was us, he says, that they were serving."[79]

Although the prophets rebuke, often harshly, the people's sin and failure to keep the first commandment, they never cease to proclaim in various ways the comforting promise of the Messiah and the kingdom he will establish. In fact, Luther does not fail to expose how every prophet carries on the task of promising and prophesying about the person and work of the Messiah passed on from Moses in their respective prefaces except for Jonah. Nonetheless, even if absent from its prologue to accompany the *Deutsche Bibel*, aside from its anticipation of the gospel spreading to the Gentiles, Luther contends for a figural reading (not opposed to its *sensus literalis*) of Jonah in his *Lectures on Jonah* (1525) that reveals how God is using this prophet to anticipate Christ's death and resurrection.[80]

In short, to affirm Christ as the literal sense of the OT, for Luther, is to recognize that the OT as Christian Scripture is foremost concerned with *was Messias treibet*. It would not be Holy Scripture given by the Triune God if its central authorial referent was not Christ as the promised Messiah. Helmer encapsulates this ontological and textual reality well when she posits, "With respect to the christological referent, the Old Testament differs from the New Testament only according to the temporal orientation to Christ. The New Testament is written from the perspective of the Christ who has come, whereas the Old Testament is the cradle of Christ, conveying the Christ who is to come."[81]

---

78. *LW* 35:265–66; WA, *DB* 11.1:2, 4.

79. *LW* 35:266; WA, *DB* 11.2:2, "wie S. Petrus rhümet. i. Petr. i. Das die Propheten habens nicht jnen selbs dargethan, was jnen offenbart ist, Sondern, Uns, Uns (spricht er) haben sie es dargethan."

80. See discussion and notes in chapter 2 under the section, "Preface to the Prophet Jonah."

81. Helmer, "Luther's Trinitarian Hermeneutic and the Old Testament," 52.

Authorial Intention as a Textual Warrant
for Christ as the *Sensus Literalis*

The claim of the messianic basis for Luther's view that all Scripture is directed to Jesus Christ stems also from the ancillary claim that this messianic
reading of the Bible is a determinate from exegesis of the scriptural text.
The point to be made is that the groundwork for Luther's observed christocentric approach to Scripture is foremost a textual conclusion generated
by his prevailing messianic account of the christological referent of both
Testaments that together form "the character of Christian Scripture" as a
whole.[82] The role of authorial intention is significant for this assertion because it grounds Luther's commitment to Christ as the Bible's center within
Scripture's literal sense.

Richard Muller correctly notes that "the transition from the Middle
Ages to the Reformation was not, certainly, a transition from precritical to
modern 'critical' exegesis."[83] A better way to describe the change is that it
was a shift "from a precritical approach that could acknowledge spiritual
senses of the text beyond the literal sense to a precritical approach that
strove to locate spiritual meaning entirely in the literal sense."[84] In many
ways, Muller's expression of the continuity/discontinuity between Medieval
and Reformation biblical interpretation is epitomized in the competing
theories on the "early" Luther's hermeneutical shift represented by Gerhard
Ebeling and James Preus previously outlined.[85] The crux of Preus's response
to Ebeling is that during his *First Lectures on the Psalms* (1513–15), Luther
moved into a position that assigned Christ to the OT's literal-historical
sense as opposed to a "prophetic" or "spiritual" one not latent in its "letter."[86]

82. This terminology draws from Seitz's insightful and dense work, *The Character
of Christian Scripture: The Significance of a Two-Testament Bible*.

83. Muller, "Biblical Interpretation in the Era of the Reformation," 14. As it regards
Luther, Hendrix admits, "It would be much easier to find Luther's place in the history
of biblical interpretation if medieval and Reformation exegesis could be sharply dis-
tinguished from each other . . . The dividing line between medieval and Reformation
interpretation of Scripture is blurred." By the end of his essay, Hendrix decides to put
Luther in a category all by himself, given the continuities shared with his Medieval interpreters and his own nuanced principles. Hendrix, "Luther against the Background
of the History of Biblical Interpretation," 229, 238; see also the fine essay, Herrmann,
"Luther's Absorption of Medieval Biblical Interpretation and His Use of the Church
Fathers," 71–90.

84. Muller, "Biblical Interpretation in the Era of the Reformation," 14.

85. See the section on "The 'Early' Luther" in chapter 1.

86. Preus defends a "promise-advent" scheme to Luther's developed hermeneutic
in the *Dictata super Psalterium*. A result of this structure is, "First, the text is interpreted

Whether Preus's alternative proposal is superior to Ebeling's concerning Luther's hermeneutic from start to finish in the *Dictata* does not deter from the reality that by the time of the Bible-prefaces, a literal-historical conception of the *sensus literalis* is Luther's approach to Scripture.

On another note, Luther's interest in the spirituality of the letter was not innovative, even if he personally experienced a shift in interpretive practice. In the book, *Biblical Poetics before Humanism and Reformation*, Christopher Ocker has convincingly evinced the case that the Protestant Reformers continued, in large part, the "textual attitude" developed in the Late Middle Ages.[87] Perhaps the most significant component of this "textual attitude" in Ocker's designation is the "association of spiritual or ultimate meaning with the literal sense."[88] Likewise, G. R. Evans has vividly described the state of the traditional fourfold method at the Reformation in her important two volume study on biblical interpretation in the Medieval period, *The Language and Logic of the Bible*, "The old image of chewing and sucking Scripture and coming to the heart of its flavor, which in the *earlier* Middle Ages had made the spiritual senses the kernel, is now adapted for the literal sense alone."[89] The *sensus literalis* now contained an expansiveness which enabled it to be the place for theological reflection and spiritual experience in Christian Bible reading.

'christologically,' but in a way different from the early treatment in the prefaces [to the *Dictata*], whereby Christ himself speaks, or the prophet describes Christ and the Church in New Testament fashion. Here, Christ is the one who is promised and awaited, so that in all times, God's word to his people is the promise: God comes to man in Christ." Preus, *From Shadow to Promise*, 195. Cf. Childs, "The *Sensus Literalis* of Scripture: An Ancient and Modern Problem," 87, "The Reformers' achievement was to offer an interpretation of the literal sense which, at least for a short time, held together the historical and the theological meaning, but shortly this unity of interpretation also broke apart." Childs is, here, anticipating the historical-critical method's restriction of the biblical text's *sensus literalis* to the "historical sense."

87. Ocker, *Biblical Poetics before Humanism and Reformation*, 216; see esp. chap. 5, "Reformation," 185–213.

88. The following is a summary of what Ocker identifies as the "textual attitude" of Late Medieval interpreters: "The textual attitude that developed in late medieval Europe consisted of an association of spiritual or ultimate meaning with the literal sense, the communion of (divine and human) writers with (past and present) readers, and a sense of continuity between all religious writers and readers." Ibid.

89. Evans, *The Language and Logic of the Bible: The Road to Reformation*, 50; italics mine. *The Road to Reformation* is on interpretive practice in the Late Middle Ages, and pursues the question of its relationship to the Reformation. She, likewise, is interested in revisiting how much of a break is actually occurring in the Protestant Reformers with their Medieval predecessors. *The Road to Reformation* is meant to be a sequel to *The Language and Logic of the Bible: The Earlier Middle Ages*.

The locus of theological substance and meaning in the literal sense pointed to an interesting turn of events for the history of biblical interpretation: the equivocation of the divine author's intended sense with the *sensus literalis*.[90] To grasp what the Holy Spirit has revealed in Scripture meant to discern the human author's intention. And, authorial intention was communicated through literary forms and practices. Hence, biblical interpretation in the Late Middle Ages that fed into the sixteenth century experienced increased attention to the textual features of the biblical text with respect to authorial roles in order to perceive divine meaning and to confirm orthodox, theological truth.[91]

Furthermore, adaptation of the theory of Aristotelian causality to biblical inspiration in Late Medieval thought freed human authors through the "formal cause" of their own writings to bring the divine author's revelatory "formal cause" from potentiality to actuality.[92] Human authors as the "efficient cause" produced the literal sense of the biblical text with their respective stylistic preferences, vocabulary, and genre apart from quenching divine intention or their divine inspiration.[93] The literal sense and the human author did not stand in the way of discerning what the Spirit as the ultimate author of Scripture had disclosed through written revelation; rather, understanding the biblical author's intention was paramount for grasping

90. Levy, "The Literal Sense of Scripture and the Search for Truth in the Late Middle Ages," 825. Levy offers an immensely informative essay on the formation of the *sensus literalis* peculiar to the Late Middle Ages. He follows the work of Thomas Aquinas, Nicholas de Lyra, Richard Fitzralph, John Wyclif, Henry Totting de Oyta, Jean Gerson, and Paul of Burgos to show the progression toward a strong affirmation of the literal sense as the divine' author's sense, which caused the *sensus literalis* to be the determination of orthodox doctrine for these theologians. Cf. Minnis, "'Authorial Intention' and 'Literal Sense' in the Exegetical Theories of Richard Fitzralph and John Wyclif," 1–31.

91. Levy, "The Literal Sense of Scripture and the Search for Truth in the Late Middle Ages," 783–89.

92. Minnis, *Medieval Theory of Authorship*, 117–18. See also Smalley on the retrieval of Aristotelian causality and its effects on Late Medieval theology and exegesis, beginning sometime in the thirteenth century in Smalley, *The Study of the Bible in the Middle Ages*, 292–308.

93. Minnis, *Medieval Theory of Authorship*, 75–103.

the divinely intended meaning.[94] The spirituality of the letter was contained in the literality of the literal sense.[95]

The purpose of the next two sub-sections is to perceive how Luther envisions the authorial task of both the divine and human authors of Scripture as ultimately to bear witness to Jesus Christ. This shared function determines the christological referent of Scripture accessible in the biblical author's literal sense. A caveat should be issued at this juncture. Due to the nature of the prefaces to the Bible, the internal practice of Luther's exegetical method is not on display. The prefaces are the fruit of prior exegesis and interpretation; therefore, presuppositions and preconditions will be of prime interest rather than an evaluation of his interpretive practices. So, the method of observation taken will be to ask, in what manner do the prefaces exhibit Luther's commitment to the *sensus literalis* as authorial intent? Moreover, how does authorial intention serve as a textual warrant for Christ as the

---

94. The search for a "spiritual" sense behind, beneath, or above the "letter" of the scriptural text no longer fit with the Late Medieval configuration of the relationship between divine and human authorship. The old "letter and Spirit" divide was already in a state of dissolution prior to Luther and his recasting of the *sensus literalis* as the grammatical-historical sense. Additionally, the "historicism" that subsequently predominated the literal sense in modern hermeneutics, that once again dislocated the "letter" from the "Spirit," was absent in both the late Middle Ages and Reformation biblical interpretation. Highlighting this missing characteristic, Ocker clarifies, "By historicism I mean pervasive 'modern' conviction of the historically conditioned quality of all human thought and action and a focus on particular and social experiences as conditions and qualifiers of the universal." Ocker, *Biblical Poetics before Humanism and Reformation*, 216.

95. Muller speaks of the theological and/or spiritual meaning as embedded in the Bible's "letter" as an aspect of continuity among sixteenth-century interpreters with their Medieval forebearers. The Reformers pushed this progression further, as he writes, "Even so, Luther, Calvin, and their contemporaries did not simply trade allegory for literal interpretation. They strengthened the shift to letter with increased emphasis on textual and philological study, and then proceeded to find various figures and levels of meaning, indicating *credenda*, *agenda*, and *speranda* embedded in the letter itself." Muller, "Biblical Interpretation in the Era of the Reformation," 12. Cf. Frei's depiction of precritical hermeneutics in exemplaries such as Luther and Calvin where the verbal sense (i.e., literal sense or grammatical-historical sense) pointed beyond itself to its religious, theological significance, that is, its subject matter. This perspective on the verbal sense/literal sense protected it from wooden "literalness." Because divine intention was communicated unhindered by human agency in the generation of biblical texts, verbal sense and the eternal reality to which it witnessed were not at odds. In Frei's assessment, "The literal or grammatical meaning, primary for Luther and Calvin, was for both men usually identical with the text's subject matter, i.e. its historical reference, its doctrinal content, and its meaningfulness as life description and prescription." Frei, *The Eclipse of Biblical Narrative*, 9, 23–24.

literal sense on the basis of a messianic reading of Scripture that norms the characterization of the Bible's theological unity?

Divine Authorship: The Holy Spirit as Witness to Christ

A full account of Luther's doctrine of biblical inspiration is not necessary to discuss his view of the Holy Spirit's authorial role in the creation of a scriptural witness where Jesus Christ is the literal sense referent. Regardless of the nature of Luther's inspiration "theory," Scripture undeniably has as its ultimate author the Holy Spirit in Luther's theology; the Bible's origin is divine.[96] As Kenneth Hagen has fervently maintained, Luther was a Medieval, Augustinian monk who inherited the tradition of Scripture as the *sacra pagina*.[97] The source and task of theology "was all wrapped up in the study of God's sacred imprint in Holy Writ."[98] On the Spirit as the source of Scripture, Luther himself a few years before his death states clearly in the treatise *On the Last Words of David* (1543), "Thus we attribute to the Holy Spirit all of Holy Scripture."[99]

This divine origin entails divine intention in the biblical text; thus, Luther naturally speaks of the Holy Spirit's authorial relationship to Scripture in various ways. In *Answer to the Hyperchristian* (1521), his third reply to Emser, Luther calls the Holy Spirit "the simplest writer and adviser in heaven and on earth. That is why his words could have no more than the one simplest meaning which we call the written one, or the literal meaning of the tongue."[100] In an early writing associated with Luther's *Judenschriften*

96. On Scripture's divine origin in Luther's theology, Sasse writes, "When we speak of Luther's understanding of the relationship between the Word and the Spirit, we have to answer the question what he taught on the inspiration of Scripture. It has to be stated that he took over the traditional doctrine of Scripture as having been given by inspiration of the Holy Spirit. He never questioned this doctrine, which was taken for granted by all Christendom. Nor did he try to improve it or develop a new one. He never asked whether his new understanding of Scripture demanded a revision or a new formulation of the old doctrine." Sasse, "Luther and the Word of God," 84.

97. Hagen, "The History of Scripture in the Church," 1–2; Hagen, *Luther's Approach to Scripture*, 15–17.

98. Hagen, "The History of Scripture in the Church," 1.

99. Luther's complete thought here reads: "Thus we attribute to the Holy Spirit all of Holy Scripture and the external Word and the sacraments, which touch and move our external ears and other senses." *LW* 15:275; WA 54:35, "Also gibt man nu dem Heiligen Geist die gantze Heilige Schrifft und das eusserliche wort und Sacrament, so unser eusserliche ohren und synne ruren oder bewegen."

100. *LW* 39:178; WA 7:650, "Der heylig geyst ist der aller eynfeltigst schreyber und rether, der ynn hymell und erden ist, drumb auch seyne wortt nit mehr den eynen

called, *That Jesus Christ was Born a Jew* (1523), Luther defends the true meaning of Isaiah 7:14 as a prediction of the virgin birth based upon how Matthew and Luke in their Gospels affirm Mary, the Mother of Jesus, as Isaiah's referent. For added comfort in the messianic interpretation of this OT passage, just as with the prophet Isaiah, so also Luther says, "God the Holy Spirit speaks through St. Matthew and St. Luke; we can be sure that He understands Hebrew speech and expressions perfectly well."[101] A final example demonstrates further the link between Scripture's literal sense and the Holy Spirit's authorial intention. In Luther's classic recipe for "a correct way of studying theology" (*eine rechte weise in der Theologia zu studirn*)—*oratio*, *meditatio*, and *tentatio*—he advises that when one meditates on Scripture, he or she should do so "not only in your heart, but also externally, by actually repeating and comparing oral speech and literal words of the book, reading and rereading them with diligent attention and reflection, *so that you may see what the Holy Spirit means* [*meinet*] *by them.*"[102]

Echoes of the Holy Spirit as Scripture's author, likewise, appear in the prefaces to the Bible. A general manifestation occurs in Luther's introductory formula for each of the OT texts that trace the messianic hope, starting with Genesis 3:15. To lead into the quotation of either Genesis 3:15, Genesis 22:18, or 2 Samuel 7:12–14, Luther begins with the pattern, "*God* promised . . . ."[103] Though subtle, Luther is attributing to God the Spirit the promise of the Messiah being spoken in the words of the quoted scriptural text. More explicitly, in a positive capacity, the Spirit's authorial role is invoked to praise the Christian use of the Psalter, when Luther ponders, "I have a notion that the Holy Spirit wanted to take the trouble himself to compile a short Bible and book of examples of all Christendom or all saints, so that anyone who

---

einfeltigsten synn haben kunden, wilchen wir den schrifftlichen odder buchstabischen tzungen synn nennen."

101. *LW* 45:208; WA 11:321, "Denn Gott der heylige geyst durch .S. Matheus und Lucas redet, wilchen wyr gewissz da fur halten, er verstehe die Ebreischen sprache und wort wol."

102. *Preface to the Wittenberg Edition of Luther's German Writings* (1539); italics mine; *LW* 34:286; WA 50:658–59, "Zum andern soltu meditirn, das ist: Nicht allein im hertzen, sondern auch eusserlich die mündliche rede und buchstabische wort im Buch jmer treiben und reiben, lesen und widerlesen, mit vleissigem auffmercken und nachdencken, was der heilige Geist damit meinet."

103. Genesis 3:15: "God gave the first promise when he said to the serpent, . . ."; Genesis 22:18: "God promised Abraham, . . ."; 2 Samuel 7:12–14: "Again God made this promise to David . . . ." *LW* 35:360; WA, DB 6:4, 6. As previously discussed, this device is part of Luther's biblical-theological hermeneutic, and Luther's manner of introducing these OT passages is borrowed from the Apostle Paul's language in Romans 1:1–2.

could not read the whole Bible would here have anyway almost an entire summary of it, comprised in one little book."[104] Conversely, in the *Preface to the Revelation of St. John* (1522), Luther alludes to the canonical criterion of Spirit-authorship for a negative evaluation of the Book of Revelation in his conclusion, "I can in no way detect that the Holy Spirit produced it."[105]

Certainly, Scripture's supreme author is the Holy Spirit for Luther. But as an author, what is the Spirit's main intent? What is his objective as Heaven's writer? First, just as the prophets and apostles have a particular office and message, so does the Holy Spirit. Commenting on John 16:13 from a sermon series on John 14–16 in 1537 about how the Spirit speaks what he is told, Luther believes that, "Here Christ defines the Holy Spirit's office and points out what and about what He is to teach."[106] Unlike false prophets and teachers, who conjure up empty interpretations of Scripture and preach from their own authority, the Spirit's message contains "absolute truth" (*lauter Warheit*) for he delivers only what he hears from God the Father and the God the Son. Given this inner-trinitarian relationship, what Christ means then, according to Luther, is "Thus He will speak exclusively of Me and will glorify Me, so that the people will believe in Me."[107]

Present in this latter statement is the perspective of the Holy Spirit as a "witness" to Christ. In his *Lectures on Hebrews* (1517–18) regarding the ratification of the "new testament," Luther identifies that "the witnesses of this testament are the Holy Spirit Himself and the apostles," with supporting evidence in John 15:25, Acts 3:15, and Acts 1:8.[108] The title or task of "witness" for scriptural authors in Luther's approach to Scripture is significant. During his *Lectures on Zechariah* (1527), Luther forms a modest theology of "bearing witness" that must be taken into account when considering his doctrine of biblical inspiration. Generally, "the word 'bear witness to' in Scripture," Luther suggests, "means as much as 'to proclaim the word of

---

104. *Preface to the Psalter* (1528), *LW* 35:254; *WA, DB* 10.1:98, 100, "Das mich dünckt, der heilige geist habe selbs wollen die mühe auff sich nemen, und eine kürtze Bibel und exempelbuch von der gantzen Christenheit odder allen heiligen zu samen bringen, auff das, wer die gantze Biblia nicht lesen kündte, hette hierynn doch fast die gantze summa verfasset yn ein klein büchlin."

105. *LW* 35:398; *WA, DB* 7:404, "und aller dinge nicht spuren kan, das es von dem heyligen geyst gestellet sey."

106. *LW* 24:362; *WA* 46:58, "Er mallet aber hiemit des heiligen Geists ampt und deutet, was und wovon er leren sol."

107. *LW* 24:363; *WA* 46:58, "Und also allein von Mir predigen und mich verkleren wird, das die leute an mich glewben."

108. *LW* 29:214; *WA* 57:213, "Secundo: testes huius testamenti sunt ipse spiritus sanctus et apostoli, . . ."

God.'"[109] Because the Holy Spirit as well as the prophets and apostles do not speak on their own authority, but generate Holy Scripture from what they "hear," biblical authors are "witnesses" to an external Word. More so in regards to Scripture's human authors, Luther adds,

> God's Word, then, is called a "witness" because God speaks to the people through men, who are His witnesses; Acts 1:8: "You shall be My witnesses." But what one bears witness to, that men do not see but only hear; and it must be believed. Therefore "bearing witness" is nothing but God's Word spoken by angels or men, and it calls for faith.[110]

That external word as God's Word is foremost God's desire to make known Jesus Christ and his gospel; therefore, the Holy Spirit as a "witness" to God's Word speaks it through the prophets and the apostles, resulting in an inspired text with a divine intention that foremost maintains christological referentiality at the level of its literal sense.[111]

Human Authorship:
Prophets and Apostles as Witnesses to Christ

Human authorship is an understood reality within Luther's approach to Scripture. Divine inspiration did not cause the loss of the human author's personality or even character.[112] Biblical authors had both a pen and a mind

109. *LW* 20:213; WA 23:550, "Das wort 'Bezeugen' ist ynn der schrifft eben so viel als 'Gotts wort verkündigen.'"

110. *LW* 20:213; WA 23:550, "Da her denn Gotts wort zeugnis heist, Darumb das Gott durch menschen redet, die seine zeugen sind, zum volck Act. .1. 'yhr seid meine zeugen.' Und was man zeuget, das sihet man nicht, sondern hörets alleine und mus gegleubt sein. Drumb ist 'zeugnis' nicht anders denn Gotts wort durch engel odder menschen gered, das den glauben fodder."

111. Exhorting the Lutheran Church to take its cue from Luther concerning a reexamination of the doctrine of inspiration, Sasse writes, "If we want to know what inspiration as the work of the Holy Spirit is, we must remember what Luther already knew, that none of the great works of the Spirit can be understood by means of human psychology. And we must ask what Jesus Christ Himself taught about the Holy Spirit and His work concerning the preservation of divine revelation. This is contained in the passages of chapters 14–16 of the Gospel of St. John on the Holy Spirit, the Paraclete. There the Biblical doctrine of inspiration is contained. There it becomes clear what the foremost task of the Holy Spirit is—*to witness to Christ.*" Sasse, "Luther and the Word of God," 91; italics mine.

112. For a brief account of the Late Middle Ages and Reformation struggle with the character and humanity of biblical authors as the divinely intended meaning was

of their own, though not autonomous from their Divine *Inspirator*.[113] This dynamic is represented in many ways throughout Luther's prefaces to the Bible.

To offer some examples, in the *Preface to the Book of Job* (1524), the author's language is commended as "more vigorous and splendid than that of any other book in all the Scriptures."[114] In the *Preface to the Old Testament* (1523), Luther appears to have a clear sense of Moses as the controlling author of the Pentateuch. At one point, Luther asks, "But why does Moses mix up his laws in such a disordered way?"[115] In response, Moses's authorial purposes are depicted as intertwined with their circumstances, "The answer is that Moses writes as the situation demands, so that his book is a picture and illustration of governing and of living."[116] Luther also points out that in the Pentateuch Moses "sometimes repeats a law so often and reiterates the same words so many times that it becomes tedious to read it or listen to it."[117]

---

increasingly assigned to the text's literal sense, see Evans, *The Language and Logic of the Bible: The Road to Reformation*, 15–19.

113. Minnis has an interesting essay on the problem that faced Medieval interpreters as the concept of authorship, that was growing with greater precision in the thirteenth and fourteenth centuries, was being applied in exegesis of Holy Scripture in contradistinction to pagan literature. What effect on "theology" would "poetic" analysis typically reserved for non-inspired authors have adapted for biblical interpretation? As Minnis poses the problem, "Here, then, was the trouble with theology. The fact that it shared certain styles and methods of literary procedure with the writings of the poets, who habitually were branded as liars, obliged generation after generation of Medieval theologians to defend the epistemological and moral credentials of their subject and the 'scientific' basis of its knowledge." Minnis, "The Trouble with Theology," 32–33.

114. *LW* 35:252; *WA, DB* 10.1:6, "Die rede aber dieses buchs ist so reysig und prechtig, als freylich keyns buchs ynn der gantzen schrifft."

115. *LW* 35:241; *WA, DB* 8:18, "Was ist aber, das Mose die gesetze so unordig unternander wirfft?"

116. *LW* 35:241; *WA, DB* 8:18, "Antwort, Mose schreybt, wie sichs treybt, das seyn buch eyn bild und exempel ist des regiments und lebens."

117. *LW* 35:241; *WA, DB* 8:18, "Dazu widder holet er zu weylen eyn gesetz so offt, und treybt eynerley wort so viel mal, das gleich verdrossen ist zu lesen und zu horen." Maxfield has provided a straightforward and illuminative account of Luther's approach to the authorial relationship between the Holy Spirit and Moses in the writing of Genesis. Maxfield shows that the way Luther conceived of the mode of inspiration forced him to remain strapped to the biblical text in his exegesis of Genesis, for to understand Moses meant to understand the Holy Spirit's intended meaning. He writes, "In practice, Luther's belief that the Holy Spirit has spoken in the text of the scripture as recorded by Moses led him to reject any stepping away from the text as written, even when it involved contradicting the witness of the church fathers or of reason." Maxfield, *Luther's Lectures on Genesis and the Formation of Evangelical Identity*, 34,

On a broader level, Luther freely entertains the idea that, for example, Proverbs, Ecclesiastes, or Isaiah were compiled into book form by others. His acceptance of compilation can be seen in the *Preface to the Prophet Jeremiah* (1532), when Luther submits, "So it seems as though Jeremiah did not compose these books himself, but that the parts were taken piecemeal from his utterances and written into a book. For this reason one must not worry about the order or be hindered by the lack of it."[118] At the end of the *Preface to the Epistles of St. James and St. Jude* (1522), Luther concludes without hesitation that "no one can deny that [Jude] is an extract or copy of St. Peter's second epistle, so very like it are all the words."[119]

In the midst of this kind of literary analysis, Luther remains persistent to discover the author's intention. Moreover, visible semblances of Luther's commitment to the grammatical-historical approach are present in his pursuit of Scripture's authorial intent communicated by its human authors. A clear expression occurs in the *Preface to the Acts of the Apostles* (1533) as Luther names the doctrine of justification by faith alone in Jesus Christ alone as "the chief intention [*meinung*] of the book and the author's [Luke's] principal reason for writing it."[120] Concerning an emphasis on grammatical interpretation, if one does not grasp Paul's language, as Luther posits in the *Preface to the Epistle of St. Paul to the Romans* (1522), then the reader "will never understand this letter of St. Paul, nor any other book of Holy Scripture."[121] When Luther introduces Isaiah in the *Preface to the Prophet Isaiah* (1528), he warns that if anyone fails to pay careful attention to the book's title in Isaiah 1:1 and the historical occasion conveyed therein, then the reader will be charged with misinterpreting the first verse, "let alone the whole prophet. . . . For it is impossible to mark or perceive the prophet's words and meaning [*meynung*] properly and clearly without this thorough understanding of the title."[122] Aside from other particulars to Micah's

---

see esp. the section "Genesis—The First Book of Moses and the Holy Spirit," 32–39.

118. *LW* 35:280–81; WA, *DB* 11.1:192, "as sichs ansihet, als hab Jeremias solche bücher nicht selbs gestellet, Sondern seien stücklich aus seiner rede gefasset und auffs buch verzeichent, Darumb mus man sich an die ordnung nicht keren, und die unordenung nicht hinder lassen."

119. *LW* 35:397; WA, *DB* 7:386, "Die Epistel aber Sanct Judas, kan niemant leugnen, das eyn austzog oder abschrifft ist aus Santc. Peters ander Epistel, so der selben alle wort fast gleych sind."

120. *LW* 35:363; WA, *DB* 6:414, "Solch stuck ist seine furnemeste meinung und ursache dieses buchs zu schreiben."

121. *LW* 35:372; WA, *DB* 7:12, "On solchen verstand diser wortter, wirstu dise Epistel sanct Pauli, noch keyn buch der heyligen schrifft nymer verstehen."

122. *LW* 35:274; WA, *DB* 11.1:16, "Er habe den titel und erste zeile noch nie

prophecy, Luther can say in his respective prologue, "Ultimately, however, his meaning [*meinung*] is that even though Israel and Judah have to go to pieces, Christ will yet come and make all things good."[123]

As one can see, authorial intention is both accessible and imperative in Luther's approach to Scripture. Because the biblical text has an author, divine and human at that, to claim a certain subject as the *sensus literalis* of the scope of the canon requires material validation from the parts to the whole. Although Luther's doctrine of the Word of God has a christological orientation, he would not make comprehensive claims such as "all Scripture points to Christ," if the textual meaning of the biblical witness did not do so at an authorial level. Authorial intention and the literal sense are inseparably connected to the theological identity of Scripture's authors.[124] Furthermore, Luther's preference for the grammatical-historical method is an interpretive approach applied to writings from authors who are more than poets and historians. The human authors of Holy Scripture have had a theological authorial office bestowed upon them from God the Spirit through which all of their writings are generated; therefore, whatever else might be said about Luther's theory of inspiration, it must be affirmed that the Reformer held to "a doctrinal content theory of inspiration," as Miikka Ruokanen has termed it.[125] What is meant by this formulation is that, "Luther understands the Bible before all as a theological or doctrinal entity."[126] In other words, the "historicism" alluded to previously cannot norm the biblical text's referentiality precisely because its authors (divine and human) are not so limited in the breadth or depth of their intentions as it regards the reality to which they have been charged to bear witness. The character of special revelation

---

verstanden, schweige denn den gantzen Propheten . . . Denn es unmüglich ist, des Propheten wort und meynung richtiglich und klerlich zuuernemen odder zu mercken, on solches des titels gründlich erkentnis."

123. *LW* 35:325; *WA, DB* 11.2:270, "Aber endlich ist das seine meinung, Wenn es gleich alles mus zu drümmern gehen, Israel und Juda, so wird doch der Christus komen, ders alles gut machen wird."

124. What is intended by "theological identity" has to do with Luther's conjunction of general, literary authorship with the theologically-defined "office" of a scriptural author. For Luther, an author of Scripture is not merely one who writes under the inspiration of the divine author. A "scriptural author" is a *special* "office" to which one is called for the purpose of completing a *particular* task, namely, to bear witness to Jesus Christ. The theological identity of Scripture's authors is explicated below in the dual offices of "prophets and apostles." In Luther's model, literary authorship and the divine calling to be a "witness" to Christ converge in the inspiration and generation of Scripture.

125. Ruokanen, "Does Luther Have a Theory of Biblical Inspiration?," 12.

126. Ibid.

that their writings disclose is intrinsically theological which tends toward Christ. On the other hand, Ruokanen's perspective should not be taken to encapsulate the total scope of Luther's view of biblical inspiration as if the authorial meaning was the singular reference of "inspiration" and not the words themselves. This study has labored to show that Luther guards against a false division of the *res* from the *verba*.[127] Futhermore, in his comprehensive study on the Reformer's bibliology, Mark Thompson has demonstrated extensively, "Luther's commitment to a biblical inspiration which extended to the very words of the text."[128]

"Prophets and Apostles"

A helpful paradigm for conceiving the theological nature of Luther's outlook on the authorial office in Scripture is his shorthand of "prophets and the apostles" for the Christian Bible in two-Testament form. This formula has a definite prehistory to Luther, as early as the end of the second century, where "prophets" equaled the OT and "apostles" stood for the NT as a way of encompassing the totality of Christian special revelation.[129] What began as a catch-all term for scriptural writings's human authors later doubled as a dualistic abbreviation for the Christian canon.[130] Luther's usage, likewise, reflects this tradition.

Speaking towards the relationship between the creeds of the ecumenical councils and Scripture for determination of the articles of the Christian faith, Luther contends, "if there were no Holy Scripture of *the prophets and apostles*, the mere words of the council would be meaningless, and its decisions would accomplish nothing."[131] Another occurrence interestingly

127. For an illuminating introduction into Luther's high esteem for language as capable of communicating the divine Word of God, where "the task of theology is that of linguistic theory," see Lüpke, "Luther's Use of Language," 143–55; also one may consult Lüpke, "Theologie als 'Grammatik zur Sprache der heiligen Schrift,'" 227–50.

128. Thompson, *A Sure Ground on Which to Stand*, 146. For a full defense that Luther held to a verbal-plenary understanding of inspiration, see esp. chap. 2, "The Very Words of God? Luther on Inspiration and the Origin of Holy Scripture," and chap. 3, "Divine Words? Luther on Inspiration and the Nature of Holy Scripture."

129. Farkasfalvy has painstakingly traced the development of the phrase "prophets and apostles" into a semi-technical formula for reference to the full scope of Christian Scripture in Farkasfalvy, "'Prophets and Apostles's: The Conjunction of the Two Terms before Irenaeus," 1; Farkasfalvy, *Inspiration and Interpretation*, 52–62.

130. Farkasfalvy, *Inspiration and Interpretation*, 61–62.

131. *On the Councils and the Church* (1539); italics mine; *LW* 41:59; *WA* 50:552, "Sonst wo die Heilige Schrifft der Propheten und Apostel thet, so würden die blossen wort des Concilij nichts schaffen, und jr urteil nichts ausrichten."

appears in Luther's 1543 preface to the Qur'an prepared by Hebrew and Arabic scholar, Theodor Bibliander.[132] In the prologue, Luther exhorts the Christian church to greater unity and certainty with the words, "There is one Church, existing perpetually ever since the time of Adam, to which God has disclosed Himself with sure and marvelous testimonies in the very Word that He gave to *the prophets and apostles*."[133] A final example of the shorthand manifests itself in Luther's praise of Scripture over and above all councils, church fathers, and any other non-inspired human writings for Christian faith, salvation, and living in the *Preface to the Wittenberg Edition of Luther's German Writings* (1539). "Therefore," he expresses, "it behooves us to let *the prophets and apostles* stand at the professor's lectern, while we, down below at their feet, listen to what they say. It is not they who must hear what we say."[134]

The purpose of highlighting Luther's marker for the Christian Bible in the formula, "prophets and apostles," is to connect the textual witness of Scripture to the theological identity of its human authorship, not just its divine author. This point is important to recognize because it squarely grounds the conviction that Christ is the Bible's literal sense in the divine inspiration of its human authors. In the vein of the ancient tradition aforementioned, Luther's reception of "prophets and apostles" can reference the Christian Bible as a two-Testament canon or it can serve as the categorical delineation of Scripture's authorial offices. And, it is this latter usage where Luther constructs a vision of a biblical author, whose task is to bear witness to God's revealed Word concerning his Son, a function derivative of the Holy Spirit's own office as a "witness" to Jesus Christ.

To begin, the "prophets" are responsible for witnessing to God's Word as the OT Scriptures. In the *Preface to the Old Testament* (1523), Moses as the author of the Pentateuch is the prophet from whom all subsequent OT

---

132. Luther had supported many efforts to publish a Latin translation of the Qur'an for the sake of increasing awareness of the total incompatibility between Islam and Christianity. Basel publisher Johannes Oporinus succeeded in 1543 in collaboration with Theodor Bibliander to print an elaborate edition that included prefaces from several Reformers such as Luther and Melanchthon, Bibliander's own annotations, polemical writings against Islam, and a history of the Ottoman Turks. For further background, see the translator's introduction to this preface, LW 60:286–88.

133. Italics mine; *LW* 60:292; WA 53:571, "Una est Ecclesia perpetua inde usque ab Adam, cui se certis et mirandis testimonijs patefecit Deus in hoc ipso verbo, quod tradidit prophetis et Apostolis."

134. Italics mine; *LW* 34:284; WA 50:657, "Als die wir müssen die Propheten und Apostel lassen auff dem Pult sitzen und wir hie nieden zu jren Füssen hören, was sie sagen und nicht sagen, was sie hören müssen."

prophets derive their office and message.[135] As variously discussed above, Luther on several occasions submitted his own definition of the office of a prophet; in fact, he wrote an entire preface devoted to this subject matter to introduce his German translation of the prophetic literature in 1532, the *Preface to the Prophets*. To avoid repetition, one may consult the multiple reviews of Luther's twofold definition of a prophet's office and message from the *Preface to the Prophets* in prior sections. He similarly reiterates in other prologues his presentation there. One such emblematic case can be found in the *Preface to the Prophet Isaiah* (1528).

Luther condenses Isaiah's prophecy into two addresses: (1) he rebukes the people for their many sins and idolatry; and (2) he prepares the people for and prophesies of the coming Christ and his kingdom.[136] Digressing from the particularity of Isaiah's dual prophetic word, Luther claims, "For all the prophets do the same: they teach and rebuke the people of their time, and they proclaim the coming and the kingdom of Christ, directing and pointing the people to him as the common Savior of both those who have gone before and those who are yet to come."[137] For a demonstration in Isaiah, Luther reflects momentarily upon the instance when Cyrus is called "God's anointed" in Isaiah 45:1.[138]

A theological understanding of Isaiah's prophetic and authorial role will not allow for a mere historical referent. Rather, Luther interprets, "For he [Isaiah] is concerned altogether with the Christ, that his future coming and the promised kingdom of grace and salvation shall not be despised or be lost and in vain because of unbelief and great misfortune and impatience amongst his people."[139] The kings listed whom God will use to destroy Babylon, including Cyrus, is a prophecy having to do with securing the people's hearts in God's promise of the Messiah. With subtle description,

---

135. "For Moses is, indeed, a well of all wisdom and understanding, out of which has sprung all that the prophets knew and said." *LW* 35:247; WA, *DB* 8:28.

136. *LW* 35:275; WA, *DB* 11.1:18.

137. *LW* 35:276; WA, *DB* 11.1:18, "Denn also thun alle Propheten, das sie das gegenwertige volck leren und straffen, daneben Christus zukunfft und reich verkündigen, und das volck drauff richten und weisen, als auff den gemeinen Heiland, beide der vorigen und zukünfftigen."

138. Isaiah 45:1, "Thus says the LORD to his anointed [מְשִׁיחַ], to Cyrus, whose right hand I have grasped, to subdue nations before him and to loose the belts of kings, to open doors before him that gates may not be closed."

139. *LW* 35:277; WA, *DB* 11.1:20, "Denn es ist yhm alles umb den Christum zu thun, das desselbigen zukunfft und das verheissen reich der gnaden und seligkeit, nicht odder durch unglauben und fur grossem unglück und ungedult, bey seinem volck verloren und umbsonst sein muste."

Luther notes that this prophetic aim is attributable to Isaiah's craft of which the prophet himself is conscious.[140] Isaiah is aware of his prophecy and the execution of his office as one who is to bear witness to Christ.[141] Applied to the OT canon, these authorial qualities are indicators that the OT's literal sense consists of a theological, christological referentiality determined by the messianic unveiling particular to stages of historical settings communicated through the prophets's intentionality dispensed in the "letter" of their sacred writings.

Lastly, even though at times the prophets will feature "more of threatening and rebuke than of comfort and promise," the prime goal of an OT prophet is to testify to the coming Messiah for the enduring faith and hope of those who await his arrival.[142] In the *Preface to the Second Epistle of St. Peter* (1522), Luther recounts Peter's exhortation "to hear the gospel alone and not the doctrines of men. For, as he says, 'No prophecy ever came by the impulse of men [2 Pet 1:21].'"[143] When one encounters Luther's complete exposition of 2 Peter 1:16–21 in his *Sermons on the Second Epistle of St. Peter* from the same year (1522), he or she will find that Luther paints a fuller picture of the nature of special revelation and divine inspiration.

Consistent with Peter's language, Luther speaks of the Spirit's disclosure of God's Word through human agents as "prophecy." The gospel of Jesus Christ that the Spirit makes known through the apostles is a "sure prophetic word" because it is the same "prophetic Word" he delivered through the prophets in the OT, though now revealed in clear light. To unite these

140. On the same prophecy, Luther posits, "It is here that he [Isaiah] does his greatest work, comforting and upholding a people yet to be, in this destruction and captivity yet to come, in order that they might not despair, as if they were vanquished and Christ's kingdom would not be coming and all prophecy were false and vain." *LW* 35:276; WA, *DB* 11.1:20.

141. Though not to be injected anachronistically back into ancient views on authorship and intention, a helpful insight from Hirsch on "meaning" as a "conscious" act is relevant to this point. In an attempt to reconnect "words" with their "authors," Hirsch advises, "The theory of semantic autonomy forced itself into such unsatisfactory, ad hoc formulations because in its zeal to banish the author it ignored the fact that meaning is an affair of consciousness not of words . . . A word sequence means nothing in particular until somebody either means something by it or understands something from it." Hirsch, *Validity in Interpretation*, 4.

142. *Preface to the Prophets* (1532), *LW* 35:268; WA, *DB* 11.1:6, "mehr drewens und straffens drinnen ist, wedder tröstens und verheissens."

143. *LW* 35:391; WA, *DB* 7:314, "Und fehet darnach an, widder die menschen leren, das Euangelion zu preysen, das man dasselb alleyn sole horen, und keyn menschen lere. Denn als er spricht, Es ist noch nie keyn prophecey von menschen willen geschehen."

two strands of God's Word, Luther clarifies that, in general, "*a prophet must really be one who preaches about Jesus Christ.* Therefore although many prophets in the Old Testament foretold future things, *they really came, and were sent by God, to proclaim the Christ.*"[144] In sum, the Word of God is "prophecy" about Christ and his gospel; the Spirit as a "witness" to God's Word about Christ inspires humans, who fulfill the office of "prophet" to express this message; this office itself is one that is to preach Christ, and for OT prophets as authors of Holy Scripture, this elect purpose entails that their writings will intently point to Jesus Christ by way of the messianic hope in their literal sense.

Just as he supplied a theological framework for assessing the office and message of an OT prophet, so also he provided one for a NT apostle. Luther offers an explicit description in the *Preface to the Epistles of St. James and St. Jude* (1522): "Now it is the office of a true apostle to preach of the Passion and resurrection and office of Christ, and to lay the foundation for faith in him, as Christ himself says in John 15[:27], 'You shall bear witness to me.'"[145] From here, Luther issues his canonical criterion, "All the genuine sacred books agree in this, that all of them preach and inculcate [*treyben*] Christ."[146] Applying this principle to the Book of Revelation in the original 1522 *Preface to the Revelation of St. John*, Luther similarly restates, "But to teach Christ, this is the thing which an apostle is bound above all else to do; as Christ says in Acts 1[:8], 'You shall be my witnesses.'"[147]

144. Italics mine; *LW* 30:165; WA 14:29, "Eyn Prophet aber sol eygentlich der seyn, der von Jhesu Christo predigt. Darumb wie wol viel Propheten ym alten Testament von zukunfftigen dingen geweyssagt haben, so sind sie doch eygentlich darumb komen und von Gott geschickt, das sie den Christum verkundigen solten." Cf. Luther's paraphrase of what the collective, authorial witness of the OT prophets are saying in his sermon on John 5:39–40 titled, "Search the Scriptures," from 1545, "But all the prophets, Moses, David, etc., have taught: '*I am merely a preacher of Christ, to testify and teach that He is coming,* etc. But I can give no one eternal life. When Christ comes, however, He will do it. Therefore, I will give Christ the glory,' they all said and taught, 'and ascribe this to His divine omnipotence and majesty, and fall at His feet, doff my cap, and yield to Him, for He is the Master and we are the pupils. I will say and confess that He alone is the Deliverer and Savior of the whole world, who can and will give eternal life to all who believe in Him.' That was the testimony and confession of all the prophets: Moses, David, Isaiah, etc." (italics mine); *LW* 58:255; WA 51:8–9.

145. *LW* 35:396; WA, *DB* 7:385, "Denn das ampt eines rechten Apostels ist, das er von Christus leiden und aufferstehung und Ampt predige, und lege desselbigen glaubens grund, Wie er selbs sagt, Joha. xv. Ir werdet von mir zeugen" (1546).

146. *LW* 35:366; WA, *DB* 7:384, "Und daryn stymmen alle rechtschaffene heylige bucher uber eynes, das sie alle sampt Christum predigen und treyben."

147. *LW* 35:399; WA, *DB* 7:404, "as Christus, drynnen widder geleret noch erkandt wirt, wilchs doch zu thun fur allen dingen eyn Apostel schuldig ist, wie er sagt Act. i.

Once again, Luther's theological conception of Scripture's authorship is depicted as the task of "bearing witness." And to be a "witness" inspired by the Holy Spirit to proclaim God's Word means to be called to an office that has as its supreme burden that of testifying to Jesus Christ. Luther has already repeatedly expressed in the *Preface to the New Testament* (1522) that the main content of the NT as a "book" (*buch*) is the "gospel." "[T]his gospel of God or New Testament is a good story and report" about Christ as the Son of God and of David in whose victorious death and resurrection is offered righteousness, life, and forgiveness of sins, and as Luther declares, it is "sounded forth into all the world by the apostles."[148] The apostles are the chosen heralds to begin the announcement of the gospel of the "new testament."[149] Their message is one that is intended to be, in the first place, orally proclaimed and preached, not written.[150] Nevertheless, the apostles put into written form their "witness" to Jesus Christ as the fulfillment of the long-promised Messiah foretold by the OT's prophetic word.[151] In this way,

---

yhr solt meyne zeugen seyn."

148. *LW* 35:358; WA, *DB* 6:4, "Also ist dis Euangelion Gottis unnd new testament, eyn gutte meher und geschren ynn alle wellt erschollen durch die Apostell, . . ."

149. As mentioned above, in his comments on Heb 9:17 from *the Lectures on Hebrews* (1517–18), Luther identifies the Holy Spirit and the apostles as "witnesses" to the "new testament" instituted by the sacrificial death of Jesus Christ. To show consistency in Luther's thought in coherence with the featured statements from the *Prefaces to James and Jude* and the first *Preface to Revelation*, one can see how he also uses the same categorical NT passages that speak toward the calling of human "witnesses" to Christ and his gospel to support this conclusion. In Luther's words, "In the second place, the witnesses of this testament are the Holy Spirit Himself and the apostles, as John 15:26 states: 'The Spirit of truth, who proceeds from the Father, He will bear witness concerning Me, and you will bear witness, because you have been with Me from the beginning.' Therefore they said in Acts 3:15: 'To this we are witnesses.' And in Acts 1:8 we read: 'And you shall be My witnesses in Jerusalem, etc.'" *LW* 29:214; WA 57:213.

150. Further reflection upon Luther's vision of the OT as properly "Scripture" and the NT as "proclamation" will take place in a later section. For now, on the orality of the NT, Luther describes in *A Brief Instruction* (1521), "And the gospel should really not be something written, but a spoken word which brought forth the Scriptures, as Christ and the apostles have done. This is why Christ himself did not write anything but only spoke. He called his teaching not Scripture but gospel, meaning good news or a proclamation that is spread not by pen but by word of mouth." *LW* 35:123; WA 10.1.1:17.

151. See also Luther's reflections on the true nature of the NT as a "living sermon" that was in second order transmitted into writings in his exposition of 1 Pet 1:10–12 from the *Sermons on the First Epistle of St. Peter* (1522), "For although both [OT and NT] have been put on paper word for word, the Gospel, or the New Testament, should really not be written but should be expressed with the living voice which resounds and is heard throughout the world . . . [T]he Gospel is a living sermon on the Christ who

the apostles's authorial intent will produce "sacred books" (i.e., Holy Scripture) where Christ is the literal sense, for as Luther claims in the *Preface to James and Jude* (1522), "*Whatever does not teach Christ is not yet apostolic, even though St. Peter or St. Paul does the teaching. Again, whatever preaches Christ would be apostolic*, even if Judas, Annas, Pilate, and Herod were doing it."[152]

In brief, the manner of Luther's presentation of the Bible's christocentricity in the prefaces to the *Deutsche Bibel* corroborated by other writings in Luther's corpus shows that he affirmed a concept of authorship, both divine and human, that was the determinative factor in establishing Scripture's *sensus literalis*. Scripture's authors received a particularly defined office with a special purpose from whence the Bible would derive its origin and subject matter in its "letter." Luther asserts that the Holy Spirit and the prophets and the apostles all share in the same identity as "witnesses" to God's Word concerning his Son, Jesus Christ. The Holy Spirit inspires the "prophets and the apostles" to participate in his mission to bear witness to the Word of God revealed in Christ. For the prophets, this charge entailed directly promising and prophesying the coming Messiah and his kingdom; for the apostles, their office was encapsulated in the proclamation and preaching of the gospel of God concerning his Son, Jesus Christ, as the fulfillment of that which God promised long ago by their counterparts in the OT Scriptures (Rom 1:1–2). With this theory of biblical authorship in hand, Scripture's literal sense must be Christ because making him known is the object of the authors' intentions consciously expressed in the Bible's material/textual witness.

The Hermeneutical Significance of Luther's View of Scripture as a Two-Testament Bible

The purpose of this section is to consider how Luther's teachings in the Bible-prefaces on the relationship between the two Testaments contributes to the messianic rationale for Christ as the *sensus literalis* of Scripture. In essence, Luther's explication of how the Old and New Testaments relate can be reduced into two forms: one is a soteriological (law and gospel) relationship and the other is hermeneutical.

---

has come." *LW* 30:19; WA 12:275.

152. Italics mine; *LW* 35:396; WA, *DB* 7:384, "Was Christum nicht leret, das ist nicht Apostolisch, wens gleich Petrus odder Paulus leret, Widerumb, was Christum predigt, das ist Apostolisch, wens gleych Judas, Annas, Pilatus und Herodes thett."

The Law and Gospel Distinction's Relationship to Luther's View of Christ as the Sensus Literalis

The law and gospel distinction pervades all of Luther's theology and writings.[153] The purview of this section is not to offer a comprehensive account of this theme.[154] The purpose will be narrowed to reflect upon the way Luther connects his law and gospel concept with the character of the biblical witness, specifically with respect to how the Old and New Testaments relate. The question to be asked is what is the correlation between Luther's description of law and gospel at work within the two-Testament character of Scripture and the messianic basis to Christ as the Bible's *sensus literalis*? Luther mainly expresses his thoughts on this topic in his *Preface to the New Testament* and *Preface to the Old Testament*; therefore, these two prologues will be the primary texts under review.

Near the start of the *Preface to the New Testament* (1522), Luther begins by juxtaposing the OT as a "book" (*buch*) of God's laws and commandments and the NT as a "book" (*buch*) of God's gospel and promises.[155] In 1523 with the *Preface to the Old Testament*, one can sense Luther's desire to bring the introductions for each Testament into coherence. He reaffirms

153. Ebeling explains that the nature of Luther's law and gospel formula is best understood as a "distinction" than as an "idea." Law and gospel in Luther's thought is not a centralizing theme or concept. It is an evaluative rubric for grasping theology's true meaning, or in Ebeling's words, "the decisive standard of theological judgment." Ebeling, *Luther: An Introduction to His Thought*, 111–13.

154. For introductions to law and gospel in Luther's theology, see Althaus, *The Theology of Martin Luther*, 251–73; Ebeling, *Luther: An Introduction to His Thought*, 110–24; Kolb, "'The Noblest Skill in the Christian Church': Luther's Sermons on the Proper Distinction of Law and Gospel," 301–18. An insightful study that includes an in-depth historical account of Luther's law and gospel distinction and its impact upon the English Protestant Reformation, see Whiting, *Luther in English: The Influence of His Theology of Law and Gospel on Early English Evangelicals (1525–35)*. A classic statement from Luther on the law and gospel distinction can be found in his 1535 *Lectures on Galatians*: "Therefore whoever knows well how to distinguish the Gospel from the Law should give thanks to God and know that he is a real theologian. I admit that in the time of temptation I myself do not know how to do this as I should. The way to distinguish the one from the other is to locate the Gospel in heaven and the Law on earth, to call the righteousness of the Gospel heavenly and divine and the righteousness of the Law earthly and human, and to distinguish as sharply between the righteousness of the Gospel and that of the Law as God distinguishes between heaven and earth or between light and darkness or between day and night. Let the one be like the light and the day, and the other like the darkness and the night. If we could only put an even greater distance between them!" LW 26:115; WA 40.1:207.

155. Editions of the *Preface to the New Testament* subsequent to 1537 for the complete *Deutsche Bibel* began with this passage. LW 35:358; WA, DB 6:2–3.

that the OT is a "book" (*buch*) of laws and the NT is "gospel or [a] book of grace" (*Euangeli odder gnade buch ist*).[156] But here in the *Preface to the Old Testament*, Luther extends his description of both Testaments beyond these differences. In addition to its teaching of grace, the NT also includes "other teachings that are laws and commandments."[157] So also the OT contains "certain promises [*verheyssung*] and words of grace" alongside its laws.[158] In other words, law and gospel transcend the Old and New Testaments, even though both parts of the Christian Bible have their own respective "chief teaching" (*heubt lere*).[159]

But how does this account of law and gospel in the Testaments relate to the messianic orientation of Christ as the literal sense of Scripture? The key for Luther is connecting each Testament to its corresponding historical period in relation to the advent of the Messiah as Jesus Christ. When this is determined, the relation between the Testaments explained through the law and gospel distinction becomes a soteriological one.[160] A guiding text for Luther in this analysis is 2 Corinthians 3:7–14, where he finds the Apostle Paul dividing redemptive history into two dispensations, one is the office of Moses and the other is the office of Jesus Christ.[161] In the OT, Moses informs God's people in Deuteronomy 18:15–19 that his "office and teaching" will only endure until the arrival of the Messiah, the new Prophet filled

156. He continues to say that the NT "teaches where one is to get the power to fulfill the law." *LW* 35:236; *WA, DB* 8:12.

157. *LW* 35:236; *WA, DB* 8:12, "Aber gleich, wie ym newen testament, neben der gnaden lere, auch viel ander lere geben werden, die da gesetz und gepot sind."

158. *LW* 35:237; *WA, DB* 8:12, "[A]lso sind auch ym alten testament neben den gesetzen, etliche verheyssung und gnaden spruche."

159. "Nevertheless just as the chief teaching of the New Testament is really the proclamation of grace and peace through the forgiveness of sins in Christ, so the chief teaching of the Old Testament is really the teaching of laws, the showing up of sin, and the demanding of good." *LW* 35:237; *WA, DB* 8:12.

160. On the soteriological relationship between the two Testaments in Luther, see Hagen, *A Theology of Testament in the Young Luther*, 29–70.

161. Luther envisions salvation history prior to the coming of Christ as the ministry of Moses and afterwards it is the age of the ministry of God's grace in Christ. Luther presents this perspective in a brief explanation of 2 Cor 3:7–14, "St. Paul teaches this in 2 Corinthians 3[:7–14], where he says that the splendor in the face of Moses is taken away, because of the glory in the face of Jesus Christ. That is, the office of Moses, which makes us to be sin and shame with the glare of the knowledge of our wickedness and nothingness, no longer causes us pain and no longer terrifies us with death. For we now have the glory in the face of Christ. This is the office of grace, whereby we know Christ, by whose righteousness, life, and strength we fulfil the law and overcome death and hell." *LW* 35:244–45; *WA, DB* 8:24.

with a new Word to whom they must listen.[162] Until then, Moses's office contained in the OT Scriptures reveals sin and condemns sinners, working with the christological purpose "to burden the conscience so that the hardened blindness would have to recognize itself, and feel its own inability and nothingness in the achieving of good. Such blindness must be thus compelled and forced by the law to seek something beyond the law and its own ability, namely, *the grace of God promised* [*verheyssen*] *in the Christ who was to come.*"[163] Underneath the direct promise in Deuteronomy 18:15–19 that Moses's office will last until the time of the Messiah, the prophets carry forth the administration of Moses, "bringing everyone to Christ through the law."[164]

To return to 2 Corinthians 3:7–14 in the *Preface to the Old Testament*, Luther translates διαθηκης (covenant) in 3:14 as "testament" to reflect his distinct theology of "testament" for representing the promissory nature of

162. On the nature of Christ as the referent of Moses's messianic promise in Deuteronomy 18:15–19, Luther writes, "For since God here promises another Moses whom they are to hear, it follows of necessity that this other one would teach something different from Moses; and Moses gives up his power and yields to him, so that men will listen to him. This prophet cannot, then, teach the law, for Moses has done that to perfection; for the law's sake there would be no need to raise up another prophet. *Therefore this word was surely spoken concerning Christ and the teaching of grace*" (italics mine); *LW* 35:246; *WA, DB* 8:26.

163. Italics mine; *LW* 35:244; *WA, DB* 8:24, "[U]nd sich uber die mass heufften das gewissen zu beschweeren, auff das die verstockte blindheyt sich erkennen muste, und yhr eygens unuermugen und nichtickeyt zum gutten muste fulen, und also durchs gesetz genöttiget und gedrungen wurde, etwas weytters zu suchen, denn das gesetz und eygen vermugen, nemlich Gottis gnade eynn kunfftigen Christum verheyssen." Notice that Christ as the goal of the law's burdening is not simply in the hope for an unidentified person or pathway to silencing the law's guilty and hopeless verdict. Rather, Luther specifies that the law's purpose is to compel its subjects to trust in God's revealed promise (*verheyssen*) of the coming Christ (*kunfftigen Christum*). This statement may seem subtle, but is nevertheless, a clear expression of the messianic dimension of Luther's construal of Christ as Scripture's *sensus literalis*, even in the function of the law and gospel across the Testaments.

164. Luther calls the prophets "administrators and witnesses of Moses and his office." *LW* 35:247; *WA, DB* 8:28, "Also das die propheten nichts anders sind, denn handhaber und zeugen Mose und seyns ampts, das sie durchs gesetz yderman zu Christo bringen." One example of how a prophet is an "administrator" of the ministry of Moses as it regards the law is Luther's description in the *Preface to the Prophets* (1532) of the second part of an OT's prophet office as that of enforcing the first commandment of the Decalogue. On the other hand, the full twofold responsibility of a prophet to promise and prophesy of the coming Christ and to preach the Mosaic Law would both be considered "administrations" of the office of Moses. *LW* 35:265–66; *WA, DB* 11.1:2.

God's relationship to humanity.[165] This decision enables him to contrast the soteriological content set forth in the OT and NT as "books." Luther believes that Paul labels the Mosaic Law in 2 Corinthians 3:14 as "the old testament" while Christ presupposes this status when he institutes "the new testament" recorded in passages such as Luke 22:20 or 1 Corinthians 11:25. In this scenario, OT Scripture is a "book" where Moses's office reigns in the ministry of the Law and the people live underneath the temporal promise of the "old testament." The inadequacy of this "old testament" to save because it rests upon "men's works" (*menschen wercken*), however, points towards the need for another "testament," a "new testament."[166] Therefore, beginning with Genesis 3:15 and onwards throughout the rest of Moses and the prophets, God promises the gospel of his Son, the hoped-for Messiah who will bring Moses's office to an end and make the "old testament" obsolete. So then, NT Scripture proclaims Jesus Christ as the complete realization of all aspects of the messianic hope in his person and work, and it announces that through his death and resurrection, the gospel of the "new testament" has been instituted and is an inheritance belonging to anyone who would believe upon him by faith alone.[167]

To summarize, Christian Scripture in two-Testament form is a unified book where law and gospel transcends each witness, though the OT emphasizes the law and the NT the gospel. In either case, both Testaments as law and gospel tend toward Christ from a messianic vantage point.[168] For the OT

165. *LW* 35:246; *WA, DB* 8:28.

166. The OT as "book of law" leads to Christ because it portrays the "old testament" promise as one that obviously "did not stand upon God's grace, but upon men's works," thus, "it had to become obsolete and cease, and the promised land had to be lost again—because the law cannot be fulfilled by works. And another testament had to come which would not become obsolete, which would not stand upon our deeds either, but upon God's words and works, so that it might endure for ever." *LW* 35:246; *WA, DB* 8:28.

167. A major difference for Luther between the "old testament" and the "new testament" is the temporality of the former and the eternality of the latter. As opposed to the "old testament" that contained temporal promises such as physical land and was facilitated by an imperfect sacrificial system, the "new testament" will endure forever because "it it is confirmed by the death and blood of an *eternal* [*ewigen*] Person, and an *eternal* [*ewiges*] land is promised and given" (italics mine); *LW* 35:246; *WA, DB* 8:28.

168. Once more, although Preus's account of the so-called "hermeneutical shift" in the *Dictata super Psalterium* has been contested, his argument for the emergence of *promissio* as the guiding principle for understanding the OT's literal sense and its identity as Christian Scripture causes him to make many points that cohere with this study on the the "later" Luther. One of these implications is that Preus believes that due to *promissio* serving as the nature of God's Word in the OT, that is, God's prophetic promise of the coming Messiah, Luther envisions a new "hermeneutical divide"

as Christian Scripture, its primary purpose of promising and prophesying of the coming Christ (gospel) alone is sufficient to make the messianic hope the basis for Christ as its literal sense.[169] Yet, Luther teaches that even in the substance of the OT as a "book of laws" serves a supreme messianic purpose in its application to reveal and to condemn sin as well as in its imperfect promise of the "old testament." NT Scripture as "gospel" corresponds to the messianic focus and anticipation of the OT as "law" insofar as it announces the establishment of the eternal "new testament" that offers righteousness, forgiveness of sins, and eternal life as an answer to the insufficiency of the "old testament" that was in effect under the "office of Moses" prior to Christ. Additionally, the NT as "gospel" is demonstrated by the apostles as in accordance with the OT as "gospel" concerning the apostolic preaching that Jesus Christ is the fulfillment of the direct promises and prophecies about the Messiah in the OT.[170]

That the NT also contains laws and commandments, as Luther explains in the *Preface to the New Testament*, is to be understood as directed towards the believer, the one who has expressed faith in Christ's Word of the gospel.[171] These teachings are to be reckoned as benefits of Christ's work, and one is only able to emulate them subsequent to acceptance of the gospel.[172] Upon

---

existent within the OT itself. Instead of the old "letter and Spirit" division that polarizes the Old and New Testaments, Luther's *promissio* (i.e., the gospel) of Christ is present in both Testaments, causing the new "hermeneutical divide" to be in the law and gospel distinction, not between the two Testaments. Even if this analysis is premature concerning Luther's approach to Scripture at the time of the *Dictata*, one can grant that Preus's conclusions are evident in the Bible-prefaces represented in Luther's view of how the Testaments relate to one another when each of them contain law and gospel. Preus, *From Shadow to Promise*, 197, 200–211.

169. Luther expresses this notion in his second point on the Christian usefulness of Moses and the Law in the OT in *How Christians Should Regard Moses* (1525). *LW* 35:168–69; WA 16:381–83.

170. *LW* 35:358–59; WA, *DB* 6:4, 6.

171. "Hence it comes that to a believer no law is given by which he becomes righteous before God, as St. Paul says in I Timothy 1[:9], because he is alive and righteous and saved by faith, and he needs nothing further except to prove his faith by works." *LW* 35:361; WA, *DB* 6:8.

172. In his reflections on the existence of laws and commandments in the NT, many parallels occur between the *Preface to the New Testament* (1522) and *A Brief Instruction* (1521). Concerning law in the NT in the *Preface to the New Testament*, Luther writes, "To be sure, Christ in the gospel, and St. Peter and St. Paul besides, do give many commandments and doctrines, and expound the law. But these are to be counted like all Christ's other works and good deeds. To know his works and the things that happened to him is not yet to know the true gospel, for you do not yet thereby know that he has overcome sin, death, and the devil" (*LW* 35:360–61; WA,

reception of Jesus Christ as a "gift," these laws and commandments instruct faith on how to work itself out through love and good deeds.[173] Thus, Christ can be followed as an "example," which according to Luther, ought to be the natural impulse of genuine faith that has truly grasped the gospel as evidence that Jesus is rightly known.[174]

Scripture and Proclamation: The Christian Bible as Witness to Christ

In addition to the soteriological relationship between the Testaments constructed through the law and gospel distinction, Luther also teaches in the Bible-prefaces that the Old and New Testaments relate in a hermeneutical way. Before addressing the logic of Luther's approach to the back-and-forth between the two Testaments, his estimation of the OT as properly "Holy Scripture" and the NT as "proclamation" must be examined. Luther presupposes these ontological states when he describes the interrelationship of the Testaments. Due to the subject matter, and as with the previous section on law and gospel, Luther's *Preface to the New Testament* and *Preface to the Old Testament* feature the most substantial discussions on this issue, and therefore, will be the primary sources from the Bible-prologues investigated while other writings will be consulted when appropriate.

The characterization of the OT as "Scripture" and the NT as "proclamation" predates the prefaces for Luther's German translation of the Bible.

DB 6:8). Cf. *A Brief Instruction*: "The fact that Christ and the apostles provide much good teaching and explain the law is to be counted a benefit just like any other work of Christ. For to teach aright is not the least sort of benefit." *LW* 35:120–21; WA 10.1.1:13.

173. Christ as "gift" and "example" is subtly present in the *Preface to the New Testament*. This paradigm for one's experience of Christ and the gospel is given full expression in *A Brief Instruction*, and is mostly assumed in the *Preface to the New Testament* given the amount of overlap between the two writings. A sampling of Luther's explication of this dualism in *A Brief Instruction* can be heard in the following statement: "The chief article and foundation of the gospel is that before you take Christ as an example, you accept and recognize him as a gift, as a present that God has given you and that is your own." *LW* 35:119; WA 10.1.1:11.

174. Luther ends the *Preface to the New Testament* on this note, "Truly, if faith is there, he cannot hold back; he proves himself, breaks out into good works, confesses and teaches this gospel before the people, and stakes his life on it. Everything that he lives and does is directed to his neighbor's profit, in order to help him—not only to the attainment of this grace, but also in body, property, and honor. *Seeing that Christ has done this for him, he thus follows Christ's example* . . . For where works and love do not break forth, there faith is not right, the gospel does not yet take hold, and Christ is not rightly known" (italics mine); *LW* 35:361; WA, *DB* 6:8, 10.

In *A Brief Instruction on What to Look for and Expect in the Gospels* (1521), Luther begins to close the preface to his *Church Postils* ironically with a plea for the Christian relevance of the OT. Luther reports about some people who would rather not have to study the Scriptures to learn about Christ, claiming that the OT is insignificant and no longer valid.[175] To them, he replies,

> Yet [the OT] alone bears the name of Holy Scripture. And the gospel should really not be something written, but a spoken word which brought forth the Scriptures, as Christ and the apostles have done. This is why Christ himself did not write anything but only spoke. He called his teaching not Scripture but gospel, meaning good news or a proclamation that is spread not by pen but by word of mouth.[176]

Instead of explicitly mentioning the New Testament here, Luther chooses to let "gospel" stand in its place. The "gospel" transmitted from oral to written form is the NT canon. As for the OT, it was always in the first place to be inscripturated. In contrast, the NT is a "spoken word," only secondarily a written one.

In the following year of 1522, Luther preached through many of the General Epistles. His exposition of 1 Peter 1:10–12 from the *Sermons on the First Epistle of St. Peter* contains multiple instances of parallel thought with *A Brief Instruction* (1521), the *Preface to the New Testament* (1522), and the *Preface to the Old Testament* (1523). In particular, Luther revisits this account of the Old and New Testament within a similar context. He tells his hearers, "Therefore we must ignore the good-for-nothing babblers who despise the Old Testament and say that it is no longer necessary."[177] What these people do not understand, Luther argues, is that the apostolic (i.e., NT) gospel is based upon Moses and the prophets.[178] This point, again, leads

---

175. *LW* 35:123; WA 10.1.1:17.

176. *LW* 35:123; WA 10.1.1:17, "ßo es doch alleyn den namen hatt, das es heylige schrifft heist, Und Eunageli eygentlich nitt schrifft, ßondern mundlich wort seyn solt, das die schrifft erfur truge, wie Christus und die Apostel than haben; Darumb auch Christus selbs nichts geschrieben, ßondern nur geredt hatt, und seyn lere nit schrifft, sonder Euangeli das ist eyn gutt botschafft odder vorkundigung genennet hatt, das nitt mit der feddernn, ßondern mit dem mund soll getrieben werden."

177. *LW* 30:19; WA 12:274, "Darumb soll man die unnützen schwetzer lassen faren, die das alt Testament verachten und sprechen, es sey nicht mehr von nötten."

178. "Thus the books of Moses and the prophets are also Gospel, since they proclaimed and described in advance what the apostles preached or wrote later about Christ." *LW* 30:19; WA 12:275.

Luther into the delineation of the OT as "Scripture" and the NT as "procla-mation." Luther explains,

> For although both have been put on paper word for word, the Gospel, or the New Testament, should really not be written but should be expressed with the living voice which resounds and is heard throughout the world. The fact that it is also written is su-perfluous. But the Old Testament is only put in writing. There-fore it is called "a letter." Thus the apostles call it Scripture; for it only pointed to the Christ who was to come. But the Gospel is a living sermon on the Christ who has come.[179]

Luther identifies the Testaments in this manner to communicate that the one who dismisses the OT Scriptures in favor of the NT has overlooked the NT's own self-awareness in relation to its antecedent witness. Or said another way, those who regard the OT as outmoded by the NT writings have eclipsed the NT's (i.e., Jesus and the apostles) own doctrine of the OT as Christian Scripture. In Luther's thought, if any part of the Christian Bible is to be given preeminence, it should be the OT because it is the Testament that is most fundamentally "Scripture" or "letter" (buchstab); without it, the NT's proclamation of the "gospel" would, indeed, be "babble."

Although the prefaces to the Testaments for Luther's German Bible do not feature the exact same discourse, his manner of speaking about the Old and New Testaments is consistent with this approach. Rehearsed at many points so far has been Luther's definition of the "gospel" from the beginning portions of the Preface to the New Testament (1522). What is reflected in Luther's language in these affirmations is the semantic connection between what the NT as a "book" does and the nature of the "gospel" as a message to be heralded, which Luther uses interchangeably with the promise of the eternal "new testament."

After stating that the OT is mainly a "book" (buch) of "laws and com-mandments" (gesetz und gepot) while the NT is mainly "a book in which are written the gospel and the promises of God," Luther makes several at-tempts to emphasize the proclamatory nature of the "gospel."[180] A collection

179. LW 30:19; WA 12:275, "Denn wie wol beydes dem buchstaben nach ist auff papyr geschrieben, so soll doch das Euangelion odder das new Testament eygentlich nicht geschrieben, sondern ynn die lebendige stym gefasset werden, die da erschalle und uberal gehört werde ynn der welt. Das e saber auch geschrieben ist, ist aufs uber-fluß geschehen. Aber das alte Testament ist nur ynn die schrifft verfasset, und drumb heysst es 'ein buchstab,' und also nennens die Apostel 'die schrifft,' denn es hatt alleyn gedeutet auff den zukunfftigen Christum. Das Euangelion aber ist eyn lebendige pre-dig von Christo, der da kommen ist."

180. LW 35:358; WA, DB 6:2, "Also ist das newe testament, eyn buch, darynnen das

of all of the descriptors for the "gospel/new testament" is as follows: "good message," "good tidings/story," "good news," "a good report," "encouraging tidings," "evangelical and divine news," and "preaching about Christ, Son of God and of David."[181] Given this emphatic portrayal of the oral nature of the "gospel" as the prime material of the apostolic writings, NT *Scripture* as written documentation of the "gospel," in Luther's assessment, still retains its subject matter's ultimate mode of expression: proclamation/preaching. Even as Scripture, the NT rightly understood ought to be foremost preached and heard.[182]

When Luther comes to pen the *Preface to the Old Testament* in 1523, he does not deviate from this construal of the Testaments. The prologue begins with another apologetic for the perduring witness of the OT for Christian readers. Luther rebukes those who reject it as ancient religious writings belonging only to the Jews as well as those who see Christian value in the OT insofar as a "spiritual sense" (*geystliche synn*) may be found.[183] Instead, Luther cites NT passages such as John 5:39 and Romans 1:2, where Christ is claimed as the literal sense of the OT's "letter."[184]

As it regards the distinction between the OT properly conceived as "Scripture" and the NT as "proclamation," Luther's aim for these apostolic declarations about the material status of the OT's textual witness is to restore a right view of the interrelationship of the Testaments based upon their true natures. Luther contends via Christ and the apostles's testimony, that what they proclaim about the Messiah as Jesus Christ and the foundation of the Christian faith is nothing other than what the OT as the Word of God has already revealed. In similar verbiage to the other writings reviewed above, Luther rhetorically asks, "And what is the New Testament but a public preaching and proclamation of Christ, set forth through the sayings of the Old Testament and fulfilled through Christ?"[185] This question concludes

---

Euangelion und Gottis verheyssung, . . ."

181. "[G]ute botschafft," "gute meher," "gutte newzeytung," "gutt geschrey," "trostliche mehre," "Euangelisch und Gotlich newzeyttung," and "predigt von Christo Gottis und Davids son." *LW* 35:358, 360; *WA, DB* 6:2, 4, 6.

182. To hear how Luther's "Scripture/proclamation" distinction applied to the Testaments figures into a more deeply rooted aspect of his Christian thought, see Kolb, "The Relationship between Scripture and the Confession of the Faith in Luther's Thought," 53–62; cf. Forde, "Law and Gospel in Luther's Hermeneutic," 240–52.

183. *LW* 35:235; *WA, DB* 8:10.

184. *LW* 35:235; *WA, DB* 8:10.

185. *LW* 35:236; *WA, DB* 8:11, "Und was ist das newe Testament anders, denn ein öffentliche predigt und verkündigung von Christo, durch die Sprüche im alten Testament gesetzt, und durch Christum erfüllet" (1545). The 1545 version adds "von

Luther's discourse on the contemporary significance of the OT for his six-teenth-century readers, whereby he depicts a union between the Testaments as "Scripture" and "proclamation" in which their interdependence cannot be put asunder.

The identities of the OT as "Scripture" and the NT as "proclamation" are complementary, inseparable, and hinge upon a messianic focal point.[186] In Luther's view, what fuels the perception of the NT as ultimately "proc-lamation" is due to the textual contours of the "gospel" itself anticipated in the OT. The apostolic preaching of Jesus Christ is the joyous announce-ment that God has made good on his promises, those "sayings" (*Sprüche*) he spoke through the prophets written in Holy Scripture (OT).[187]

READING THE NT IN LIGHT OF THE OT

To order reflection upon the hermeneutical relationship between the Tes-taments by beginning with how the OT shapes the NT mirrors Luther's pattern in the prefaces to the Bible. Although his translation, prefaces, and publication of the NT precedes his work on the OT, Luther never gives the impression that the NT has superseded or is superior to the OT. On the contrary, Luther vigorously battles against any form of subordination of the Old Testament to the New.

In the *Preface to the Old Testament* (1523), Luther states forthrightly, "The ground and proof of the New Testament is surely not to be despised, and therefore the Old Testament is to be highly regarded."[188] The assertion

---

Christo;" everywhere else the sentence is unchanged from the 1522 original.

186. For an example of understanding Luther's "Scripture" and "proclamation" distinction of the two Testaments in service to Christ its center because of Luther's christological doctrine of the Word of God, see Lotz, "*Sola Scriptura*: Luther on Bibli-cal Authority," 260–66. Lotz's overview of Luther's christocentric doctrine of Scripture helpfully brings together with clarity many strands of the Reformer's multifaceted perspective; however, Lotz represents an interpretation that ascribes the basis for Luther's view of Christ as the center of Scripture to the christological orientation of his understanding of the Word of God. Although it can be granted that this aspect of Luther's bibliology does exist and has its own implications, assessments such as Lotz's underestimate the exegetical determination at work in Luther's position by assuming that his conviction on this matter is foremost the result of a dogmatic or doctrinal formulation rather than a product of grappling with the "letter" and "literal sense" of the biblical text.

187. *LW* 35:236; WA, *DB* 8:11.

188. *LW* 35:236; WA, *DB* 8:10, "So wenig nu des newen testaments grund und beweysung zuurachten ist, so theur ist auch das alte testament zu achten." During his exposition of 1 Pet 1:10–12 in the *Sermons on the First Epistle of St. Peter* (1522),

that the OT is the "ground" (*grund*) and "proof" (*beweysung*) of the NT is reinforced for Luther by the apostles's own admission. This declaration follows an occurrence of the Reformer's biblical-theological hermeneutic as evidence for Christ as the literal sense of the OT. In an effort to raise estimations of the OT, Luther draws upon John 5:39, 1 Timothy 4:13 (allusion), Romans 1:2, 1 Corinthians 15:3–4, and 1 Peter 1:10–12 (allusion) as NT endorsements of the OT's indispensable importance for the gospel.

Each of these NT texts are to be heard as directives from the apostles pointing biblical readers back to the OT Scriptures to "search" them in order to see where and how God promised Christ through the prophets. These scriptural proofs indicate that the apostles "themselves base the New Testament upon [the OT] mightily, proving [the NT] by the Old Testament and appealing to it, as St. Luke also writes in Acts 17[:11], saying that they at Thessalonica examined the Scriptures daily to see if these things were so that Paul was teaching."[189] Luther's reference to the Bereans in Acts 17:11 is upheld as an ideal practice for biblical readers already patterned within the NT itself that highly values the authoritative status of OT Scripture; it is an approach that reads the OT diligently to discern how the Holy Spirit spoke through the prophets about the person and work of Jesus Christ to verify the apostolic preaching of the gospel as in accordance with the Word of God revealed in the first Testament.[190] For Luther, the apostles's assumption that the gospel and their writings required accordance with Israel's Scriptures serves as indisputable proof that the OT witnesses to Christ in its own uniquely Christian voice, that is, its literal sense.[191]

Luther similarly asserts, "From all this you see how painstakingly the apostles always pointed out the basis [*grund*] and the proof [*bewerung*] of their preaching and teaching . . . The apostles were filled with the Holy Spirit and were certain that they had been sent by Christ and that they preached the true Gospel. Yet they humbled themselves and did not want to be believed unless they proved [*bewereten*] completely from Scripture that what they said was true." *LW* 30:22–23; *WA* 12:278.

189. *LW* 35:236; *WA, DB* 8:10, "[W]eyl sie selbs das newe testament so mechtiglich grunden und beweren durchs alte testament und sich drauff beruffen, wie auch S. Lucas act. 17. schreybt, das die zu Tessalonich teglich forsscheten die schrifft, ob sichs so hielte, wie Paulus lerete."

190. In today's church culture, to be a "Berean" is commonly associated with someone who submits to *sola Scriptura*, making this label mainly about the authority of Scripture. Luther, however, sees Acts 17:11 more precisely as a demonstration of the commitment to the OT text as a witness to Christ in its literal sense. Acts 17:11 is also a recurring passage that appears in the various manifestations of Luther's biblical-theological hermeneutic when contending for Christ in the OT.

191. Seitz captures this aspect of the OT's material ground and influence on the NT's witness similar to Luther, when he explains, "The Second [New] Testament does

Later in the *Preface to the Old Testament*, Luther continues to underscore the importance of the OT for the church's reception of the NT
as Christian Scripture. Moses himself has already written an "exceedingly
evangelical book" (*fast eyn euangelisch buch*) with Genesis, and in Deuteronomy 18:15–19, he is consciously aware that his office will cease when the
Messiah appears.[192] The wielding of the law certainly predominates Moses's
ministry, however, his ultimate purpose is to drive his readers and hearers
to have faith and hope in God's promise of the Messiah to come and in the
gospel of the eternal "new testament" he will proclaim that will bring an end
to the law's impossible burden. Therefore, Moses establishes the manner of
the rest of Holy Scripture's witness. All prophetic authors that follow him
carry on his legacy *per se*, as "administrators and witnesses of Moses and his
office."[193] The bequeathment of the office of Moses to the prophets definitely
involves the preaching of the law, but as Luther reveals in his Bible-prefaces
to the prophets, it ultimately entails bearing witness to the coming Messiah. Furthermore, Moses's foundational status is extended even beyond the
prophets to the NT in Luther's statement, "For Moses is, indeed, a well of all
wisdom and understanding, out of which has sprung all that the prophets
knew and said. Moreover even the New Testament flows out of it and is
grounded [*gegrundet*] in it, as we have heard."[194]

Luther's adamant resolve to persuade others of Christ as the *sensus
literalis* of the OT's "letter" by reaching all the way back to Moses and the
Pentateuch can be seen in the first biblical text treated in *Avoiding the Doctrines of Men* (1522), a writing contemporaneous to the first Bible-prefaces.
Luther begins with Deuteronomy 4:2, where Moses prohibits any additions
or subtractions to the Word he speaks. Some people will wonder, then,

---

not give record of what it seeks to tell in a detached idiom, . . . It speaks of a special
action in time, but it can only describe this action with reference to prior acts recorded
in the First Testament. In order to do this persuasively and formally it grandly takes
up the language—allusively, or by citation of specific words, phrases, sentences—of
the First Testament. The status of the Second Testament is therefore a deeply accorded
one: it says what is says by recourse to the language of the first, in order to state what
it judges to be the decisive act of God." Seitz, *The Character of Christian Scripture*,
137–38.

192. *LW* 35:237 246; WA, *DB* 8:12, 26.

193. *LW* 35:247; WA, *DB* 8:28, "Also das die propheten nichts anders sind, denn
handhaber und zeugen Mose und seyns ampts, . . ."

194. *LW* 35:247; WA, *DB* 8:28, "Denn freylich Mose eyn brun is taller weyscheyt
und verstands, daraus gequollen ist alles was alle propheten weisst und gesagt haben,
dazu auch das newe testament eraus fleusset und dreyn gegrundet ist, wie wyr gehort
haben."

according to Luther, what to make of the prophetic writings that followed as well as the NT? He replies with the following interpretation:

> Nevertheless nothing new has been added, for the same thing that is found in the books of Moses is found also in the others.... Throughout them all there is one and the same teaching and thought. And here we can challenge them to show us one word in all the books outside those of Moses that is not already found in the books of Moses. For this much is beyond question, that *all the Scriptures point to Christ alone.* Indeed in John 5[:46] Christ says, 'Moses wrote of me.' Therefore everything in the other books is already in the books of Moses, as in a basic source.[195]

Many observations could be made from this selection, but two will suffice for present purposes. First, Luther teaches that the full scope of the biblical witness flows out of Moses as the forerunner for all "witnesses" of God's Word, and therefore, the NT as Christian Scripture is necessarily dependent upon the already spoken and received OT Scriptures as its "ground" and "proof." Second, when Luther has the opportunity to describe the content of Moses's message that is adopted by all prophets and apostles who come after him, Luther does so by drafting John 5:46 as scriptural proof that Moses's prime objective was to witness directly to Christ. Here again, Luther draws from his pool of texts that function as the pillars of his biblical-theological hermeneutic in order to demonstrate how he arrives at the conclusion that Christ is the central (authorial) meaning of the Bible's testimony. Moreover, assumed in his usage of John 5:46 in support of the statement, "all the Scriptures point to Christ alone," is that the manner of Moses's "writing" about Christ is his promising and prophesying of the Messiah. If the rest of the OT's prophetic authors and the NT apostles are simply following Moses's lead, then to say that "all the Scriptures point to Christ alone" is to affirm the messianic basis for asserting that Christ is the Bible's literal sense.

Luther's language in the prefaces to the NT writings reflects the perspective that the OT "proves" what they proclaim. As has been evidenced at several points thus far, the definition(s) of the "gospel" that opens the *Preface to the New Testament* (1522) claims to be the exact fulfillment of the same "gospel" God promised through the messianic hope in the OT. To

---

195. Italics mine; *LW* 35:132; WA 10.2:73, "Eß ist aber nichts newes datzu than, ßondern eben dasselb, das yn Moses bücher steht, das steht yn den andern ... Eß ist aber alles die selbige eynige lere und meynung. Und hie ist zu trotzen wider sie, Das sie yn allen büchern außer Moses bücher eyn wortt tzeygen, das nicht tzuvor yn Moses buch erfunden werd. Denn das ist ungetzweyfflet, das die gantze schrifft auff Christum allein ist gericht. Nuh spricht Christus Joan. 5.: Moses hat von mir geschriben, darumb ists alles yn Moses büchern alß ym hewbt bryve, was yn andern büchern ist."

support his NT summary of the gospel's message, Luther does not resort to NT texts; instead, he traces direct messianic predictions (Genesis 3:15; 22:18; 2 Samuel 7:12–14, etc.) that he upholds as indicative of the OT's witness to Jesus Christ.[196] In the *Preface to the Epistle of St. Paul to the Romans* (1522), Luther regards the Apostle Paul's teaching about the righteousness of God and justification by faith alone in Christ alone as principle parts of the NT "gospel" that were "witnessed to beforehand by the law and the prophets," alluding to Romans 3:21.[197] Likewise, in the *Preface to the Epistle of St. Paul to the Galatians* (1522), Luther says that Paul "proves" (*bewert*) all of his teaching in the epistle's first two chapters on salvation and justification through Christ alone with God's promises in the OT Scriptures.[198] And last, in the *Preface to the First Epistle of St. Peter* (1522), Luther highlights that Peter also follows this pattern by showing that the salvation in Christ he preaches "was first proclaimed by the prophets" in an implicit reference to 1 Peter 1:10–12.[199]

READING THE OT IN LIGHT OF THE NT

Whenever Heinrich Bornkamm says in *Luther and the Old Testament* that to follow Luther step-for-step in his "christological-prophetic" interpretation of the OT would require contemporary interpreters "to carry the concepts of the New Testament revelation into the Old Testament and put them in the mouths of the patriarchs and writers," he misses the hermeneutical exchange between the Testaments in Luther's formulation of how they work together to form a single, unified Christian Scripture as the Word of God.[200]

196. *LW* 35:358–60; WA, *DB* 6:2, 4, 6.

197. *LW* 35:373; WA, *DB* 7:14, "und zuuor durchs gesetz und propheten betzeuget ist."

198. *LW* 35:384; WA, *DB* 7:172.

199. *LW* 35:390; WA, *DB* 7:298, "sondern zuuor durch die propheten verkundigt sey."

200. Bornkamm, *Luther and the Old Testament*, 263. Similarly in a critical assessment of Luther "for today," so to speak, Klein seems to find little worth incorporating from Luther's "precritical" interpretation. Besides approving basic contextual, literary interpretation exemplified in Luther or supposing him to be a precursor of modern-critical judgments of the canon, Klein dismisses the most central aspect of Luther's hermeneutic. In his list of Luther's practices contemporary readers must leave behind, Klein says that to read the OT *without* Luther "means that we recognize that the Old Testament does not literally proclaim Christ." Throughout the essay, Klein repeatedly indicates that Luther, as well as others in the precritical tradition of biblical interpretation, implement exegesis that is "excessively christological" for his taste. Unfortunately, Klein does Luther an injustice in his desire to appropriate Luther's *promissio* (he

From the previous section, to grant Bornkamm's recommendation would immediately undermine the apostolic notion of "accordance" with the OT as necessary to verify the truth of the gospel of God concerning his Son, Jesus Christ. If the NT is not in the historical, eschatological horizon of the OT's "letter," then how could the first Testament possibly serve as the "ground" or "proof" of the second Witness?

On the matter of Luther's reading the Old Testament in light of the New, Bornkamm's assessment would definitely lead to the accusation of "Christianization," since the NT's language and theology are not, supposedly, on the tongues or pens of Moses and the prophets. This account of how Luther envisions the Testaments's interrelationship, however, does not do justice to the hermeneutical implications of Luther's theology of Christian Scripture that has a two-Testament form. Perhaps the most pronounced statements on the issue of engaging the OT from the vantage point of the NT actually occur in the *Preface to the Old Testament* (1523).[201]

After Luther begins the *Preface to the Old Testament* with a plea for the Christian-theological vitality of the OT's "letter" by referencing the same apostolic perspective from various NT passages, he explains the purpose of such texts (e.g., Romans 1:2, 1 Corinthians 15:3-4) as the apostles's insistent aim to point its audience back to the OT Scriptures.[202] The goal in this apostolic prescription is to awaken other readers to the reality of the OT as "the swaddling cloths and the manger in which Christ lies."[203] "Simple and lowly," Luther says these "swaddling cloths" may seem, "but dear is the treasure, Christ, who lies in them."[204] The "swaddling cloths" imagery is

---

accepts Preus's thesis in *From Shadow to Promise*) perspective on God's Word in the OT as if this part of Luther's methodology retained any substance or was retrievable in the least bit, if Christ is emptied from the *promissio*'s eschatological horizon and absent from the literal sense of the OT's "letter." Klein, "Reading the Old Testament with Martin Luther—and without Him," 103.

201. It seems likely that the cause for greater treatment on the relationship between the two Testaments in the *Preface to the Old Testament* (1523) than in the *Preface to the New Testament* (1522) has to do with Luther's desire to bring into coherence both "witnesses" for a unified reading of Christian Scripture now that vernacular translations of the Bible in German are appearing in print from both parts of the Bible.

202. Though this clause is in immediate reference to Peter's words in 1 Peter 1:10–12, it can be seen as an explanation of the intent of all of the preceding verses: John 5:39; 1 Timothy 4:13; Romans 1:2; 1 Corinthian 15:3–4; and 1 Peter 1:10–12. *LW* 35:235; *WA, DB* 8:10, "So weyset uns auch S. Petrus mehr denn eyn mal enhyndern ynn die schrifft."

203. *LW* 35:236; *WA, DB* 8:12, "Hie wirstu die windeln und die krippen finden, da Christus ynnen ligt."

204. *LW* 35:236; *WA, DB* 8:12, "Schlechte und geringe windel sin des, aber theur ist

connected to Luther's hermeneutical reflection on how the NT informs a proper reading and interpretation of the OT. Several of Luther's other writings, all in close proximity to the time of the prefaces to the New and Old Testaments (1522–23), will help to disclose more of the Reformer's interpretive conclusions in relation to this metaphor.

Towards the final portions of *A Brief Instruction on What to Look for and Expect in the Gospels* (1521), Luther features an excursus on the hermeneutical relationship between the Testaments. He asserts that the purpose for which "the gospels and epistles of the apostles" were written was so that they could be "our guides" (*tzeyger*) into the OT.[205] In their "guidance," Luther says, they "direct us to the writings of the prophets and of Moses in the Old Testament so that we might there read and see for ourselves how *Christ is wrapped in swaddling cloths and laid in the manger*, that is, how he is comprehended in the writings of the prophets."[206] For scriptural proof to corroborate this claim, Luther next moves through many of the key texts from his biblical-theological hermeneutic in the following order: John 5:46, 39; Romans 1:1–2; Acts 17:11; 1 Peter 1:10–12; Acts 3:24; Luke 24:45; and John 10:9, 3.[207] He, then, closes the excursus with a statement that functions as an inclusio in connection with how this section began: "Thus it is ultimately true that the gospel itself is *our guide [tzeyger] and instructor [unterrichter] in the Scriptures*, just as with this foreword I would gladly give instruction and point you to the gospel."[208]

New Testament-"guided" reading of the Old, for Luther, is aligning one's own theology of the nature of the first Testament's witness to Christ with the apostles's as displayed through the multiple NT texts that Luther repeatedly cites in this context. The OT Scriptures imaged as Christ's "swaddling cloths" is meant to portray the antecedent presence of its christological

---

der schatz Christus, der drynnen ligt."

205. *LW* 35:122; WA 10.1.1:15, "Syntemal die Euangeli und Epistel der Apostel darumb geschrieben sind, das sie self solche tzeyger seyn wollen, . . ."

206. Italics mine; *LW* 35:122; WA 10.1.1:15, "und uns weyßen ynn die schrifft der propheten und Mosi des allten testaments, das wyr alda selbs leßen und sehen sollen, wie Christus ynn die windel thucher gewicklet und yn die krippen gelegt sey, das ist, wie er ynn der schrifft der propheten vorfassett sey."

207. On how John 10:9, 3 fits into a defense of Christ in the OT, Luther teaches, "And Christ, in John 10[:9, 3], declares that he is the door by which one must enter, and whoever enters by him, to him the gatekeeper (the Holy Spirit) opens in order that he might find pasture and blessedness." *LW* 35:123; WA 10.1.1:16–17.

208. Italics mine; *LW* 35:123; WA 10.1.1:17, "Alßo das endlich war ist, wie das Euangeli selbs tzeyger und unterrichter ist ynn die schrifft, gleych wie ich mit dißer vorrede gerne das Euangelium tzeygen und unterricht geben wollt."

referentiality independent of some form of injection of the NT's concepts and doctrines back into the OT's textual bloodstream. If contemporary readers allow Christ and the apostles in the NT writings to be their "guides" and "instructors" in the Scriptures (i.e., OT), then the OT will be brought into the clear and bright light of the gospel, a light that will reveal the literal sense of the OT as Christian Scripture with apostolic authority and certainty for what it is, namely, God's promises of the Messiah through the prophets contained in the Holy Scriptures (Rom 1:1–2). In actuality, Luther's rhetorical question posed a few years later in the *Preface to the Old Testament* (1523) prevents any such notion that he considers himself to be forcing the NT upon the OT. To his pondering of the manner of the NT's "public preaching and proclamation of Christ," he submits that the substance of the apostles's message is garbed in none other than "the sayings [*Sprüche*] of the Old Testament."[209] In other words, the NT's language and concepts concerning Christ and the gospel are taken from the OT.[210] The NT's mode of Christian-theological expression originates in the Christian, literal sense voice of the OT Scriptures.

This approach to reading the OT in light of the NT works from Luther's presupposition of the OT as the "ground" and "proof" of the NT. Thus, when an interpreter approaches the first Testament from the NT's horizon, the backwards move is one of illumination, not implantation. The key difference is that the former exposes what is already latent within the biblical text as opposed to the latter which inserts intention and meaning into the text that is foreign to the OT. On the one hand, Luther affirms a simple, plain sense grammatical-historical witness to the Messiah as Jesus Christ prior to his coming.[211] On the other hand, upon Christ's finished work and complete

---

209. The complete excerpt from Luther is: "And what is the New Testament but a public preaching and proclamation of Christ, set forth through the sayings of the Old Testament and fulfilled through Christ?" *LW* 35:236; WA, *DB* 8:11, "Und was ist das newe Testament anders, denn ein öffentliche predigt und verkündigung von Christo, durch die Sprüche im alten Testament gesetzt, und durch Christum erfüllet" (1545).

210. This notion concerning the way in which the NT articulates its theology, especially its Christology, in accord with the Scriptures (OT), is the point Behr has attempted to demonstrate in his chapter, "The Scriptural Christ," found in Behr, *Formation of Christian Theology: The Way to Nicaea*, 49–70; cf. with the approach taken in Bauckham, *God Crucified: Monotheism and Christology in the New Testament*.

211. In a sermon from the *Church Postils*, "The Gospel for the Sunday after Christmas, Luke 2[:33–40]" (1522), Luther acknowledges that, "Although there is hidden here a deeper meaning, it is enough to say for the present that the prophecies [*prophetien*] and statements [*sprüche*] of Scripture present Christ in a straightforward manner and offer him to everybody, and do not keep him for themselves, just as we do with what we carry in our arms." *LW* 52:106–07; WA 10.1.1:386. Later in the same sermon,

fulfillment of God's promises through the prophets concerning his Son, the NT now offers the biblical reader an unveiled OT ripe with direct referentiality to Christ.[212] In this way, a Christian's interpretive journey will always be one which understands the Scriptures backwards through the cross.[213]

Along these lines, in the sermon, "The Gospel for Christmas Eve, Luke 2[:1–14]" from 1522, Luther again draws upon this imagery. "[T]he law and the prophets," Luther warns, "cannot be preached or recognized properly, unless we see Christ wrapped up in the Scriptures."[214] Subsequent to the first advent and the full disclosure of the gospel in Jesus Christ that God promised beforehand through the OT, assurance of right interpretation of the first Testament as Christian Scripture comes by way of the NT. Without the "guidance" of the NT, Luther admits that it will often seem as though the OT does not speak of Christ. For Luther, then, this experience only reinforces the interpretive state of affairs that "the New Testament, the gospel, must explain, reveal, and illumine, as has been pointed out."[215] He goes on to

---

Luther makes a similar judgment as it regards those in the OT who "heartily believed in the Christ who was to come because of clear statements [*klare sprüch*] from God's word, understood without recourse to allegory [*figurn*]." *LW* 52:127; WA 10.1.1:417.

212. Immediately prior to the analogy of the OT as Christ's "swaddling cloths" in the *Preface to the Old Testament* (1523), Luther evokes the imagery of OT Scripture as the "richest of mines which can never be sufficiently explored," where God has deposited his divine wisdom in simple speech, awaiting those who would empty their pride, become fools, and see how these Scriptures as the Word of God reveal the promised Christ. These kind of interpreters, for Luther, will be those who approach the OT with a NT or apostolic-"guided" reading. *LW* 35:236; WA, *DB* 8:10, 12.

213. This "backwards" motif is also prescribed by Behr in his promotion of a pre-critical approach to theological method. Like Luther, Behr argues that the starting point for Christian theology is the cross, which provides the proper interpretive equipment for perceiving how the NT's gospel and Christian theology is in accord with the Scriptures (i.e., OT). Behr writes, "The disciples did not simply come to understand Christ in the light of the Passion. Rather, only when turned again (or were turned by the risen Christ) to the scriptures (meaning what we now call the 'Old Testament') did they begin to see there all sorts of references to Christ, specifically to the necessity that he should suffer before entering his glory, which they then used in their proclamation of Christ. In other words, the scriptures were not used merely as a narrative of the past, but rather as a thesaurus, a treasury of imagery, for entering the mystery of Christ, the starting point for which is the historical event of the Passion. In this it is not so much scripture that is being exegeted, but rather Christ who is being interpreted by recourse to the scriptures." Behr, *The Mystery of Christ: Life in Death*, 17.

214. *LW* 52:22; WA 10.1.1:81, "Szo sehen wyr, das auch gesetz und propheten nitt recht geprediget noch erkennet werdenn, wyr sehenn denn Christum drynnen gewicklet."

215. *LW* 52:22; WA 10.1.1:81, "ßondern das new testament, das Euangeli, muß antzeygen, offenen und erleuchten, wie gesagt ist."

depict the apostles as "angels" whose voice biblical readers must heed as was necessary for the shepherds in order to find the promised Christ.[216] First hearing Christ in the gospel proclaimed by the NT is a prerequisite for the endowment of the ability to see "how beautifully the entire Old Testament is attuned solely to him and makes sense so sweetly that man must give himself up captive in faith; then he realizes how true are the words which Christ says in John 5[:46]: "Moses has written of me; if you believed him you would also believe me."[217]

Another aspect of this New Testament-"guided" reading of the Old is the interpretive role of the Holy Spirit. Luther's exposition of 2 Peter 1:16–21 from the *Sermons on the Second Epistle of St. Peter* (1522), describes the illuminating effect of the gospel upon the material witness of the OT as another manner of speaking of the Holy Spirit's interpretation of the OT as opposed to human "wisdom and reason" (*klugheyt und vernunfft*) that assumes it has the capacity to discern the true meaning of the God-revealed and inspired Scriptures.[218] Sheer human "reason and wisdom" (*vernunfft und klugheit*) are unreliable tools for arriving at the divine intention of Scripture in its "letter."[219] Instead, Luther asserts, "The Holy Spirit Himself must expound Scripture. Otherwise it must remain unexpounded."[220] This understanding about Scripture, whether OT or NT, is Peter's point in 2 Peter

216. "First the gospel must be heard, and one must believe the appearance of the angel and his voice. Had the shepherds not heard from the angels that Christ was lying there, they might have looked at him a thousand and another thousand times and yet they would not have found out from that that the child was Christ." *LW* 52:22; *WA* 10.1.1:81.

217. *LW* 52:22; *WA* 10.1.1:81–82, "wie feyn das gantz allt testament auff yhn alleynn stymmet und reymet sich ßo lieblich, das der mensch sich muß ynn glawben gefangen geben, und wirtt ynnen, wie war das sey, das Christus Joan. 5. sagt: Moses hatt von myr geschrieben, wenn yhr demselben glewbtet, ßo glewbtet ihr auch myr."

218. In his comments on 2 Pet 1:19, Luther describes the "gospel" as the Word of God that brings light to interpretive darkness over the Scriptures, "It is God's Word, the Gospel, that we have been redeemed from death, sin, and hell through Christ. He who hears this has lighted the light and the lamp in our hearts to enable us to see. The Gospel illumines us and teaches what we should know. But where it is missing, we rush in and want to find the road to heaven with a self-invented way of life and self-invented works. Concerning this you cannot judge and see by means of your light that it is darkness. Consequently, since they do not want to have or accept the light, they must remain in darkness and blindness; for the light teaches us everything we should know and everything that is necessary for our salvation. This the world does not recognize by means of its wisdom and reason." *LW* 30:165–66; *WA* 14:30–31.

219. *LW* 30:166; *WA* 14:31.

220. *LW* 30:166; *WA* 14:31, "Der heylig geyst sol es selbs auslegen odder sol unausgelegt bleiben."

1:21, according to Luther. Scripture is "prophecy" from God, not from man; its prophetic and apostolic writings possess a divine origin, not a human one. Luther's hermeneutical logic, then, is that if the *sensus literalis* of Scripture is its divinely intended sense, then the Spirit's direct witness to Christ through the authorial intentions of the prophets and the apostles are not epistemologically accessible or recognizable apart from a confessional faith in Christ that submits itself to the pattern of the apostolic preaching that extols and expounds the gospel of Jesus Christ as in accordance with the Holy Scriptures (i.e., OT), those writings wherein God revealed beforehand about the gospel concerning his Son through his prophets.

In sum, reading the Old Testament in light of the New, in Luther's approach, is the natural outworking of the Testamental reality of God's written Word having taken the form of two interdependent witnesses. The NT is the necessary "guide" for the proper interpretation of the OT as Christian Scripture because the second Testament is the literal sense of the first. Luther conveys this notion in a strikingly clear statement from his comments on 1 Peter 1:10–12 in the *Sermons on the First Epistle of St. Peter* (1522), by clarifying, "The prophets have a special way of speaking, but they mean [*meynen*] exactly what the apostles preach."[221] Even so, as the NT issues forth its distinct witness to Christ, it constantly reaches back to the OT for its "ground" and "proof" because of the self-awareness that its own voice would be speechless apart from it. As Luther teaches in another sermon from the *Church Postils* in 1522 on John 1:1–14, "For the New Testament is nothing but a revelation of the Old."[222]

The hermeneutical relationship between the Testaments in Luther's thought is a dialectical one, where the OT proves the NT and NT illumines the OT. In many ways, each one has a role in interpreting the other, creating Scripture's remarkable unity through the diversity of its witness. Luther's explanation of the interplay between the Testaments and their indissoluble union as co-witnesses to the same Word of God concerning Jesus Christ occurs almost predictably in moments that feature his contention for Christ as the *sensus literalis* of the Bible based upon the messianic hope promised and fulfilled across the entire landscape of Scripture by the inspired prophets and apostles. Said differently, Luther's reflections on the hermeneutical implications of Christian Scripture in a two-Testament form find their fullest and richest expression in his discussions on how the biblical text's

---

221. *LW* 35:24; WA 12:279, "Die propheten haben eyn sonderliche weyße zü reden, meynen aber eben das, das die Apostel predigen."

222. *LW* 52:41; WA 10.1.1:181, "enn das new testament ist nit mehr denn eyn offinbarung des allten."

preoccupation with the Messiah causes all of Scripture to be about Jesus Christ.

4

The Messiah in the OT
and Christ as the *Sensus Literalis* of Scripture
in Luther's Treatise *On the Last Words of David*

LUTHER'S 1543 TREATISE *ON THE LAST WORDS OF DAVID: 2 SAMUEL 23:1–7* is widely recognized among scholars as perhaps the one writing within the Reformer's corpus that is singularly concerned with prescribing his approach to the christological-exegesis of Scripture. Without a doubt, Luther intended this work to provide and to demonstrate central principles for Christian biblical interpretation.[1] Yet in spite of its exegetical purview, the treatise still takes a polemical posture. That the treatise incorporates both of these dynamics has made this writing difficult to classify.[2]

1. At the end of the introductory section of the treatise, Luther states up front his objective: "In brief, if we do not apply all diligence to interpret the Hebrew Bible, wherever that is feasible, in the direction of the New Testament, in opposition to the interpretation of the rabbis, it would be better to keep the old translation (which, after all, retains, thanks to the New Testament, most of the good elements) than to have so many translations just because a few passages presumably have a different reading or are still not understood. This only confuses the memory of the reader, hinders his study, and leaves him in greater uncertainty than he was before. To illustrate this, I have decided to discourse on the last words of David, not according to the German translation, in which I followed all the others to avoid the impression that I considered myself the only smart person. No, now I am going to be stubborn and follow none but my own spirit." *LW* 15:270; WA 54:30.

2. An example of this difficulty can be observed in the publishing decisions of the American Edition of *Luther's Works*. Volume 47, *The Christian in Society, vol. 4,* focuses on the theme of polemics and contains two of the commonly associated "anti-Jewish" writings, *Against the Sabbatarians* (1538) and *On the Jews and Their Lies* (1539). Given the tendency to view *On the Last Words of David* as an additional "anti-Jewish" tract following *On the Jews and Their Lies*, one would expect it to appear in vol. 47 as well. Instead, *On the Last Words of David* is treated as one of Luther's "exegetical writings," and is included in vol. 15, subsequent to his *Notes on Ecclesiastes* and *Lectures on Song*

Typically, *On the Last Words of David* is categorized as one of Luther's final *Judenschriften*, that is, treatises or other writings of his that appear to be directly against the Jews.[3] Some Luther scholars, however, have downplayed this designation for *On the Last Words of David*. From his book on *Luther's Last Battles*, Mark Edwards admits in the chapter, "Against the Jews," that the tract includes various "critical asides" directed towards rabbinical exegesis, but in the end, it "just happens not to be a polemical treatise. Instead, it is a detailed discussion of those passages in the Old Testament that he believed attested unequivocally to the Christian Trinity and to the incarnation of the Word in Jesus Christ."[4] Mickey Mattox also recognizes that the treatise has a history of inclusion with Luther's "anti-Jewish" writings; however, even with its occasional word of warning against Jewish interpretation of the OT, *On the Last Words of David*, "did not at all take the form of an extended argument with the Jews."[5]

Contrary to Edwards and Mattox, John Slotemaker opts for an approach that resists what he considers to be a false dichotomy between exegetical and polemical works within Luther's writings.[6] In his article, "The Trinitarian House of David," Slotemaker classifies *On the Last Words of David* as "polemical exegesis," and sees the treatise as the possible culmination of "a cohesive exegetical argument put forth throughout this series of *Judenschriften* that is simultaneously exegetical and theologically polemical."[7] Slotemaker makes a compelling case for the "polemical exegesis" label,

---

of Solomon.

3. Standard writings of Luther that are identified as *Judenschriften* are: *That Jesus Christ was Born a Jew* (1523; *LW* 45:199–229; *WA* 11:314–36), *Against the Sabbatarians* (1538; *LW* 47:65–98; *WA* 50:312–37), *On the Jews and Their Lies* (1539; *LW* 47:137–306; *WA* 53:417–552), *On the Ineffable Name and On the Lineage of Christ* (1543; *WA* 53:579–648), and *On the Last Words of David* (1543; *LW* 15:265–352; *WA* 54:28–100). For additional works from Luther pertaining to his Jewish polemics as well as a helpful introduction to the vast and complex field of research on "Luther and the Jews," see Schramm and Stjerna, eds., *Martin Luther, the Bible, and the Jewish People: A Reader.*

4. Edwards, *Luther's Last Battles*, 134.

5. Mattox, "From Faith to the Text and Back Again: Martin Luther on the Trinity in the Old Testament," 294–95. Mattox goes on to affirm, "Instead, it offered one example after another of how to discern the authentic grammatical and theological meaning of the Old Testament as Luther understood it. In short, it modeled the way Luther believed Christian exegetes informed by the latest developments in biblical studies ought to read the text."

6. Slotemaker, "The Trinitarian House of David: Martin Luther's Anti-Jewish Exegesis of 2 Samuel 23:1–7," 248–49.

7. Ibid., 249–50.

especially in light of the fact that *Against the Sabbatarians* (1538) and *On the Jews and Their Lies* (1539), both as "usual suspects" under the *Judenschriften* title, feature early attempts by Luther to interpret 2 Samuel 23:1–7 in support of trinitarian and christological interpretation of the OT.[8] Furthermore, visible evidence occurs in Luther's "introduction," "conclusion," and scattered elsewhere, that points to the likelihood that *On the Last Words of David* is motivated by polemical interests, specifically against Jewish and rabbinic interpretations of the OT that were holding sway over Christian Hebraists.[9] Uncritical appropriation of such interpretive practices and the *interpretations* themselves, for Luther, not only threatened to undermine the proper relationship between the two Testaments of the Christian Bible, but the foundation of the gospel as well.

Still, Kenneth Hagen's warning should be heeded that, "To call a writing something, gives it a frame of meaning; to call it what it is gives it an accurate frame; to call it something other than what it was historically to be casts it into a foreign frame of reference."[10] Hagen questions the validity of the *Judenschriften* title, and whether such a genre actually exists within Luther that matches the contemporary assumption behind this modern construction.[11] Ultimately, Hagen rejects the term as suitable for representing the Medieval and sixteenth-century historical context within which Luther composes the often associated writings.[12] As it regards *On the Last Words of David* in particular, he believes the term fails to do justice to the overarching thrust of the treatise. Clearly the tract is meant to counter rabbinical exegesis of the OT, but if the moments when Luther addresses Jewish interpreters, rabbis, or Hebraists are unduly stressed, "then the point of the whole would be missed; this book could hardly be understood as an attack on Jews. In terms of genre, the book as a whole is a thoroughgoing expositio

---

8. On the development of Luther's handling of 2 Samuel 23:1–7 in these two treatises leading up to *On the Last Words of David* (1543), see ibid., 241–48.

9. Friedman defines "Christian-Hebraism" as "the use of Hebrew, rabbinic, or Cabbalistic sources for Christian religious purposes, . . ." Friedman, *The Most Ancient Testimony*, 1. See also Burnett, *Christian Hebraism in the Reformation Era (1500–1660)*.

10. Hagen, "Luther's So-called *Judenschriften*: A Genre Approach," 131.

11. As is standard procedure for Hagen, he conducted his research through meticulous textual criticism applied to the Weimar edition of Luther's works, and discovered that the term *Judenschriften* first appeared in 1920 in reference to certain writings that appeared to be "anti-Jewish" in nature. Among them was *On the Last Words of David*. Ibid., 137.

12. Ibid., 155–57.

of a theological topic, the Trinity, which is based on a detailed exegesis of the Last Words of David and a collage of biblical passages."[13]

Both Hagen's caution against illegitimate framing of the treatise and Slotemaker's characterization of it as "polemical-exegesis" should be duly noted. To some degree, one would be hard-pressed to locate a writing within Luther's corpus where any form of polemics is totally absent. Nevertheless, the overall aim of *On the Last Words of David* is to display for fellow believers how Luther reads the OT as distinctly Christian Scripture. Normally, this treatise is heard against the backdrop of other *Judenschriften*, so it seems that examining it within the context of the Bible-prefaces would produce a fresh reading. If the exegetical method on display in *On the Last Words of David* becomes foremost characterized as "anti-Semitic," then Luther is not allowed to have a Christian approach to interpreting the Scriptures outside of being primarily predetermined by socio-political norms as opposed to one that is dictated by the biblical text.[14]

Luther intended the prefaces to the Bible to give a theological introduction to Scripture and to offer instruction on Christian biblical interpretation. In this presentation, Luther exhibits a messianic approach to Christ as the Bible's *sensus literalis*, therefore, it only seems fitting that the one other writing from Luther's works that promotes itself in the same way should be investigated in order to evaluate the consistency of Luther's prescribed

13. Ibid., 147. Obviously the study to follow will challenge Hagen's comment that *On the Last Words of David* is principally a defense of trinitarian doctrine. Although the Trinity is a major focal point of the treatise, a better reading of the work would see Luther's affirmation of the Trinity as a secondary matter to his goal to demonstrate that Christ is the literal sense of the OT Scriptures on the basis of the messianic promise.

14. A case in point is the title of Slotemaker's essay, "The Trinitarian House of David: Martin Luther's *Anti-Jewish Exegesis* of 2 Samuel 23:1–7" (italics mine). The irony is that Slotemaker argues for the exegetical and polemical sides of this treatise to have equal footing, however, he proves Hagen's warning true about the impact a title can have on framing the interpretation of a writing in his decision to label Luther's interpretive practice in *On the Last Words of David* as "anti-Jewish exegesis." Although Slotemaker is connecting this treatise with preceding *Judenschriften* because of the development of Luther's interpretation of 2 Samuel 23, the polemical tone of *On the Last Words of David* never rises to a level that merits the "anti-Jewish" label. If viewed in relation to a core hermeneutic already explicated in non-*Judenschriften* writings such as the prefaces to the Bible, could not Luther's reading of the OT in *On the Last Words of David* (and elsewhere) be regarded positively as an exemplification of a stabilized methodology for Christian biblical interpretation and theology as opposed to being framed as an interpretive method enshrined in a cultural response considered beyond retrieval? To what degree does defense of Jesus Christ as the Messiah on the basis of the OT as distinctly *Christian* Scripture against Jews who are influencing believers with their confessionally *non*-Christian interpretation become "anti-Jewish" and not simply a confessional-Christian approach, even if part of the argument is supersessionist?

interpretive method. The three main characteristics of the hermeneutic deduced from the prefaces to the Bible covered in chapter 3 will be applied to *On the Last Words of David* to gauge the endurance and importance of these foundational elements to his "Christ-centered" reading of Scripture beyond their service to Luther's *German Bible*.

The Messiah in the OT and Luther's Biblical-Theological Hermeneutic

The aim of this section is to identify occurrences or semblances of the biblical-theological hermeneutic found within Luther's prefaces to the Bible that underscore the messianic rationale for concluding that Christ is the *sensus literalis* of Scripture. The theme of "the Messiah in the OT" permeates the entire treatise, so the caveat must be given that evaluation of every scriptural text Luther deems as "messianic" will not take place, since this study's thesis revolves around investigation of the messianic dimension of Luther's holistic approach to Scripture. The validity of Luther's designation of any given biblical passage as messianic is not in question; rather, what is under consideration is to what extent does Scripture's own preoccupation with the messianic hope produce Luther's christocentric view of the Bible?

Similar to his opening address in the *Preface to the Old Testament* (1523), Luther seeks to reverse views of the OT that dismiss Christ present within its "letter." Before engaging the actual text of 2 Samuel 23:1–7, Luther begins *On the Last Words of David* with caution and concern for the growing interests in Jewish and rabbinic OT interpretation. If Jewish translation and exegesis of the Hebrew OT are to be given the greatest weight for Christian approaches, then "a uniform Bible" (*eintrechtigen Bibel*) is beyond achievement.[15] Even though these sources may offer general aids for translating and dealing with grammatical issues, such positives are insufficient grounds for granting them interpretive authority as it concerns the true sense of the OT Scriptures. Despite the Jews's historical priority, Luther believes Christians are in a better place to interpret the OT rightly, even if they remain ignorant on some of the finer points of the Hebrew language. According to Luther,

---

15. *LW* 15:267; *WA* 54:28. A sublte presupposition disclosed from Luther in this initial section is the distinguishing of the Jews's Hebrew Bible from "our Bible" (*unser Bibel*). The distinction is that the Jews's Bible consists of only the Old Testament since they reject the New Testament whereas Christians confess a "uniform" or "unified" canon composed of both Old and New Testaments as Christian Scripture. As will be shown subsequently, interpretation of the OT from a starting point that rejects the NT and denies Jesus Christ as the Messiah cannot be a trusted source for proper, theological exegesis of the first part of Holy Scripture as God's Word in Luther's thought.

"The reason for that is this: We Christians have the meaning [*synn*] and import [*verstand*] of the Bible because we have the New Testament, that is, Jesus Christ, who was promised [*verheissen*] in the Old Testament and who later appeared and brought with Him the light and the true meaning [*verstand*] of Scripture."[16]

For scriptural proof of the claim to be privy to the OT's "true meaning," Luther quotes Jesus, whom he believes makes the selfsame assertion in John 5:46 and Luke 24:44–45. This move mirrors Luther's practice at various points in the Bible-prefaces, especially the *Preface to the Old Testament*. The biblical-theological hermeneutic from which he regards the "uniform" testimony of the Bible is guided by its own intertextual pronouncements, and in this case, Jesus's teachings in John 5:46 and Luke 24:44–45 have explicitly to do with the material substance of the OT's "letter." It is Luther's conviction that biblical texts such as these contain "the all-important point on which everything depends. Whoever does not have or want to have this Man properly and truly who is called Jesus Christ, God's Son, whom we Christians proclaim, must keep his hands off the Bible—that I advise. He will surely come to naught."[17] In these few excerpts, one can see that in the context of affirming Christ as the literal sense meaning of the OT, Luther substantiates his case through scriptural proofs that he understands as referencing the specific messianic hope God promised through the prophets later announced by the NT writings as fulfilled in Jesus Christ.[18]

16. *LW* 15:268; WA 54:29, "Ursache ist die, Wir Christen haben den synn und verstand der Biblia, weil wir das Newe Testament, das ist Jhesum Christum haben, welcher im alten Testament verheissen und hernach komen, mit sich das liecht und verstand der schrifft bracht hat."

17. *LW* 15:268; WA 54:29, "Denn da steckts, da ligts, da bleibts. Wer diesen man, der da heist Jhesus Christus, Gottes son, den wir Christen predigen, nicht recht und rein hat, noch haben wil, der lasse die Bible zu frieden, das rate ich, Er stösst sich gewislich."

18. Gow regards Luther's appeal to isolated OT texts as direct messianic prophecies of Jesus Christ as another feature of his "colonial" campaign to arrest the Hebrew Bible from the free use of the Jews. He posits, "Christological readings of Hebrew Bible texts rarely coincide with Jewish interpretations; and in Luther's case, Christ-centered readings had a directly polemical function that colonized and appropriated Hebrew Bible texts." Gow, "Christian Colonialism: Luther's Exegesis of Hebrew Scripture," 243. Gow's argument merits in-depth analysis beyond the scope of this work insofar as it reduces Luther's OT interpretation to a sociopolitical phenomenon. In the meantime, one hopeful aim of this present study, which stands upon Luther's hermeneutic foremost accounted for in his prefaces to the *Deutsche Bibel*, is to correct such exaggerations, by grounding some of the most significant components of Luther's Christian approach to the Scriptures, particularly the OT, in sources external to their occurrences within highly polemical writings such as the so-called *Judenschriften*, where

Another significant occurrence of Luther's biblical-theological hermeneutic manifests itself as the underpinning of his messianic exegesis of 2
Samuel 23:1–7. After a brief exposition of the first three verses, Luther has
already submitted that in them David has confessed through the Holy Spirit
"the two sublimest doctrines of our faith so aptly," namely, that there is one
God in three Persons, and that one of them, the Son, will become a man to
be the Messiah.[19] Even though depiction of the distinct persons within the
Godhead is a grand textual feature for Luther in this passage, he is mainly
interested in strengthening confidence about David's cognizance of his direct witness to the particulars of God the Son's messianic identity as the future God-man.[20] To reassure his readers that David is certainly aware of his

---

many scholars are hesitant to separate Luther's hermeneutical principles that privilege
the view of Christ as the literal sense of the Hebrew Bible from the context of his
deplorable rhetoric.

19. *LW* 35:277; *WA* 54:36, "Darinnen er fein bekennet die zween höchsten artickel,
. . ." The trinitarian context of Luther's messianic account of 2 Samuel 23:1–7 is the subject of Slotemaker's analysis of the Reformer's exegetical method in *On the Last Words
of David*. To some degree, Soltemaker sees the trinitarian disputation which occupies a
significant portion of this treatise as the actual focal point of Luther's interpretive demonstration. Yet by the end of his essay, he concludes that Luther's trinitarian-exegesis is
not an end in itself. Slotemaker contends that "Luther thinks it is necessary to formu-
late the trinitarian argument in 2 Samuel 23:2–3 in order to justify the messianic reading of 2 Samuel 23:5." Slotemaker, "The Trinitarian House of David," 251–53. This keen
insight is worth further consideration, however, held against this present study the
justification for a messianic-christological referent in David's "last words" has more to
do with the communion of human and divine authorship in Scripture than locating
biblical texts where all three of the distinct Persons of the Trinity can be seen bearing
witness through the scriptural text to God the Son. Nevertheless, it does seem the case
that Luther gravitates to passages within the OT where "God is speaking about God"
in order to show that when inner-trinitarian dialogue is recorded in Scripture, one can
always expect that God the Father and God the Spirit are intently bearing witness to
God the Son as the promised Messiah who will be the God-man. On this note Helmer's
essay proves immensely valuable. See Helmer, "Luther's Trinitarian Hermeneutic and
the Old Testament," 51–65. The topic of "Luther and the Trinity" has been Helmer's
specialization within Luther studies. See also her published dissertation, Helmer, *The
Trinity and Martin Luther: A Study on the Relationship between Genre, Language, and
the Trinity in Luther's Works (1523–1546)*; and Helmer, "God from Eternity to Eternity:
Luther's Trinitarian Understanding," 127–46.

20. Concerning David as "the sweet psalmist of Israel," in 2 Samuel 23:1, Luther
concludes that because of David's assurance that the Messiah, whom God promised
would come through the line of Jacob in Genesis 49:10 is the same Messiah promised to arise from his offspring, David must be composing songs primarily about this
coming one. Luther says that David boasts that "he did not keep this certain promise of the Messiah to himself nor for himself," and that he "glories in the fact here
that he has indited many exquisite, sweet, and melodious psalms about the promised

genealogical connection to the coming Messiah concurrent with his office as a prophet and psalmist for the sake of this Messiah, Luther contends that David has based his "last words" upon the messianic promise God made to him in 2 Samuel 7:11–16 also recorded in 1 Chronicles 17:10–14.[21] This intertextual connection points to a deeper theological reading of the OT present within Luther's unprecedented christological-exegesis of 2 Samuel 23:1–7.

The connection of 2 Samuel 23:1–7 with 2 Samuel 7:11–16 and 1 Chronicles 17:10–14 to Luther's biblical-theological hermeneutic is established in relation to Genesis 3:15.[22] Later in the treatise after he has allotted space for a detailed exposition of 1 Chronicles 17:10–17 (as a representative for the same promise in 2 Samuel 7), Luther directs his gaze towards Moses in order to push the messianic foundation of the OT's witness to Christ all the way back to the patriarch of the prophets. In a section where he strives to show how Moses's prophetic word about the Messiah coheres with NT Christology, he invokes Genesis 3:15 as a means to harmonize John's teaching about the Divine Word through whom all things were created, yet who

---

Messiah, which should be sung in Israel to the praise of God and, in fact, have been sung there, in which, simultaneously, both excellent prophecy and a lofty meaning has been preached and imparted to the people of Israel." Even the Psalter's "sweetness" receives its flavor from its messianic purpose because it is intended to uplift hearts overburdened with sin, adversity, and death, which only comes through consolation of the coming Messiah and his salvation. "To such hearts the Book of Psalms," Luther reflects, "is a sweet and delightful song because it *sings of and proclaims the Messiah* even when a person does not sing the notes but merely recites and pronounces the words" (italics mine); *LW* 15:272–73; WA 54:33.

21. *LW* 15:279; WA 54:38.

22. Although 2 Samuel 7:11–16 (the Davidic covenant) does not receive overwhelming attention in the Bible-prefaces, it does, nonetheless, appear in an important place within the prologues as a part of the observed biblical-theological scheme for a messianic reading of the OT. In the *Preface to the New Testament* (1522), Luther includes this text in his demonstration that God has, indeed, promised the apostolic gospel of Jesus Christ through the prophets in the OT. As reviewed several times thus far, in order to prove that the OT witnessed to the same content of the NT's proclamation of Christ and his gospel, Luther offers a messianic chain of OT texts tracing the "seed" (*samen*) promise: Genesis 3:15; 22:18; and 2 Samuel 7:12–14 (*LW* 35:359–60; WA, *DB* 6:4, 6). For further evidence that this text holds a firm spot within Luther's unbroken line of messianic promises, one will find it utilized as such in one of the earliest so-called *Judenschriften*, *That Jesus Christ Was Born a Jew* (1523). Here again, Luther outlines the clear messianic "seed" (*samen*) promises as evidence that Jesus Christ as the Incarnate, Son of God and of David, was directly promised and prophesied in the OT Scripture's messianic portrait. To argue this case in a defined opening portion of the treatise, Luther's choice texts are: Genesis 3:15; 22:18; 2 Samuel 7:12–14; and Isaiah 7:14. *LW* 45:201–13; WA 11:316–25.

became flesh in John 1:1–14 with Moses's account of the Divine Word in Genesis 1, though with no apparent "fleshly" or incarnate counterpart.[23]

As is his pattern, Luther explains how Genesis 3:15 contains more than a mere promise of a shadowy future Messiah. Neither is it about a "silly little snake, such as eat little frogs, but a snake that devours the entire world."[24] Luther understands the prophecy of "the seed of the woman" (*Des Weibes same*) in its development throughout the OT as an indicator that the Messiah would be both God and man.[25] The next major stage in the promise of this messianic "seed" in Luther's discourse is Genesis 22:18 and God's promise to Abraham that through this same "seed" (*samen*), the Gentiles will be blessed through removal of sin's curse.[26] Luther, then, condenses the course of this messianic prophecy leading up to the virgin birth by summarizing, "Here the promise [*verheissung*] of the Seed [*Samen*] of the woman is renewed, and henceforth it is to be known as Abraham's Seed [*Samen*]. Later it was called David's Seed [*samen*], and finally the Virgin's Seed [*samen*]. Therefore the blessing in the Seed [*samen*] of Abraham here means the same as earlier [Gen. 3:15]: The Seed [*same*] of the woman shall crush the serpent's head."[27]

At this point, Luther has established a general link with God's promise to David that the Messiah would come from his "seed" with the initial "gospel" promise made to Adam and Eve in Genesis 3:15. Upon further reflection concerning the "seed" promise in these messianic passages and others, which he believes reveal the Incarnate identity of the Messiah, Luther claims to have brought Moses, John, Paul, and the entire NT in agreement on its doctrine of God and its Christology.[28] Christians can arrive at this unified

23. *LW* 15:317; WA 54:69–70.

24. *LW* 15:317; WA 54:70, "Das ist nicht ein schlecht alber schlengelin, das frösschlin frisset, Sondern die gantzen Welt verschlinget."

25. *LW* 15:317; WA 54:70.

26. *LW* 15:323–24; WA 54:75–76.

27. *LW* 15:324: WA 54:76, "Und ist hiemit die verheissung von des Weibes Samen vernewet, und sol nu Abrahams Samen heissen, wie er weiter hernach Davids samen und zu letzt der Jungfrawen samen worden ist, Darumb heist hie Segen in dem samen Abraham eben so viel, als droben. Der same des Weibes sol der Schlangen den Kopff zu tretten." In a similarly worded passage only a few lines later, Luther exults in this promise, "We sing and say: In the Seed of Abraham, of David, of the woman Mary we have remission of sin, ablution of sin, redemption from sin, liberation from death and every other evil; for it is He 'whom God made our Wisdom, our Righteousness, and Sanctification and Redemption' (1 Cor. 1:30), our Blessing, our Consolation, our Life, and our Joy in eternity. May God be praised for this forever. Amen." *LW* 15:324–25; WA 54:76.

28. *LW* 15:326; WA 54:77.

vision of the Bible's theological witness, Luther says, because they listen to and understand Christ's words in John 5:46, where it is taught that "[Moses] indeed wrote of Christ throughout his entire book, in which he speaks of God and Messiah."[29] From this interpretive horizon, Luther claims that Christians are also able to make sense of Jesus's curious statement in John 8:56 that Abraham saw his (i.e., Christ's) day and rejoiced.[30] Luther explains, "Where did he see it? In this verse, where he heard that his Seed [*same*] was to be God and man, who would bless all Gentiles, redeem them from sin and death, and give eternal life and holiness and blessedness. *He felt the same joy which David experienced above, in 1 Chron. 17:16, when the same Son was promised [verheissen] him.*"[31]

Here in this last excerpt is now revealed a direct relationship between the messianic interpretation of David's "last words" in 2 Samuel 23:1–7 and Genesis 3:15. As highlighted above, Luther's immediate rationale for David's intended messianic referent in his "last words" is that David grounded them upon the prior promise God made to him in 2 Samuel 7:11–16 and 1 Chronicles 17:10–14. The latter passage (expanded to incorporate 1 Chronicles 17:10–17) is the one Luther chooses to exposit in order to revisit the original messianic covenant God made with David. When Luther finally draws back and invokes his broader biblical-theological hermeneutic, it causes him to anchor the OT's literal sense, messianic witness to Jesus Christ (as verified in John 5:46) in the promise of the coming "seed of the woman" made to Adam and Eve (Genesis 3:15), to Abraham (Genesis 22:18), and to David (1 Chronicles 17:16). In sum, Luther attests that 2 Samuel 23:1–7 must have a messianic referent, and thereby, a christological one, because David is working from God's messianic promise delivered in 1 Chronicles 17:10–17. A major factor that enables this reading of 2 Samuel 23:1–7 comes from the defining role Genesis 3:15 plays in determining the ultimate subject matter of the OT as it is maintained throughout its "letter" (Abraham, David, etc.) expectant of the first advent.[32]

29. *LW* 15:326; WA 54:77–78, "Freilich geschrieben, durch sein gantzes Buch, wo er von Gott redet und von Messia."

30. *LW* 15:326; WA 54:78.

31. Italics mine; *LW* 15:326; WA 54:78, "Wo sahe er jnen? In diesem spruch, da er höret, wie sein same sole Gott und Mensch sein, der alle Heiden segenen, von Sünden und Tod erlösen, ewiglich, Lebendig, Heilig und selig machen solt, gleich wie droben David, j. Paral. 17. Even die selbige freunde hatte, da jm der selbe Son auch verheissen ward."

32. An additional pivotal passage that figures prominently in *On the Last Words of David* as it concerns Luther's conviction that the driving narrative of the OT is in the direction of the Messiah is Genesis 49:10. This text underwent significant treatment

Aside from the pervasive citation of various biblical texts from the OT and NT, Luther's sweeping statements near the end of *On the Last Words of David* strongly evince that it is his messianic reading of Bible as a whole that determines his view of Christ as Scripture's *sensus literalis*. At the culmination of Luther's lengthy discourse on the Trinity and Christ in the OT, Luther emphasizes the necessity for this type of approach to both Testaments as Christian Scripture, especially the OT, because God desires to be known truly through right apprehension of his self-disclosure in the biblical text.[33] Furthermore, Luther says,

> God is particularly concerned about our knowledge of the revelation of His Son, as seen throughout the Old and the New Testament. All points to the Son. *For Scripture is given for the sake of the Messiah*, or Woman's Seed [*samens*], who is to remedy all that the serpent has corrupted, to remove sin, death, and wrath, to restore innocence, life, paradise, and heaven.[34]

---

in *On the Jews and Their Lies* (1539) to argue against any notions that Jews should continue waiting for the appearing of their Messiah. Luther interprets Gen 49:10 as a messianic prediction that that the "scepter" or "government" of the Jews will remain in the land of Judah until the Messiah's advent. Once the Messiah comes, then the people of God will expand to all nations. Since the Jews at the time of the sixteenth century, had not had real possession of Judah or Jerusalem since the first century and the time of Jesus Christ, whom the NT and Christians confess as the OT's Messiah, Luther uses Genesis 49:10 both to confirm the NT's claim that Jesus of Nazareth is the Messiah and to expose the futility of the Jews's ongoing messianic hope. For more on the significance of Genesis 49:10 and other central messianic biblical texts in Luther's christological-exegesis, so to speak, of the OT in *On the Jews and Their Lies*, see Maser, "Luthers Schriftauslegung in dem Tractat 'Von den Juden und ihren Lügen' (1543)," 78–82.

33. "We must know the Divine Majesty aright, lest we believe blindly and wildly, as Jews, heretics, and Mohammed do, that God is but one Person. God resents that. He wants to be acknowledged as He reveals Himself." *LW* 15:338; *WA* 54:88. Previously in the treatise, Luther indicated that God reveals himsef not without purpose. Based upon John 17:3, Luther frames God's self-disclosure in Scripture in soteriological terms. He writes, "[I]t is certain that God wants to be known by us, here on earth by faith, yonder by sight, that He is one God and yet three Persons. And according to John 17:3, this is our everlasting life. *To this end He gave us His Word and Holy Scripture*, attested with great miracles and signs. We must learn from it. To attain that knowledge of God, it is surely necessary that He Himself instruct us, that He reveal Himself and appear to us. By ourselves we could not ascend into heaven and discover what God is or how His divine essence is constituted." *LW* 15:306–7; *WA* 54:61.

34. Italics mine; *LW* 15:338; *WA* 54:88, "Und sonderlich ists Gott zu thun umb die offenbarung und erkentnis seines Sons, durch die gantze Schrifft, Alts und Newen Testaments, Alles gehets auff den Son, Denn die Schrifft ist gegeben umb des Messia, oder Weibs samens willen, der alles wider zu recht bringen sol, was die Schlange verderbt

As one can see, when Luther clarifies what it means that "all points to the Son" in the Christian Bible across both of its Testaments, he does so by the assertion that Scripture foremost exists to witness to the Messiah, the "seed of the woman" first promised in Genesis 3:15.[35]

---

hat, Sünde, Tod, Zorn weg nemen, Unschuld, Leben, Paradis und Himelreich wider bringen." Cf. Luther's similar, yet more limited designation in *On the Jews and Their Lies* (1539), "As it happens, not only the Jew but all the world is obliged to know that *the New Testament is God the Father's book about his Son Jesus Christ.* Whoever does not accept and honor that book does not accept and honor God the Father himself. For we read, 'He who rejects me rejects my Father' ... *[F]or this is God the Father's book [Buch], it is the word about his Son Jesus Christ.* It will not avail them [the Jews] but rather prejudice their case if they plead ignorance or rejection of the book [*Buch*]. For it is incumbent on all to know God's book [*Buch*]. He did not reveal it to have it ignored or rejected; he wants it to be known, and he excuses no one from this" (italics mine); *LW* 47:280; *WA* 53:532. Luther connects God's active self-revelation to humanity with the reason for which Scripture (specifically the NT in this instance) was given. Viewed from this perspective, Scripture as God's "book" about his Son, Jesus Christ, features God the Son as its central subject matter because he is the person within the Triune Godhead through whom humans by faith have access to the One, True, and Living God. A comparsion made with the statement in *On the Last Words of David* above shows that God's *NT* "book" about his Son, Jesus Christ serves as an indispensable segment of the complete Word of God in Scripture that was given for the sake of making known the Messiah. Therefore, if Scripture's full witness is lacking by way of dismissal of the second Testament, which Luther claims is undoubtedly the God of Israel's "book" about the Son of God, the Messiah, then not only will OT interpretation be distorted, but even more so, encountering God in the Scriptures for relationship and salvation will be rendered impossible. In this scenario, neither God, Christ, the gospel, nor Scripture are rightly known, and this result betrays the very purpose for which God has not remained hidden or silent.

35. In *Against the Sabbatarians* (1538), an earlier treatise often associated with the *Judenschriften*, Luther also contends extensively for the NT's proclamation of Jesus Christ as the direct fulfillment of the OT's messianic promises and prophecies. Although differently expressed, Luther offers an appraisal of God's promise of the Messiah in the OT that places it at a level above all other meanings and themes in Scripture. In Luther's interpretation of the OT, if the Messiah has, indeed, not yet come, causing the Jews to be still waiting for the Messiah's first advent, then God has forgotten to keep his promise. Luther asks, "Why, then, should God forget his promise so woefully in this exile or let it fail of fulfillment or be so hostile to them, since they have no sin which they can name, and *yet this promise of the Messiah is the most glorious and the mightiest promise, upon which all other prophecy, promise, and the entire law are built?* For the other promises such as those pertaining to Egypt, the wilderness, and Babylon, are to be esteemed very small in comparison with *this chief promise of the Messiah*" (italics mine); *LW* 47:77; *WA* 50:322. The single statement offers much for reflection in relation to Christ as the literal sense of Scripture on the basis of the Bible's messianic hope and portrait. Restricted in this case to the OT, Luther grants supremacy to the promise of the Messiah and places all other aspects of the OT's textual witness, whether historical prophecies or even the law, at its service.

In addition to this telling claim, Luther makes two other such comprehensive statements concerning Christ as the *sensus literalis* of Scripture. First, and still within the same discussion, Luther offers a variation of the sentiments expressed above, when he affirms, "Thus all of Scripture, as already said, is pure Christ, God's and Mary's Son. Everything is focused on this Son, so that we might know Him distinctively and in that way see the Father and the Holy Spirit eternally as one God."[36] A faithful reading of this passage will be against the statement above where Luther affixes the Messiah as the focal point of Scripture's testimony; this contextual interpretation will lead once more to the conclusion that to declare that "all of Scripture" points to or is "focused" on Christ the Son of God (fully God) and of Mary (fully man) is to uphold that Scripture was "given for the sake of the Messiah, or Woman's Seed."[37]

The second and last variation comes only a few pages later during a polemical address to the Hebraists to loose the OT from rabbinic clutches, for "[t]hey are prone to equivocate with words and sentences to suit their stupid interpretation, even though the letter harmonizes readily with the New Testament, and it is certain that Jesus Christ is Lord over all. *To Him Scripture must bear witness, for it is given solely for His sake.*"[38] In this instance, the same idea is communicated as in the previous two iterations, namely, that God the Holy Spirit has revealed Scripture for the utmost purpose of bearing "witness" to Jesus Christ. So, then, if left untampered, Luther believes the OT will "harmonize" (*reimet*) naturally in its "letter" (*Buchstabe*) with the NT's proclamation of the gospel, which demonstrates that the literal sense of both Testaments has to do with the identity of the Messiah as God the Son.

In short, Luther's construal of Christ as the *sensus literalis* of Scripture is motivated by observance that the biblical text's primary objective is to promise and to make known Jesus Christ, the Incarnate Son of God and Son of David, through whose person and work the serpent's head will be crushed, the curse of sin removed, and eternal life bestowed upon all who receive him by faith alone. This account and approach to the Bible's

---

36. *LW* 15:339; WA 54:88–89, "Also ist nu die gantze Schrifft, wie gesagt, alles Eitel Christus, Gottes und Marien Son, Alles ists zu thun umb den selben Son, das wir jn unterschiedlich erkennen, und also den Vater und den Heiligengeist, Einen Gott ewiglich sehen mügen."

37. *LW* 15:338; WA 54:88.

38. *LW* 15:343; WA 54:92, "[W]o sie daheimen sind, und die Vocabula und Sententz gerne Equivocirn auff jren tollen verstand, da doch der Buchstabe gerne mit dem newen Testament sich reimet, Und gewis ist, das Jhesus Christus der HERR uber alles ist, denn die Schrifft sol zeugnis geben, als die allein umb seinen willen gegeben ist."

"uniform" theological witness to God in Christ is in complete coherence with the vision he cast in the prefaces to the Bible, particularly the *Preface to the New Testament* (1522) and the *Preface to the Old Testament* (1523).

Authorial Intention as a Textual Warrant for Christ as the *Sensus Literalis* of Scripture

As was shown in his prefaces to the Bible, Luther's ambition to depict Jesus Christ as the ultimate subject matter of the Bible's witness is driven by his engagement with the biblical text in pursuit of its authorial intention. Put another way, one should not expect Luther to assign a so-called "center" or literal sense to Scripture if he was not convinced that his ascription was in unison with what the biblical authors meant in their writings. This precondition for determination of Scripture's *sensus literalis* is the product of the attempt to grapple with the Christian commitment to divine and human authorship.

On the Last Words of David features multiple instances where Luther affirms Scripture's divine origin. A straightforward example cited previously can be seen in his comment, "Thus we attribute to the Holy Spirit *all* [*gantze*] of Holy Scripture . . . ."[39] Later, Luther seems to refer back to this statement, when he recalls, "We heard before that *Holy Scripture is spoken by the Holy Spirit* in keeping with the words of David: 'The Spirit of the Lord has spoken by me.'"[40] And once more, he offers in a subsequent discussion a similar rendition, "It has been stated often enough above that *Holy Scripture is given through the Holy Spirit.*"[41]

For Luther, Scripture's divine origin entails divine authorial intention. On the other hand, even though it is "divine," Scripture is, nonetheless, a literary document composed by human authors. Yet, in spite of its "human" dimension, the Bible's theological substance does not originate with man, nor does its rationale for coming into existence as written special revelation. Nevertheless, as has been noted from Christopher Ocker's study on the "textual attitude" of the Late Middle Ages and the Reformation, the doctrine of biblical inspiration exemplified in Luther allowed for the communion

---

39. Italics mine; *LW* 15:275; WA 54:35, "Also gibt man nu dem Heiligen Geist die gantze Heilige Schrifft, . . ."

40. Italics mine; *LW* 15:280; WA 54:38, "[W]ie wire droben gehört, das die Heilige schrifft, durch den Heiligen geist gesprochen ist, nach dem spruch David: 'Die geist des HErrn hat durch mich geredet.'"

41. Italics mine; *LW* 15:292; WA 54:48, "[W]ie droben offt gesagt, das die heilige Schrifft durch den Heiligen Geist gesprochen ist."

of divine and human authors, bringing the collapse of the old "letter and Spirit" divide or the separation of the "literal" and "spiritual" meanings.[42] This development is on display all throughout *On the Last Words of David*, and thus, examples of how divine and human authorship provide authorial intent to the biblical text that warrants designating Christ as Scripture's *sensus literalis* will be examined together.

The overall aim of Luther's desire to publish a treatise on 2 Samuel 23:1–7 is to demonstrate how the Hebrew OT bears witness to Jesus Christ at the level of its "letter" contrary to the alternative interpretations from Jewish and rabbinic sources. Luther believes that David's "last words" are an attempt to exult in the promise of the Messiah. Perhaps the central reason for this view is reflected in Luther's own translation of 2 Samuel 23:1, "The oracle of David, the son of Jesse, *the oracle of the man who is assured of the Messiah of the God of Jacob*, the sweet psalmist of Israel."[43] King David's greatest boast is his "assurance" of the Messiah, the one who has been promised to come from David's offspring. Luther tries to capture this sense as he paraphrases David's thoughts, "And what is it that he lauds so highly? He says: 'In the first place it is that I am the man to whom God promised the Messiah of the God of Jacob, that the Messiah will descend from me, from my blood, from my tribe and family.'"[44] In other words, this interpretation is what Luther understands as the "intention" or "meaning" of not simply David's "words," but of David himself. These "last words" are David's "last will and testament," according to Luther.[45] And, David has chosen to utter

42. Ocker, *Biblical Poetics before Humanism and Reformation*, 216. Cf. Helmer who addresses this authorial communion manifest in *On the Last Words of David*, wherein Luther, nonetheless, grants ultimate determination of meaning/intention to the divine author, especially as it concerns the inner-trinitarian disclosure. Helmer frames this matter within the *verba* and *res* dynamic, "For Luther, authorial agency must be divine because of the subject matter that is eternal. When Luther describes the text from the perspective of its eternal referent, he attributes authorship to the Holy Spirit . . . On the other hand, Luther ties access into the mystery to historically concrete sites. The literal speech of the prophets, apostles and church is valorized because the Spirit is responsible for creating these tangible means to access the mystery. The referent opens up historical speech to unseen things, thereby establishing the dignity of the speech's written records." Helmer, "Luther's Trinitarian Hermeneutic and the Old Testament," 55.

43. Italics mine; *LW* 15:270–71, 345; WA 54:31, 94, "Es sprach David, der Son Jsai, Es sprach der man, der von dem Messia des Gottes Jacob versichert ist, Lieblich mit Psalmen Israel."

44. *LW* 15:271; WA 54:32, "Was ists denn, das er rhumet? Erstlich ists, (spricht er) das ich der Man bin, dem Gott verheissen hat den Messia des Gottes Jacob, das der selbe von mir, von meinem blut, stam und hause komen wird."

45. "[B]ut they are his last will and testament. We Germans call this *Seelrecht*, on

them as a celebratory testimony to the Messiah who will come through his bloodline; they are David's "final word" on the legacy he wishes to leave.

These reflections occur within Luther's brief explanation of 2 Samuel 23:1. Thus, in the first verse of David's "last words," Luther finds conscious, human authorial intent conveyed through 2 Samuel's "letter" about the Messiah, i.e., its literal sense. Conversely, in 2 Samuel 23:2, Luther observes David identifying the Holy Spirit as the divine source of this messianic revelation: "The Spirit of the Lord has spoken [*geredt*] by me, His Word [*rede*] is upon my tongue [*zunge*]."[46] Yet even more precisely, David describes the Holy Spirit as a "speaker," the one who directs David's own "speech." This second verse serves an important role in Luther's messianic interpretation of David's "last words" because it answers the question of how David is able to speak of an explicit Christian-theological referent in the first verse.[47]

To start his initial comments on 2 Samuel 23:2, Luther writes, "In the first place, he [David] mentions the Holy Spirit. *To Him he ascribes all that is foretold [weissagen] by the prophets.*"[48] Luther supports this view by quoting 2 Peter 1:21, "No prophecy [*weissagung*] ever came by the impulse of man; but moved by the Holy Spirit, holy men of God spoke [*geredt*]."[49] From here, Luther asserts that the Creed derives its verbiage concerning the Holy Spirit in the clause, "Who spake [*geredet*] by the prophets."[50] This affirmation brings Luther to the conclusion aforementioned, "Thus we attribute to the Holy Spirit all of Holy Scripture and the external Word and the sacraments, which touch and move our external ears and other senses."[51] In short, Lu-

---

which a person is willing to die and which is to be executed unaltered after his death. The jurists call it a 'last will.'" *LW* 15:270; WA 54:31, "Sondern sein Testament, und das wir Deudschen heissen seel recht, darauff einer sterben wil, das es nach seinem tode also geschehen und bleiben sol. Ultima Voluntas heists bey den Juristen."

46. *LW* 15:275; WA 54:34, "Der Geist des HERR hat durch mich gerdt. Und seine rede ist durch meine zunge geschehen."

47. Luther also notes that David "begins to talk about the exalted Holy Trinity, of the divine essence" in 2 Samuel 23:2. *LW* 15:275; WA 54:34.

48. *LW* 15:275; WA 54:34, "Erstlich nennet er den Heiligen Geist, dem gibt er alles, was die Propheten weissagen."

49. Luther's full statement here is: "And to this and to similar verses St. Peter refers in 2 Pet 1:21, where he says: 'No prophecy ever came by the impulse of man; but moved by the Holy Spirit, holy men of God spoke.'" *LW* 15:275; WA 54:34, "Und auff diesen, und der gleichen sprüch, sihet S. Petrus 2. Pet. j.: 'Es ist noch nie keine weissagung aus menschlichem willen erfurbracht. Sondern die heiligen Menschen Gottes haben gerdt aus eingebunge des Heiligen Geistes.'"

50. *LW* 15:275; WA 54:35, "Der durch die Propheten geredet hat."

51. *LW* 15:275; WA 54:35, "Also gibt man nu dem Heiligen Geist die gantze Heilige Schrifft und das eusserliche wort und Sacrament, so unser eusserliche ohren und

ther interprets David in 2 Samuel 23:2 as an affirmation of the viewpoint that characterizes the Holy Spirit as more than merely the source of divine knowledge; he is a divine "speaker," who speaks God's Word through divine inspiration of prophets and apostles. In this way, he is also a divine author with a divine intention expressed through the agency of human authorship.

In Luther's estimation, David's point in 2 Samuel 23:2 is that his boast in 2 Samuel 23:1 about the Messiah is to be attributed to the Holy Spirit's speaking through him. Herein lies the significance of Luther's understanding of 2 Peter 1:21. According to Luther, Peter teaches that the biblical text in its "letter" is able to contain the theological and/or "spiritual" meaning from God because the *modus operandi* of the doctrine of inspiration consists of the Holy Spirit speaking by way of the prophets's speaking.[52] On David's claim to be the voice through whom God the Spirit communicates, Luther remarks that normally this would be "a glorious and arrogant arrogance" (*ein herrlicher hohmütiger hohmut*) except for the fact that "David, the son of Jesse, born in sin, . . is he who has been *called to be a prophet* by the promise of God."[53] The literal sense of David's "last words" picture and promise the Messiah because of the "communion" he experiences with the Holy Spirit as divine inspiration gives way to biblical authorship.[54]

The language Luther uses here for David's "prophetic calling" mirrors that of the Bible-prefaces, particularly the depiction of the office of a prophet in many of the OT prologues, and of course, the *Preface to the Prophets* (1532). David's intent in 2 Samuel 23:2, according to Luther, is that he wants to be clear that he is not speaking as a mere man, a "son of Jesse," but instead, his "last words" of rejoicing in the Messiah are voiced from his prophetic office.[55] David receives this office from the Holy Spirit, and likewise, adopts

---

synne ruren oder bewegen."

52. See Helmer, "For Luther, access to the inner-trinitarian mystery is granted soley by the third person of the Trinity. In the Old Testament, the Spirit's inspiration of the prophets serves to open up the trinitarian *res*." Helmer, "Luther's Trinitarian Hermeneutic and the Old Testament," 54.

53. The complete quotation serves as a contrast with the possible criticism that David is acting arrogantly, or perhaps, presumptuously in the announcement that the Holy Spirit has spoken through him: "David, the son of Jesse, born in sin, is not such a man, but it is he who has been *called to be a prophet* by the promise of God" (italics mine); *LW* 15:275; *WA* 54:35, "Das wird nicht sein David, Jsai son, in sunden geborn, sondern der zum Propheten durch Gottes verheissung erweckt ist."

54. Ocker, *Biblical Poetics before Humanism and Reformation*, 216.

55. Helmer comments on this distinction in relation to the Spirit's inspiration, who causes the human words of David to be divinely "prophetic" within their "letter" and literal sense, "The self-same Spirit inspires the human author of the Psalms, David, so that he speaks not anymore as the 'Son of Jesse, born in sin,' but as the one awakened

the same charge: to witness to Christ. David fulfills this prophetic-authorial office in his scriptural writings, whether the psalms or presently in the case of his "last words." For this office to produce a biblical text where the *sensus literalis* or the authorial intention of David in 2 Samuel 23:1 is the NT's proclamation of the Messiah as Jesus Christ, the Incarnate Son of God and Son of David, is only possible because this "prophecy" has come from God the Spirit, whose own authorial office is to bear witness to the messianic identity of God the Son. Luther expresses this unity between the divine and human authors, when he adds, "Therefore these words [*wort*] of David are also those of the Holy Spirit, which He speaks [*redet*] with David's tongue [*zunge*] . . . ."[56] In this statement, Luther reveals the one-mindedness at work in the generation of Scripture between its authors; David's words (*wort*) are, indeed, his words, but they are also simultaneously the Holy Spirit's words, which the Spirit communicates with David's "tongue" (*zunge*).

Luther formulates this divine and human authorial relationship similarly with other OT prophets in *On the Last Words of David*. For instance, concerning his interpretation of Daniel 7:13–14 as a passage that portrays the Messiah as both God and man, Luther says that the Holy Spirit "speaks [*redet*] these words through Daniel."[57] Likewise, in support of his view that Jeremiah 30:8–9 purports the doctrine of the Messiah's Incarnation, Luther identifies the source of this divine truth as "the Holy Spirit, who speaks [*redet*] these words through Jeremiah and teaches us to believe and understand them, . . ."[58] Luther's approach to biblical authorship allows him to attribute the intention and meaning of the text to both the human author/prophet or the Spirit without any contradiction. Yet, Scripture's ultimate meaning, its literal sense, is set in motion by the Spirit as its divine author. Human authors are privy to the theological and spiritual meaning of their inspired

---

by God to be a prophet. The Spirit creates the historical actuality of access into the divine subject matter." Helmer, "Luther's Trinitarian Hermeneutic and the Old Testament," 54.

56. *LW* 15:276; WA 54:35, "Darumb sind diese wort Davids auch des Heiligen geistes, die er durch seine zunge redet, . . ." Cf. Luther's comments on Isaiah 60:19–20, "Who is it who speaks [*redet*] these words by the tongue [*zungen*] of Isaiah? Without a doubt, God the Holy Spirit, who speaks [*redet*] by the prophets, introducing the Person of the Father, who, in turn, speaks [*redend*] of the eternal Light, that is, of His Son, Jesus of Nazareth, the Son of David and of Mary." *LW* 15:290; WA 54:47.

57. *LW* 15:291; WA 54:48, "So is der Heilige Geist da, ders durch Daniel redet, . . ."

58. The complete quotation reads, "And the Holy Spirit, who speaks these words through Jeremiah and teaches us to believe and understand them, must be the third Person present here." *LW* 15:298; WA 54:54, "Hie bey mus der Heilige geist die dritte Person sein, der solchs durch Jeremia redet, und uns leret, das wirs gleuben und verstehen."

writings, but this cognizance is not a result of their own esoteric ascension into the heavens. "For such sublime and mysterious things," Luther reminds, "no one could know if the Holy Spirit would not reveal them through the prophets. It has been stated often enough above that Holy Scripture is given through the Holy Spirit."[59]

In sum, Luther discerns in 2 Samuel 23:1–2 both human and divine authorial intention directly referencing the coming Messiah in the "letter" of the biblical text. The Spirit speaks by way of the prophet's "tongue," or one could say, the prophet's "pen" without the human author suffering the loss of personality or self-awareness of his textual meaning. This binary relationship preserves the literal dignity of Scripture's "letter" because the literary expression of the human author is the instrumental means by which the Holy Spirit witnesses to God's Word. The *sensus literalis* of David's "last words" in 2 Samuel 23:1–7 is Jesus Christ insofar as David himself recognizes his life's greatest and "sweetest" task as to promise, prophesy, and exalt in the coming Messiah. This messianic interpretation is what Luther considers a "christological-exegesis" of an OT passage such as 2 Samuel 23:1–7, and it is epistemologically viable because of the pneumatological orientation of biblical authorship,[60] where the Spirit has spoken the divine *res* by the *verba* of "the prophets and the apostles, through whom God proclaims His Word to us."[61]

---

59. *LW* 15:291; WA 54:48, "Denn solch hoch heimlich ding kundte niemand wissen wo es der Heilige Geist nicht durch die Propheten offenbart, wie droben offt gesagt, das die heilige Schrifft durch den Heiligen Geist gesprochen ist."

60. On the Spirit's epistemological function in grounding the referential dignity of the external text, see Helmer, "Luther's Trinitarian Hermeneutic and the Old Testament," 55–56; see also Seitz, "The Trinity in the Old Testament," 36–39. In relation to this study, Seitz closes his essay with this reflection: "Luther was right to argue that any account of the Trinity must be based on a proper understanding of the semantics of Old Testament sense-making, and not to be conceived either as later historical developments or located in the Church's authority to see something, and so warranting the Trinitarian talk from within its own sense-making. The Holy Spirit 'spake by the prophets' and so revealed from the Old Testament the majesty of YHWH, the Lord, upholding this majesty and showing it to be properly understood as a Trinity of Persons in One God." Ibid., 38–39.

61. *LW* 15:327; WA 54:78, "als Propheten und Aposteln befolhen, durch welche er sein wort uns verkundigt." Luther's usage of the shorthand "prophets and apostles" also occurs repeatedly in *On the Last Words of David*. Just as in the Bible-prefaces, this phrase can refer to the totality of Christian Scripture in its two-Testament form or it can refer to Scripture's dual authorial offices. Luther's vision for "prophets and apostles," likewise, includes a theological perspective on biblical authorship, and therefore, for instance, the psalmist David composes psalms out of his prophetic office for the main purpose of bearing witness to Jesus Christ, which in his case entails speaking

The Hermeneutical Relationship
between the Testaments

In the Bible-prefaces, Luther articulated several dimensions to his view of the Christian Bible's formal shape as a single Word of God that appears in two Testaments. Elements of his two-Testament understanding of the Bible such as the characterization of the OT as properly "Scripture" and the NT as "proclamation" or the notion of the law and gospel's transcendence across the canon are present in the background of *On the Last Words of David*. Due to the exegetical nature of the treatise, Luther's understanding of the herme-neutical relationship between the Testaments features most prominently.[62] Dialectical movement from the Old Testament to the New and vice versa is fundamental to Luther's argument for Christ as the direct referent of the OT Scriptures; therefore, the hermeneutical significance of the character of God's Word contained equally in two Testaments will be the focus of this section to evince that what Luther proposed in the prefaces to the Bible is still at work as late as 1543 here in *On the Last Words of David* as a method for discerning Christ as the *sensus literalis* of Scripture.

Luther's messianic approach to the christological exegesis of 2 Samuel 23:1–7 must be understood as the practice of biblical interpretation in the context of the Christian Bible. In other words, Luther's confession that both the Old and the New Testaments are the Word of God and Holy Scripture causes him to engage the individual "parts" or "texts" of the Bible in a con-textual relationship within the full scope of the scriptural witness. This point

---

of the promised Messiah. See for example Luther's thoughts at the end of his long dis-course regarding how the messianic referentiality of David's "last words" in 2 Samuel 23:1–7 are based upon 1 Chronicles 17, "However, since this is such fine subject matter and we, unfortunately, are such a small number together with *the apostles and proph-ets, who concern themselves with Christ,* the crucified David and eternal God, we want to discourse further on David's last words before we conclude them and take leave of them" (italics mine); *LW* 15:299; WA 54:54. Notice Luther's qualification of "the apos-tles and prophets"; they are defined as those "who concern themselves with Christ." This understanding coheres with the manner of his presentation in the prefaces to the Bible concerning the primary function of the office of a prophet or an apostle, namely, one who is principally charged with the task of bearing witness to Jesus Christ, the Son of God and Son of David.

62. In chapter 3, although each aspect of Luther's thought concerning the signifi-cance of Christian Scripture consisting of two Testaments has "hermeneutical" im-plications, this section is referring to the hermeneutic of the interpretive exchange between the Testaments for biblical interpretation in contradistinction to the "sote-riological" dynamic of the Old and New Testaments's interrelationship understood through law and gospel. See chapter 3, "The Law and Gospel Distinction's Relationship to Luther's View of the *Sensus Literalis.*"

must not be overlooked or else the tendency to reduce Luther's hermeneutic to "Christianization" or to dismiss it as "anti-Semitic" could be easily
committed. As previously noted, Luther begins *On the Last Words of David*
making this distinction front and center.

In essence, Luther warns against permitting those who reject the complete Word of God contained in both the Old and New Testaments to serve
as authoritative interpreters of an isolated portion such as Jewish and rabbinic commentators on the OT. Because the two Testaments are inextrica-
bly intertwined in Luther's hermeneutic, one cannot be rightly understood
without the other. Hence his caveat that a "uniform Bible" (*eintrechtigen
Bibel*), that is, a two-Testament Christian Bible, would be unattainable if
normative interpretation of the OT was yielded to those who deny the Messiah as Jesus Christ, the one whom Luther hears the NT proclaiming as the
Bible's ultimate "meaning" (*synn*) and "import" (*verstand*).[63] Luther goes on
to clarify this assertion by explaining that Jesus is he "who was promised
[*verheissen*] in the Old Testament and who later appeared and brought with
Him the light and the true meaning [*verstand*] of Scripture."[64] Therefore, if
the OT's material purpose is primarily to "promise" the coming Christ, as
Luther believes, then when interpreted without the corresponding fulfillment of its witness (i.e., the NT), the true literal sense meaning of Hebrew
OT as the prophetic Word of God will remain in darkness until the bright
"light" (*liecht*) of Jesus Christ is shone upon it.

Reading the NT in Light of the OT

The central aspect of what it meant to read the NT in light of the OT in
the prefaces to Luther's *Deutsche Bibel* involved understanding the OT as
the "ground" and "proof" of the NT's proclamation of Jesus Christ and
the gospel.[65] Although not restated in exact terms, other semblances appear concerning the notion that the OT sets the tone of the entire biblical
witness, thereby requiring the NT in its ontological identity as revealed
Christian Scripture to be in accord with the first Testament. Perhaps one
of the most significant components leading Luther to this perspective in
the Bible-prefaces was the consideration of Moses as the figurehead of the
prophets's and apostles's message. Luther, likewise, in *On the Last Words of*

63. *LW* 15:267–68; WA 54:28–29.

64. *LW* 15:268; WA 54:29, "welcher im alten Testament verheissen und hernach
komen, mit sich das liecht und verstand der schrifft bracht hat."

65. See for instance the *Preface to the Old Testament* (1523), *LW* 35:236; WA, *DB*
8:10.

David reiterates his view on Moses's influence upon the biblical canon as a determinative factor for discerning Christ as Scripture's *sensus literalis*.

Upon completion of his intertextual argument for a messianic reading of 2 Samuel 23:1–7 based upon 1 Chronicles 17:10–17, Luther decides to offer further assurance of Christ in the OT's "letter" through its prophetic word about the Messiah. This aim brings a transition in *On the Last Words of David* from focus upon King David's execution of his prophetic office to Moses, "the fountainhead, the source, the father, and teacher of all prophets."[66] Luther's polemical rhetoric is on display in his stated goal to "test [Moses] to see whether we find him to be a Christian, whether he supports our position."[67] Luther, then, invokes Jesus's claim in John 5:46 that "Moses wrote of Me" for scriptural warrant to investigate just how much of a NT "Christian" the OT's Moses really is.[68] Luther is persuaded that if he can convince his audience that Moses considered his chief task as that of promising and prophesying not only of a future Messiah in general, but one who would appear as God in the flesh, then every prophet subsequent to him can be agreed upon to have shared in this same purpose. Luther admits this logic when he writes, "And if he wrote of Christ, he must, of course, have prophesied [*geweissagt*] and proclaimed [*gepredigt*] Him and enjoined all prophets who followed him to write [*Schreiben*] and to preach [*Predigen*] of Christ."[69]

Luther's interpretive quest for "Moses the Christian" predominates the remaining substance of *On the Last Words of David* until he returns at the end to a brief verse-by-verse exposition of 2 Samuel 23:1–7. Throughout this section, Luther's objective is to show how Moses's doctrine of God and of the Messiah is entirely consistent with NT expressions of the Trinity and Christology, using passages from John and Paul as prime test cases. It is also within this discourse (as examined above) that Luther's recourse to his biblical-theological hermeneutic rooted Genesis 3:15 and the OT promise of the messianic "seed" serves as a harmonizing device to manifest the theological coherence of the Testaments's separate witnesses to Christ. Once he is convinced that he has sufficiently substantiated his case for Moses's "Christian"

---

66. *LW* 15:299; *WA* 54:55, "den heubtbrun, Quelle, Vater und Meister aller Propheten."

67. *LW* 15:299; *WA* 54:55, "ob er sich wolle lassen einen Christen machen, und uns beystehen."

68. *LW* 15:299; *WA* 54:55, "weil Christus selbs jnen Teuffet, Joh. 5 und spricht: 'Moses hat von mit geschrieben.'"

69. *LW* 15:299; *WA* 54:55, "Hat er von jm geschrieben, so hat er freilich von jm auch geweissagt, gepredigt und befohlen allen Propheten nach jm, von Christo zu Schreiben und zu Predigen."

identity, Luther begins to conclude with a parallel set of thoughts to his initial comments about Moses as the pacesetter for the canonical scope of Scripture's witness.

Although Moses may seem unsuspecting "cowled and attired in the Old Testament, as though he were no Christian but a devout monk," this garb is the "swaddling cloths" wherein Christ the treasure is to be found, to mix Luther's metaphors.[70] Continuing the imagery of Moses's "outer appearance," Luther adds, "Moses lets the rest boast of the Law and circumcision; he goes along with them dressed in this cowl, but his heart, his faith, and his profession are always Jesus Christ, God's Son, etc."[71] In other words, throughout his entire OT occupation, Moses is fixed upon his calling to drive hearts towards and to make known Jesus Christ, the Son of God who would become flesh in fulfillment of the first Testament's messianic portrait. How this relates to the guiding principle of the OT as the "ground" and "proof" of the NT pertains to the impact Moses has upon the material substance of the rest of Holy Scripture. Just as he intimated at the beginning of this discourse, Luther teaches that every subsequent OT prophet derives his office and message from Moses. This relationship among the prophets leads Luther to reason, "And if we have Moses, the teacher and the chief, on our side, then his disciples, the prophets, will follow him in crowds and join us; for they do not believe, profess, and teach differently than Moses, their teacher, does."[72]

Whenever John aligns Jesus Christ with the Divine Word through whom all things were created in John 1:1–17 or similarly Paul in Colossians 1:15–17, Luther says that Moses "hears" (*Höret*) and "approves" (*bekennet*) them.[73] Because God the Son goes on to be revealed in Moses's writings, notwithstanding the whole OT, as the coming Messiah and as the Person of the Godhead by whom God created all things, Moses provides the doctrinal truth which the apostles certify and announce as fully revealed. Stated differently, John and Paul's Christology teaches that Jesus is the Messiah,

70. *LW* 15:335; WA 54:85, "Schadet nicht, das er dazu mal noch in der Kappen steckt, und im alten Testament gekleidet daher gehet, als sey er nicht ein Christ, Gleich wie ein fromer Münch." On the OT Scriptures as Christ's "swaddling cloths," see *LW* 35:236; WA, *DB* 8:12.

71. *LW* 15:335; WA 54:85, "Also lesst Mose den andern hauffen sich des Gesetzes und Beschneittung rhümen, gehet jmer mit in solcher Kappen, Aber sein hertz, glauben und bekentnis ist Jhesus Christus, Gottes Son a."

72. *LW* 15:335; WA 54:85, "Haben wir nu Mosen, das ist, den Meister und obersten, So werden seine Jünger die Propheten mit hauffen jm nach zu uns fallen, Denn sie nichs anders gleuben, bekennen und leren, weder Mose jr Preceptor thut."

73. *LW* 15:312–13; WA 54:66.

the Incarnate One, and is the one at work in creation because Moses does. Seen from this vantage point, to claim that David, an OT prophet who is to follow Moses's lead, has chosen to craft his "last words" as an exaltation in the distinct messianic promise God made to him and his offspring is to be expected.

Reading the OT in Light of the NT

Luther unashamedly reads the Old Testament in light of the NT due to his commitment to the church's confession of a bipartite formal shape of Christian Scripture. To reiterate, Luther does not divide these voices according to the logic of "letter and Spirit" that polarizes one witness from the other, but rather the Reformer perceives hermeneutical interplay and interdependence as inherent to their relationship resultant from both Testaments's ontological self-understanding as the living and abiding Word of God, though having been voiced from different sides of the cross, so to speak. Within this framework, a biblical reader should be compelled by the biblical witness to reconcile the first Testament with the second, since the latter offers itself as authoritative Scripture insofar as it is accords with the former. This "accordance" is not merely one which is "in accord with" an established, stand alone body of work, but even further is one which "is according to" the anticipation of its antecedent testimony.[74] Thus, what the NT teaches about

---

74. Farkasfalvy calls attention to the tendency to regard Paul's confessional kerygmatic statement in 1 Corinthians 15:3–4 as "meaning an unspecified 'agreement' with the Scriptures rather than the fulfillment of prophecies." This interpretation is facilitated by translation of the Greek preposition κατα as "in accordance with" rather than "according to." Though the former is a possible rendering, Farkasfalvy seems to opt for the latter translation. Given the specificity of what Paul claims to be approved by the Scriptures (i.e., the OT) concerning the person and work of Jesus Christ, "the text's reference to the Scriptures cannot be reduced to some vague agreement." On the other hand, Farkasfalvy still advocates for an "accordance" that is *in toto* with the entire OT canonical witness. He writes, "Since εν πρωτοις modifies the act of giving ('I passed on'), we must also conclude that not only the Messiah's death, burial, and resurrection, but also their scriptural attestation are 'of first importance.' This is why we should prefer to interpret 1 Corinthians 15:3–4 as referring not only to one or just a few scriptural attestations, but to scripture in its totality." In this way, Christ is the sum of the OT's witness, but this formulation encompasses the reality that the OT Scriptures contain direct prophetic utterances about Jesus as the Messiah which find their intended fulfillment in him (Luke 24:27–47). Farkasfalvy, *Inspiration and Interpretation*, 14–15. Cf. Seitz, "'In Accordance with the Scriptures': Creed, Scripture, and 'Historical Jesus,'" 55–57, who stresses the idea of "accordance" more so as "congruence" with the unique nature of the OT's revelation about God and his redemptive plans. Seitz clarifies, "This accordance is not about scattered proof texts, but about a

the foundational elements of the gospel and the Christian faith (the *regula fidei*) governs OT interpretation because with Christ's first advent, Jesus himself and the apostles claim to have brought resolution to the immediate eschatological horizon of the first Testament. Because "the New Testament is nothing but a revelation of the Old" for Luther, the guide to right and certain interpretation of the OT Scripture's literal sense is the NT.[75]

Before his concluding exposition of the full text of 2 Samuel 23:1–7, Luther closes the main substance of *On the Last Words of David* with the plea for interpreting the OT as *Christian* Scripture, for "it behooves us to recover Scripture from them [Jewish interpreters] as from public thieves wherever grammar warrants this and harmonizes [*reimet*] with the New Testament. *The apostles furnish us with many precedents for this.*"[76] Luther does not list these apostolic "precedents" (*Exempel*), but in light of the study on the Bible-prefaces, one can imagine that Luther has envisioned here many of his standard scriptural proofs for a NT-"guided" reading of the OT such as: Luke 24; John 5:39, 46; Romans 1:1–2; 3:21; and 1 Peter 1:10–12. At the end of the treatise, this exhortation bookends well with Luther's intro-ductory contention for the pathway to a "uniform" (*eintrechtigen*) Christian Bible equipped with "the meaning and import of the Bible . . . the New Tes-tament, that is, Jesus Christ."[77]

---

much broader skein of convictions." He continues, "'In accordance with the scriptures' means: related to claims about God and God's promises as presented in the Old Testa-ment scriptures—not to individual proof texts about the details of Jesus's death, burial, and resurrection. To speak of God raising Jesus is to ask how such raising fits into a larger scriptural description of God's plans with the world." Seitz makes a compelling case for the broader "in accordance with" perspective, but Farkasfalvy's conviction for the necessity to anchor 1 Corinthians 15:3–4 in a more concrete textual foundation of specific prophetic reference in the OT Scriptures in addition to confessing Christ as comprehensively accorded with God's self-disclosure in the first Testament seems to account best for all the implications of 1 Corinthians 15:3–4. Seitz's position does not deny the existence of explicit prophecies about Christ, but it seems his desire not to emphasize a one-to-one linear connection between the Testaments as an explana-tion of "accordance" has to do with his larger commitment to a canonical approach to Christian Scripture that resists reduction to promise-fulfillment and salvation-history (*Heilgeschichte*) as models for biblical theology.

75. *LW* 52:41; WA 10.1.1:181, "[D]enn das new testament ist nit mehr denn eyn offinbarung des allten."

76. *LW* 15:344; WA 54:93, "Darumb man als von öffentlichen dieben wider nemen sol die Schrifft, wo es die Grammatica gerne gibt und sich mit dem Newen Testament reimet, wie die Aposteln uns Exempel reichlich gnug geben."

77. *LW* 15:268; WA 54:29, "den synn und verstand der Biblia, . . . das Newe Testa-ment, das ist Jhesum Christum."

Following the declaration that Christians have the right understanding of the OT's literal sense in the NT's apostolic preaching of Christ, Luther raises the issue of which should be given priority, the *verba* or the *res*? In response, Luther declares,

> If I were offered free choice either to have St. Augustine's and the dear fathers', that is, the apostles's, understanding [*verstand*] of Scripture, together with the handicap that St. Augustine occasionally lacks the correct Hebrew letters [*buchstaben*] and words [*wort*], . . . I would let the Jews with their interpretation [*verstand*] and their letters [*buchstaben*] go to the devil, and I would ascend into heaven with St. Augustine's interpretation [*verstand*] without their letters [*buchstaben*].[78]

Although Luther seems to grant preeminence to the *verstand*, that is, the reality (*res*) and/or meaning to which the text (*verba*) refers, over Scripture's "letter" (*buchstabe*), this interpretive choice should not be mistaken as evidence of the perspective that accuses Luther of imposing a dogmatic and historically anachronistic reading upon the OT. Augustine and other Church Fathers represent, for Luther, biblical interpreters who have listened attentively to the "apostolic precedents," which reveal that the NT is none other than that which God has promised and prophesied by the prophets in the OT. The NT, not church tradition and dogma, is the *sensus literalis* (i.e., *verstand, res*) of the OT's "letter" (i.e., *buchstabe, verba*).[79] So long as the

78. *LW* 15:268; WA 54:29, "Wenns nu solt wundschens und wehlens gelten, Entweder, das ich S. Augustini und der lieben Veter, das ist der Apostel verstand in der schrifft solt haben, mit dem mangel, das S. Augustinus zu weilen nicht die rechte buchstaben oder wort in Ebreischen hat, . . . wo zu ich wehlen würde, ich liesse die Jüden mit jrem verstand und buchstaben zum Teüffel faren und füre mit S. Augustin verstand on jre buchstaben zum Himel."

79. In his examination of Luther's interpretive approach in *On the Last Words of David*, Mattox offers many valuable insights on Luther's indebtedness to the "Catholic" tradition of whose creedal formulations he had not abandoned as a Reformer. From this angle, Mattox credits the *regula fidei* as the cause for Luther's prioritization of the *res* over the *verba*. Mattox further elaborates, "Unlike some other sixteenth-century interpreters, then, Luther could never content himself to find and defend an irreducible minimum of clear and incontrovertible texts in support of central Christian claims. To the contrary, he wanted to show that the truth of the Nicene faith had been inscribed far and wide into every letter of Holy Scripture, and to insist that the explicit recognition of this truth should illuminate and inform every authentically Christian act of biblical interpretation." Mattox, "From Faith to the Text and Back Again: Martin Luther on the Trinity in the Old Testament," 302. Mattox also revists many of same conclusions concerning Luther's exegesis in *On the Last Words of David* within a broader analysis of his interpretive approach in, Mattox, "Luther's Interpretation of Scripture: Biblical Understanding in Trinitarian Shape," 51–57. Certainly, Luther approached Scripture

Testaments embody an inherently interdependent hermeneutical relationship, reading one in light of the other is in no way a violation of the discrete witness of the other; in fact, it is imperative in Luther's approach. Thus, to interpret the OT in denial of the NT's veracity as the Word of God and as the realization of the OT Scriptures's future-oriented witness creates an interpretive methodology that will leave the real meaning (*verstand*) of the OT's "letters" (*buchstaben*) constantly out of reach, no matter how well someone may be trained in Hebrew vocabulary, grammar, and syntax.[80]

---

within a *regula fidei* frame of mind as a confessional, orthodox Christian, but Mattox's assessment does not seem to do full justice to Luther's own hermeneutical practices or prescriptions. For instance, although Mattox suggests that Luther would shy away from reliance upon scriptural proofs in support foundational Christian truths, *On the Last Words of David* proves to the contrary. An entire study on how scriptural proofs figure into Luther's exegetical method could be developed squarely upon this single treatise insofar as they permeate every aspect of his argumentation from start to finish. Additionally, what Mattox describes as Luther's interest in the "Nicene faith" should actually be applied to the New Testament. As has been argued thus far, Luther repeatedly recommends the NT, not the *regula fidei* or even the "Creed," as the hermeneutical tool for "harmonization" and "illumination" of the OT. Luther's ambition is to reveal that the *NT* is what is "inscribed far and wide into every letter of Holy Scripture." Mattox's substitution of the "Nicene faith" for the NT neglects not only Luther's straightforward assertions about the NT that pervade *On the Last Words of David*, but it also fails to recognize that for Luther there exists between the Testaments an inherent hermeneutical exchange, whereby a "uniform" Bible is achieved that discloses a Christian theology not so coincidentally represented in the *regula fidei*.

80. Luther further stresses this dilemma, "Furthermore, since the Jews repudiate this Christ, they cannot know [*wissen*] or understand [*verstehen*] what Moses, the prophets, and the psalms are saying, what true faith is, what the Ten Commandments purport, what tradition and story teach and prove. But according to the prophecy in Is. 29:12, Scripture must be to them what a letter [*brieff*] is to an illiterate. Indeed, he may see the letters [*buchstaben*], but he is ignorant of their significance." *LW* 15:269; *WA* 54:30. Luther's choice to speak of "Moses, the prophets, and the psalms" is likely a subtle allusion to Luke 24:44, where Jesus specifically refers to these three to represent the totality of OT Scripture and its witness to him. If Christ is not received by faith as the long-expected Messiah along with the apostolic writings that make up the NT canon, then, according to Luther, the entire OT will be lost to its interpreters. They will miss the reality to which the "letters" point and be blinded to the biblical text's true literal sense meaning, one that is not only the divinely intended sense, but even is that which the prophets and the apostles are trying to communicate. Cf. with Gow who recognizes that despite Luther's interest in Hebrew, one's skill with the language was not what he considered as the most important tool for the "right" interpretation of Israel's Scriptures. Instead Luther most valued "Christian truth" for properly reading the OT. This recognition, of course, is still placed within a negative connotation within Gow's larger thesis on Luther's "colonization" agenda for the Hebrew Bible against the Jews. Gow, "Christian Colonialism: Luther's Exegesis of Hebrew Scripture," 251–52.

In order to preserve the "meaning of Christ" (*synn Christi*), Luther exhorts Christian readers all throughout *On the Last Words of David* "to interpret the Hebrew Bible, wherever that is feasible, in the direction of the New Testament."[81] For example, Luther translates the last clause of 1 Chronicles 17:17 as, "Thou hast regarded me as in the form of a Man who is God the Lord on high."[82] After providing justification for this rendering of the Hebrew, Luther, as expected, expounds upon David's deliberate attempt to articulate that the Messiah from his offspring will be both lowly man and exalted Lord and God.[83] If there is any doubt concerning this interpretation of 1 Chronicles 17:17, then one can find assurance in the truth "[t]hat [this] is the doctrine and belief of the New Testament" manifest in its proclamation of Jesus of Nazareth as the Incarnate Messiah who is also God the Son, "one God and three distinct Persons together with the Father and the Holy Spirit."[84]

At this point, Luther digresses to his recurring petition for reading the Old Testament in light of the New. Given his translation of 1 Chronicles 17:17, Luther encourages his readers to see how "David's words [*wort*] in

81. *LW* 15:269–70; WA 54:30, "Summa, wenn wir unsern vleis nicht dahin keren, das die Ebreische Biblia, wo es jmer sich leiden wil, zum verstand des Newen Testaments zihen."

82. *LW* 15:286; WA 54:44.

83. Luther writes, "With these words David clearly states that his Son, the Messiah, will surely be true Man, in form, manner, and size like any other man (Phil. 2:7), and yet up above and on high, where there is no manner of men, where only God is and governs, He is to be God the Lord." *LW* 15:286; WA 54:44.

84. *LW* 15:287; WA 54:44, "Das is die lere und Glauben des Newen Testaments . . . , mit dem Vater und Heiligen geist, ein Einiger Gott und drey unterscheidliche Personen." See also the important declaration from Luther for understanding in part the rationale for *On the Jews and Their Lies* (1539): "However, although we perhaps labor in vain on the Jews—for I said earlier that I don't want to dispute with them—we nonetheless want to discuss their senseless folly among ourselves, *for the strengthening of our faith and as a warning to weak Christians* against the Jews, and, chiefly, in honor of God, in order to prove that our faith is true and that they are entirely mistaken on the question of the Messiah. *We Christians have our New Testament, which furnishes us reliable and adequate testimony concerning the Messiah*" (italics mine); *LW* 47:177; WA 53:450. The manner with which Luther goes on to vindicate the NT as "reliable" testimony of the Jews's Messiah is by demonstrating that the messianic portrait of the OT Scriptures in their "letter" is undeniably Jesus of Nazareth, whom the apostles in the NT proclaim as the Christ with recourse to the first Testament's witness. This understanding of the NT provides an appropriate hermeneutical control on OT interpretation in Luther's view, since in its self-understanding as the Word of God from the same God of Israel who spoke into existence the first Testament witnesses to a "Messiah" that is specified as none other than the Messiah promised to the Jews in the Hebrew Bible.

this passage amply reflect that meaning [*verstand*] in accord with the general usage of the Hebrew tongue [*sprachen*]."[85] Therefore, instead of searching for an alternative "meaning" (*verstand*) from other sources, Christians equipped with a NT-"guided" reading must accept "this as the only correct one [*verstand*] and look upon all other interpretations [*deutung*] as worthless human imagination."[86] Christian interpretation of the OT can be applied in this way with certainty, for "[t]he New Testament cannot err, nor can the Old Testament where it harmonizes [*reimet*] and agrees with the New Testament."[87] What Luther reveals here is a twofold commitment: First, he wishes for the Hebrew to contribute to Christian doctrine with its own voice (even if his translation is contestable). And second, his resolve to demonstrate the Christian-theological referent in the OT's "letter" incorporates utilization of the NT as a guide and/or corrective for interpretive (or even translation) decisions due to its claim as the fullness of the OT's prophetic word. Even at this point, Luther does not jettison the Hebrew or the "grammatical" aspect of his exegetical method; his conclusions, whether related to translation or theological interpretation, remain anchored in the scriptural text. This sort of hermeneutical usage of the NT is not a reading of it back into the OT, but instead is an exemplification of "Scripture as its own interpreter" to resolve whatever problems or obscurities that might exist between the theological witness of the Testaments.

On a related passage, Luther offers a similar account. The messianic-christological referent of 1 Chronicles 17 is so certain for Luther that he

85. *LW* 15:287; WA 54:44, "David's wort, an diesem ort, solchen verstand gerne geben, nach aller art Ebreischer sprachen."

86. *LW* 15:287; WA 54:44, "sonder diesen den einigen, allein rechten verstand, Alle ander deutung fur Menschlichen nichtigen dunckel."

87. *LW* 15:287; WA 54:44, "Das newe Testament kan nicht feilen, Also das Alte Testament auch nicht, wo sichs reimet, und dem newen ehnlich ist." On the surface, this statement seems to hint at the possibility within Luther's doctrine of Scripture for some parts of the OT to be able to "err" (*feilen*), except for those parts that "harmonize" (*reimet*) with the NT. Luther's actual point within the full context of *On the Last Words of David* is that without the "guidance" of the NT, 1 Chronicles 17:17 may be translated and interpreted in a manner that works against the real messianic and trinitarian meaning conveyed through the "letter" in Luther's rendering of the verse. He notes the existence of other translation options, ones often preferred by Hebraists. But Luther shows that with the NT, one can choose with confidence the more difficult translation that would seem to disclose a contradictory truth, namely, that David refers to his son as both a man *and* God in the same sentence. In fact, as shown above, he suggests that his translation is the most natural wording of the Hebrew. Therefore, what may seem like an interpretive problem in the plain sense of the Hebrew, Luther assures his readers that the NT confirms that the OT means exactly what it says, as unbelievable as it may sound.

contends that, "The prophets that followed David, as well as David himself, derived much proof of Christ's deity and of His humanity from this."[88] An indisputable example of this sort of intertextuality, according to Luther, is Psalm 110. Like 1 Chronicles 17, Luther sees David disclosing in this psalm a messianic profile that is synonymous with the NT's doctrine of the Incarnation. Luther, then, shows how Jesus himself supports this interpretation in Matthew 22:43–44, when the Pharisees are asked how David is able to call his "son" Lord in Psalm 110. Echoing Matthew 22:46, Luther says, "they were unable to make reply."[89]

Christian interpreters, however, "have the New Testament," and thus, can respond in confidence with the right understanding.[90] The NT with its gaze set backwards upon the OT as it makes its own claims about the Triune God and the Messiah as Jesus Christ provides "enough reason here to interpret [*verstand*] the Old Testament as we do."[91] All other attempts outside of the NT's "guidance" to make sense of the supposed problematic in Psalm 110 "will inevitably go awry."[92] In Luther's assessment, consideration of other "interpretations" (*verstand*) blatantly ignores the plain sense witness of the NT clearly demonstrated in the fact that,

> Christ Himself appears on the scene with His apostles, who testify [*zeugen*] and prove [*zeigen*] with an abundance of words [*worten*] and works [*werken*] that this is the meaning [*verstand*]. This psalm is, furthermore, one of the passages in which the three distinct Persons dwelling in one Godhead are proclaimed, which is the only interpretation [*verstand*] of the prophets and of Christians, given by the Holy Spirit.[93]

Notice here that allowing the NT to facilitate the correct "interpretation" (*verstand*) to Jesus's query in Matthew 22:43–44 concerning what Psalm 110 reveals is not an advocation for an added level of meaning or a deeper

---

88. *LW* 15:294; WA 54:50, "Denn die Propheten nach David, und er selbs auch viel draus genomen haben, von Christo, das er Gott und Mensch sey."

89. *LW* 15:294; WA 54:51, "Kundten sie jm nichts antworten."

90. *LW* 15:295; WA 54:51, "Wir haben aber das Newe Testament."

91. *LW* 15:295; WA 54:51, "Wir Christen gnug haben, das Alte Testament auff unsern verstand zu zihen."

92. *LW* 15:295; WA 54:51, "Sondern alle ander verstand mus feilen."

93. *LW* 15:295; WA 54:51, "So ist Christus selbs da, mit seinen Aposteln, die zeugen und zeigen uns diesen verstand mit reichen worten und wercken, Und ist dieser Psalm auch der örter einer, da die drey Personen unterschiedlich in einer Gottheit verkundigt sind, welchs allein der Propheten und Christen verstand ist, durch den Heiligen geist gegeben."

"sense" to be discovered. Rather, Christ and the apostles hear the discourse in Psalm 110 as a direct prediction that the Messiah from David's offspring will be both God and man. This meaning is David's literal sense, his authorial intent, in the composition of this particular psalm. Moreover, David is able to communicate this teaching because the Holy Spirit is speaking through his speaking. Thus, in Luther's approach to this dimension of the hermeneutical exchange between the Testaments, the NT directs biblical readers to an understanding and/or interpretation (*verstand*) of the OT that is the one which the Holy Spirit has divinely intended through the authorial practices of the prophets. Because the selfsame Spirit has also inspired the NT witness to be God's Word, the "apostolic precedents" promise a "uniform" Bible, so long as biblical readers yield to their instruction.

Luther repeats this process of argumentation numerous times throughout *On the Last Words of David* as a critical aspect of his exegetical program for OT interpretation. Post the first advent, if one is struggling to find Christ spoken of in the OT's "letter," Luther wonders why, since contemporary Christians have the unique privilege of approaching the OT Scriptures with the literal sense interpretation of its promises and prophecies already supplied by the apostles inscripturated in the NT canon. At this level, the struggle to maintain the confession of the ontological reality of the OT as *Christian* Scripture also entails a fight for the integrity of the gospel of Jesus Christ and the validity of the NT as equally Christian Scripture and the Word of God.[94]

As Luther articulates how this hermeneutic works, he must not be misheard as advancing an imposition of the New Testament upon the Old so as to flatten the first Testament's unique witness. Instead, the NT is to serve as a light of definite Christian revelation from God the Holy Spirit that shines into the dimly lit stable, exposing a manger wherein beneath the illumined "swaddling cloths" has lain all along Jesus Christ, the promised Messiah. Luther conveys in his own "last words" to this treatise that, if scriptural exegesis is engaged in this manner, "Then we will again find and recognize our dear Lord and Savior clearly and distinctly in Scripture. To Him, together with the Father and the Holy Spirit, be glory and honor in eternity. Amen."[95]

94. Helmer recognizes that Luther believes the gospel is at stake in the preservation of the OT Scriptures's ability to reveal distinctly Christian theology within the semantics of its own "letter," when she writes, "Without this testament's [OT] living voice, the whole gospel would become dead history." Helmer, "Luther's Trinitarian Hermeneutic and the Old Testament," 65.

95. *LW* 15:352; WA 54:100, "amit wir den lieben HERRR und Heiland hell und klar in der schrifft finden und erkennen, Dem sey Lob und Her sampt dem Vater und Heiligen Geist in Ewigkeit, Amen."

5

Conclusion

THE PURPOSE OF THIS STUDY HAS BEEN TO PENETRATE TO THE HEART OF
what is ultimately responsible for Luther's so-called "christocentric" view
of the Bible. The claim advanced has been that Luther affirms Christ as the
sensus literalis of Scripture primarily due to the Bible's preoccupation with
the messianic hope. It is Luther's conviction that Scripture's fixation upon
Jesus Christ as its central subject matter is a reality about the literal sense
referent of the biblical text in its "letter."

The tendency within Luther scholarship has been to explain the
"Christ-centeredness" of Luther's reading of the Bible as a byproduct of his
christologically-oriented doctrine of the Word of God or his attempt to read
the New Testament *back* into the Old. Chapter 1 surveys the major fronts on
the landscape of studies concerning Luther's biblical interpretation. Since
the earliest of the Bible-prefaces is dated at 1522, it was necessary to situate
their contribution to the portrait of Luther as a biblical interpreter within
the context of established research on the contrast in approaches from a
generally defined division between the "early" and "later" Luther.

The main theme within "early" Luther studies has revolved around the
question of a "hermeneutical shift" in the Reformer's interpretive method.
Whatever the case may be on this supposed "shift," the prefaces to the Bible
appear subsequent to any of the datings respective to the various proposals. By 1522, it can be assumed that Luther's hermeneutic has reasonably
stabilized. The Bible-prefaces, therefore, in their span from 1522 until his
death in 1546, offer suitable source material for gathering a holistic account
of Luther's approach to Scripture both in terms of their genre and their historical setting.

The field of scholarship on the "later" Luther's practice of biblical
interpretation has long been dominated by Heinrich Bornkamm's seminal
work, *Luther and the Old Testament*. With the aid of Christian Helmer's

essay, "Luther's Trinitarian Hermeneutic and the Old Testament," chapter 1 recounted the deficiencies in Bornkamm's assessment of the nature of Luther's "christological" interpretation of the OT. In essence, Bornkamm represents the general charge of "Christianization" leveled against Luther as it regards his "christocentric" reading of the OT Scriptures. This perspective suggests that Luther infuses the OT with the NT's concepts and doctrines, or even possibly the major tenets of the Christian faith (e.g., the *regula fidei*, justification by faith), in order to give the OT a distinctly "Christian" voice. The problem with this interpretation is that Luther argued quite the opposite, and ironically, much of his labor to defend the OT as Christian Scripture was to show how the NT takes its cue from the former rather than the reverse.

The goal of chapter 2 is to interact with each of the prefaces to the Bible in their chronological development in order to display Luther's pervasive account of the Bible's christocentricity in terms of its messianic witness and to discern key hermeneutical components that undergird the Reformer's approach. The central components are explored in chapter 3. First, the Bible-prefaces reveal that Luther's understanding of the Messiah in the OT norms the character of the rest of Scripture's witness to Christ. Moreover, the prefaces manifest a pattern of argumentation particularly observable in cases where he digresses to contend for Christ as the literal sense of Scripture. In these moments, Luther typically employs a biblical-theological hermeneutic supported by a chain of messianic promises in the OT and scriptural proofs from the NT that work together to evince that "all Scripture points to Christ." When this interpretive activity occurs, Luther's explanation for "Christ in the OT" or "Christ as the center of Scripture" is set within the context of the Bible's promise and fulfillment of the messianic hope in the person and work of Jesus Christ.

Next, the prefaces to the Bible demonstrate that Luther's interpretive conclusions come from his discernment of the biblical text's meaning. Luther affirms divine and human authorship of Scripture, and he offers a theologically defined perspective on their authorial roles through his concept of the "office" of "bearing witness." The Holy Spirit and the prophets and apostles share in this distinct "office," which Luther teaches is one that is solely given to testify to the Messiah as God the Son. Therefore, the scriptural text refers to Jesus Christ in the literal sense of its "letter" as the intended meaning expressed by both its human and divine authors.

The final hermeneutical implication from the prefaces explicated in chapter 3 is Luther's conception of the relationship between the Old and New Testaments. Ultimately, the OT is "Scripture" and the NT is "proclamation" because what the former promised by the prophets is now heralded by the apostles as realized. Even the purpose of the law and gospel distinction as it transcends the Testaments serves the messianic portrait of Christ as the principle focal point of Scripture in its two parts by driving hearts either to the coming or the arrived Messiah, Jesus Christ. Last, the Bible-prefaces advocate an approach that reads each Testament in light of the other. The OT is the "ground" and "proof" of the NT's proclamation of the gospel of Jesus Christ, and the NT "guides" the interpreter to discern how the OT text witnesses to Christ as the Messiah in the literal sense of its "letter." Luther has envisioned the hermeneutical interplay between the Testaments as one that illumines the messianic-christological literal sense referent of the full scope of the biblical witness in Scripture's bipartite form as the Word of God.

Chapter 4 features an excursus on Luther's 1543 treatise, *On the Last Words of David: 2 Samuel 23:1–7*, for the purpose of observing the presence and application of the hermeneutical implications taken from the prefaces to the Bible in a non-prefatory setting. When investigated against the background of the Bible-prefaces instead of the *Judenschriften*, does *On the Last Words of David* disclose consistency in Luther's interpretive method precisely within an entire treatise devoted to the demonstration of his "christological-exegesis"? The evidence in chapter 4 answers in the affirmative insofar as each of the major components highlighted in chapter 3 serves as fundamental pillars not only to his messianic interpretation of 2 Samuel 23:1–7, but also to Luther's comprehensive judgments where Christ is upheld as Scripture's *sensus literalis* because of his messianic identity.

What emerges from this overall study agrees with the consensus that Luther has a "Christ-centered" view of and approach to the Bible. But as it regards statements about the ultimate meaning of the Bible as the written Word of God, this study diverges from other majority voices in its claim that Luther assigns Christ to Scripture's *sensus literalis* because of the textual "pressure" he experiences exerted by the Bible itself that leads to the assumption of this primary referent. To put it another way, to make a declaration about the essence of Scripture as the Word of God is in the first place a textual matter, not a dogmatic one, for Luther.[1] Thus, it is Luther's exegetical and interpretive wrestling with the "letter" of Scripture, especially the OT's, that brings him to this formulation.

Hopeful prospects for further research in light of this examination of the prefaces to the Bible could take several forms. First, if the Bible-prefaces offer a coherent account of the central principles of Luther's biblical

---

1. For an approach that grounds Luther's "christocentric" view of Scripture in the Reformer's christological understanding of the doctrine of the Word of God, see Lotz, "*Sola Scriptura*: Luther on Biblical Authority," 28–73.

hermeneutic and theology, then analyzing them directly in relation to the corresponding sermons and lectures that in many ways produced Luther's summarized perspectives on the individual books and groupings of the Bible would be worthwhile. Of course, additional insights could be gained from comparing the prefaces to the translation theory at work in Luther's *Deutsche Bibel*, but to overlook the reality that many of the prefaces flow directly out of Luther's exegetical endeavors simultaneous to their origin would be remiss. This approach would be especially fruitful regarding the prefaces to the prophets, where it is certain that most of the prologues were heavily influenced by Luther's OT lectures from 1523 to 1532. In this way, the details of Luther's exegetical practices could be further illumined, thereby closing the sometimes apparent gulf between acknowledgments of Luther's "principles" of biblical interpretation and investigations of what he actually does in his engagement with the biblical text. In other words, this method could prevent the shortcoming explanation of "Luther the exegete" as really "Luther the dogmatic theologian."

Aside from hermeneutical presuppositions, certain themes arise in the prefaces to the Bible that should merit further attention concerning Luther's biblical theology. An obvious starting point would be an in-depth study on the Messiah in Luther. Given the significant role the promise and identity of the Messiah plays within Luther's approach to both the Old and New Testaments, it comes as a surprise that little research has centered on this topic.[2] One will find it included in broader treatments of Luther's Christology, but given its preeminence within Luther's OT and NT theology, there seems to be significant space and material for a great deal more of research on this matter.[3] In addition to the Messiah, other related biblical-theological themes prominent in the prefaces that would prove to be valuable lines of

2. Up this point, I have yet to discover a single essay or monograph devoted to the subject of "Luther and the Messiah" in English or German Luther studies. However, despite my extensive search, it is possible that one exists that I have either overlooked or have simply failed to encounter.

3. Admittedly, Siggins does seem to prioritize Luther's affinity for messianic-Christology in his book, Siggins, *Martin Luther's Doctrine of Christ*, 16–47. In contrast, the terms "Messiah" or "messianic" do not even appear in the "index" of Lienhard's highly regarded work on Luther's Christology, *Luther, Witness to Jesus Christ: Stages and Themes of the Reformer's Christology*, 407–12.

study are: Israel and the "kingdom of Christ,"[4] covenant and testament,[5] and Luther's definition of the "gospel" based upon Romans 1:1–4.[6]

Beyond Luther studies, current interests in the appropriation of pre-critical hermeneutics and the practices of the theological interpretation of Scripture and theological exegesis would find great benefit through increased ressourcement of Luther that is perhaps taken for granted or eclipsed by others such as Augustine, Aquinas, or Calvin. With respect to the present enthusiasm for biblical theology, the prefaces reveal that the Reformer should have a much stronger presence within contemporary discussions and proposals on the significance of a two-Testament Christian Bible. As this study has shown, Luther's approach consists of several dimensions, but particularly relevant is his explication of the hermeneutical exchange between the Testaments that cannot simply be reduced to a "promise-fulfillment" scheme.[7]

On this note, one could ponder how Luther would respond to a modern query such as the one posed by Rolf Rendtorff in his essay, "Must 'Biblical Theology' be Christian Theology?"[8] Rendtorff asks, "Can there be a theological interpretation of the Old Testament or Hebrew Bible that is not linked to, nor evaluated from, the point of view of the New Testament

4. Optimal source material for this study would be Luther's exegesis of the OT's prophetic writings, particularly the Minor Prophets.

5. Hagen's, *A Theology of Testament in the Young Luther: The Lectures on Hebrews* has become an authoritative work on Luther's "theology of testament," but it is limited to the "early" Luther. The prefaces shows signs of this same *testamentum* theology, and thus, Hagen's thesis should be carried "further up and further in" to see how it takes shape as a formative piece of Luther's biblical theology in his "later" writings, especially in the OT prefaces, sermons, and lectures.

6. Though another analysis of the "gospel" in Luther may seem redundant, given the priority that is often allotted to the doctrine of justification to many impressions of Luther's understanding of the "gospel," an examination of how Luther stands upon Rom 1:1–4 to supply a biblical-theological definition of the "gospel" as Jesus Christ, the Son of God and Son of David, would not only bring further clarity to Luther's own thought, but would also serve as a wise voice that is anchored in the biblical text in contemporary discussions on the question of "What is the gospel?"

7. One of the leading voices on how to conceive of the relationship between the Testaments is Christopher Seitz. In his recent work, *The Character of Christian Scripture: The Significance of a Two-Testament Bible*, Seitz shows many signs of coming to recognize that Luther has already grappled extensively with this aspect of the formal and material shape of Christian Scripture in a way that follows closely with the canonical approach to biblical theology he is advancing. Seitz, *The Character of Christian Scripture*, see esp., 68–69, 209–10.

8. Rendtorff, "Must 'Biblical Theology' be Christian Theology?," 40–43.

or Christian theology?"[9] In light of the prefaces to the Bible, Luther's answer would be undoubtedly, "Nicht!" For Luther, pursuit of a *via media* for Jewish and Christian relations on Jewish terms would likely arouse an appendix to the *Preface to the Old Testament* or a sequel to *On the Last Words of David*. In Luther's approach, reading the OT Christianly is not a new "contextualized"[10] interpretive experience of the "Hebrew Bible"[11] as a result of Christian reception and its being joined together with the NT in a biblical canon. Luther reads the OT *as* Christian Scripture because he believes it *is* Christian Scripture. To interpret the OT otherwise exhibits the spiritual inability to hear the Spirit speaking through the prophets in their "letter" of God's witness to Jesus Christ, Lord and Messiah. This type of approach, according to Luther, poses a threat to the foundation of the gospel and to the identity of Christ. Furthermore, the "apostolic precedents" refer back to the OT not merely because they find a general "accordance" with a prior spoken Word of God. On the contrary, the apostles point backwards in order to make clear that the OT's promise of the Messiah gave birth to the NT's proclamation of Jesus Christ, the Son of God and Son of David.

The messianic focal point of Scripture provides the rationale for Luther's insistence that Christ is the *sensus literalis* of the Christian Bible, both Old and New Testaments. At this point, Luther finds more common ground with a different OT theologian, John Sailhamer. In his article, "The Messiah and the Hebrew Bible," Sailhamer closes with this final word:

> What I have tried to suggest is that it can be argued that the books of the OT are messianic in the full NT sense of the word. The OT is the *light* that points the way to the NT. The NT is not only to cast its light back on the Old, but more importantly, the light of the OT is to be cast on the New. The books of the OT were written as the embodiment of a real, messianic hope—a hope in a future miraculous work of God in sending a promised Redeemer. This was not an afterthought in the Hebrew Bible.

9. Ibid., 42.

10. OT theologian Moberly advances the view that reading the OT as Christian Scripture should be understood as a Christian "contextualized" interpretation of Israel's Scriptures. In short, Moberly recommends that the only viable way to find "Christ in the all the Scriptures" is through a "spiritual" sense or understanding. Here he endorses Lubac's program for precritical ressourcement as the best way forward for Christian interpretation of the OT. Obviously in Moberly's case, Christ in the OT's literal sense is historically off limits. Moberly, "Christ in All the Scriptures? The Challenge of Reading the Old Testament as Christian Scripture," 94–100.

11. On how the choice of titles for Israel's Scriptures figures into this discussion, see Seitz, "Old Testament or Hebrew Bible? Some Theological Considerations," 61–74.

This was not the work of final redactors. I believe the messianic thrust of the OT was the *whole* reason the books of the Hebrew Bible were written.[12]

Luther heartily agrees,

God is particularly concerned about our knowledge of the revelation of His Son, as seen throughout the Old and the New Testament. All points to the Son. *For Scripture is given for the sake of the Messiah*, or Woman's Seed, who is to remedy all that the serpent has corrupted, to remove sin, death, and wrath, to restore innocence, life, paradise, and heaven.[13]

---

12. Sailhamer, "The Messiah and the Hebrew Bible," 23; italics original.

13. Italics mine; *LW* 15:338; WA 54:88, "Und sonderlich ists Gott zu thun umb die offenbarung und erkentnis seines Sons, durch die gantze Schrifft, Alts und Newen Testaments, Alles gehets auff den Son, Denn die Schrifft ist gegeben umb des Messia, oder Weibs samens willen, der alles wider zu recht bringen sol, was die Schlange verderbt hat, Sünde, Tod, Zorn weg nemen, Unschuld, Leben, Paradis und Himelreich wider bringen."

Bibliography

Aland, Kurt. "Luther as Exegete." *Expository Times* 69 (1957) 45–48, 68–70.

Althaus, Paul. *The Theology of Martin Luther*. Translated by Robert C. Schultz. Philadelphia: Fortress, 1966.

Augustine, *On Christian Teaching*. Translated by R. P. H. Green. Oxford: Oxford University Press, 1997.

Barr, James. "Luther and Biblical Chronology." *Bulletin of the John Rylands University Library of Manchester* 72 (1990) 51–67.

Bauckham, Richard. *God Crucified: Monotheism and Christology in the New Testament*. Grand Rapids: Eerdmans, 1998.

Behr, John. *Formation of Christian Theology: The Way to Nicaea*. Vol. 1. Crestwood, NY: St. Vladimir's Seminary Press, 2001.

———. *The Mystery of Christ: Life in Death*. Crestwood, NY: St. Vladimir's Seminary Press, 2006.

Bluhm, Heinz. "Luther's German Bible." In *Seven-Headed Luther: Essays in Commemoration of a Quincentenary 1483–1983*, edited by Peter Newman Brooks, 177–94. Oxford: Oxford University Press, 1983.

Boehmer, Heinrich. *Road to Reformation: Martin Luther to the Year 1521*. Translated by John W. Doberstein and Theodore G. Tappert. Philadelphia: Fortress, 1946.

Bornkamm, Heinrich. *Luther and the Old Testament*. Translated by Eric W. and Ruth C. Gritsch. Edited by Victor I. Gruhn. Philadelphia: Fortress, 1969.

———. *Luther in Mid-Career, 1521–1530*. Edited and with a foreword by Karin Bornkamm. Translated by E. Theodore Bachman. Philadelphia: Fortress, 1983.

———. *Luthers Vorreden zur Bibel*. Göttingen: Vandenhoeck & Ruprecht, 1989.

Brecht, Martin. *Martin Luther*. Vol. 1, *His Road to Reformation, 1483–1521*. Translated by James L. Schaaf. Philadelphia: Fortress, 1985.

———. *Martin Luther*. Vol. 2, *Shaping and Defining the Reformation, 1521–1532*. Translated by James L. Schaaf. Minneapolis: Fortress, 1990.

———. *Martin Luther*. Vol. 3, *The Preservation of the Church, 1532–1546*. Translated by James L. Schaaf. Minneapolis: Fortress, 1993.

Burnett, Stephen G. *Christian Hebraism in the Reformation Era (1500–1660): Authors, Books, and the Transmission of Jewish Learning*. Library of the Written Word. Leiden: Brill, 2012.

Childs, Brevard S. "The *Sensus Literalis* of Scripture: An Ancient and Modern Problem." In *Beiträge zur alttestamentlichen Theologie: Festschrift für Walther Zimmerli zum 70. Geburtstag*, edited by Herbert Donner, Robert Hanhart, and Rudolf Smend, 80–93. Göttingen: Vandenhoeck & Ruprecht, 1977.

Dockery, David S. "Martin Luther's Christological Hermeneutics." *Grace Theological Journal* 4 (1984) 189–203.

Dunn, Kevin. *Pretexts of Authority: The Rhetoric of Authorship in the Renaissance Preface*. Stanford: Stanford University Press, 1994.

Ebeling, Gerhard. "Die Anfänge von Luthers Hermeneutik." *Zeitschrift für Theologie und Kirche* 48 (1951) 172–230.

———. "The Beginnings of Luther's Hermeneutics." Translated by Richard B. Steele. *Lutheran Quarterly* 7 (1993) 129–58, 315–38, 451–68.

———. *Luther: An Introduction to His Thought*. Translated by R. A. Wilson. Philadelphia: Fortress, 1970.

———. "The Meaning of 'Biblical Theology.'" In *Word and Faith*. Translated by James W. Leitch, 79–97. Philadelphia: Fortress, 1963.

———. "The New Hermeneutics and the Early Luther." Translated by Mrs. James Carse. *Theology Today* 21 (1964) 34–46.

Edwards, Mark U., Jr. *Luther's Last Battles: Politics and Polemics, 1531–46*. Ithaca, NY: Cornell University Press, 1983.

———. *Printing, Propaganda, and Martin Luther*. 1994. Reprint, Minneapolis: Fortress, 2005.

Erasmus. "The *Paraclesis*." In *Christian Humanism and the Reformation: Selected Writings of Erasmus with His Life by Beatus Rhenanus and A Biographical Sketch by the Editor*, edited by John C. Olin, 97–108. 3rd ed. New York: Fordham University Press, 1987.

Evans, G. R. *The Language and Logic of the Bible: The Earlier Middle Ages*. Cambridge: Cambridge University Press, 1984.

———. *The Language and Logic of the Bible: The Road to Reformation*. Cambridge: Cambridge University Press, 1985.

Farkasfalvy, Denis. *Inspiration and Interpretation: A Theological Introduction to Sacred Scripture*. Washington, DC: Catholic University of America Press, 2010.

———. "Prophets and Apostles": The Conjunction of the Two Terms before Irenaeus." In *Texts and Testaments: Critical Essays on the Bible and Early Church Fathers: A Volume in Honor of Stuart Dickson Currie*, edited by W. Eugene March, 109–34. San Antonio: Trinity University Press, 1980.

Felber, Stefan. "Vischer, Wilhelm (1895–1988)." In *Dictionary of Major Biblical Interpreters*, edited by Donald K. McKim, 1011–16. Downers Grove, IL: InterVarsity, 2007.

Forde, Gerhard O. "Law and Gospel in Luther's Hermeneutic." *Interpretation* 37 (1983) 240–52.

Frei, Hans W. *The Eclipse of Biblical Narrative: A Study in Eighteenth and Nineteenth Century Hermeneutics*. New Haven: Yale University Press, 1974.

Friedman, Jerome. *The Most Ancient Testimony: Sixteenth-Century Christian-Hebraica in the Age of Renaissance Nostalgia*. Athens: Ohio University Press, 1983.

George, Timothy. "'A Right Strawy Epistle': Reformation Perspectives on James." *Review & Expositor* 83 (1986) 369–82.

Gleason, Randall. "'Letter' and 'Spirit' in Luther's Hermeneutics." *Bibliotheca Sacra* 157/628 (2000) 468–85.

Gow, Andrew C. "Christian Colonialism: Luther's Exegesis of Hebrew Scripture." In *Continuity and Change: The Harvest of Late-Medieval and Reformation History,*

Essays Presented to Heiko A. Oberman on His 70th Birthday, edited by Robert J. Bast and Andrew C. Gow, 229–52. Leiden: Brill, 2000.

Greene-McCreight, Kathryn E. *Ad Litteram: How Augustine, Calvin, and Barth Read the "Plain Sense" of Genesis 1–3.* Issues in Systematic Theology. New York: Lang, 1999.

———. "Literal Sense." In *Dictionary for Theological Interpretation of the Bible*, edited by Kevin J. Vanhoozer et al., 455–56. Grand Rapids: Baker, 2005.

Gritsch, Eric W. "Luther as Bible Translator." In *The Cambridge Companion to Martin Luther*, edited by Donald K. McKim, 62–72. Cambridge Companions to Religion. Cambridge: Cambridge University Press, 2003.

Hagen, Kenneth. "The History of Scripture in the Church." In *The Bible in the Churches: How Various Christians Interpret the Scriptures*, edited by Kenneth Hagen, 1–28. Milwaukee: Marquette University Press, 1994.

———. "Luther, Martin (1483–1546)." In *Dictionary of Major Biblical Interpreters*, edited by Donald K. McKim, 687–94. Downers Grove, IL: InterVarsity, 2007.

———. *Luther's Approach to Scripture as Seen in His "Commentaries" on Galatians, 1519–1538.* Tübingen: Mohr/Siebeck, 1993.

———. "Luther's So-called *Judenschriften*: A Genre Approach." *Archiv für Reformationsgeschichte* 90 (1999) 130–58.

———. *A Theology of Testament in the Young Luther: The Lectures on Hebrews.* Studies in Medieval and Reformation Thought 12. Leiden: Brill, 1974.

Hahn, Fritz. "Faber Stapulensis und Luther." *Zeitschrfit für Krichengeschichte* 57 (1938) 356–432.

Harnack, Adolf. *History of Dogma.* Vols. 6–7. Translated from the 3rd German ed. by Neil Buchanan. Gloucester, MA: Smith, 1976.

Helmer, Christine. "God from Eternity to Eternity: Luther's Trinitarian Understanding." *Harvard Theological Review* 96 (2003) 127–46.

———. "Luther's Trinitarian Hermeneutic and the Old Testament." *Modern Theology* 18 (2002) 49–73.

———. *The Trinity and Martin Luther: A Study on the Relationship between Genre, Language, and the Trinity in Luther's Works (1523–1546).* Mainz: von Zabern, 1999.

Hendrix, Scott H. *Ecclesia in Via: Ecclesiological Developments in the Medieval Psalms Exegesis and the Dictata super Psalterium (1513–1515) of Martin Luther.* Studies in Medieval and Reformation Thought 8. Leiden: Brill, 1974.

———. "Luther against the Background of the History of Biblical Interpretation." *Interpretation* 37 (1983) 229–39.

Herrmann, Erik. "Luther's Absorption of Medieval Biblical Interpretation and His Use of the Church Fathers." In *The Oxford Handbook of Martin Luther's Theology*, edited by Robert Kolb, Irene Dingel, and L'ubomír Batka, 71–90. Oxford Handbooks. Oxford: Oxford University Press, 2014.

Hirsch, E. D., Jr. *Validity in Interpretation.* New Haven: Yale University Press, 1967.

Jünghans, Helmar. "Interpreting the Old Luther (1526–1546)." *Currents in Theology and Mission* 9 (1982) 271–81.

Klein, Ralph W. "Reading the Old Testament with Martin Luther—and without Him." *Currents in Theology and Mission* 36 (2009) 95–103.

Kolb, Robert. "'The Noblest Skill in the Christian Church': Luther's Sermons on the Proper Distinction of Law and Gospel." *Concordia Theological Quarterly* 71 (2007) 301–18.

————. "The Relationship between Scripture and the Confession of the Faith in Luther's Thought." In *Kirkens bekjennelse I historisk og aktuelt perspektiv: Festskrift til Kjell Olav Sannes*, edited by Torleiv Austad, Tormad Engelviksen, and Lars Østnor, 53–62. Trondheim: Tapir Akademisk, 2010.

Kooiman, Willem J. *Luther and the Bible*. Translated by John Schmidt. Philadelphia: Fortress, 1961.

Kümmel, Werner G. "The Continuing Significance of Luther's Prefaces to the New Testament." *Concordia Theological Monthly* 37 (1966) 573–81.

Levy, Ian Christopher. "The Literal Sense of Scripture and the Search for Truth in the Late Middle Ages." *Revue d'Histoire Ecclésiastique* 104 (2009) 783–827.

Lienhard, Marc. *Luther, Witness to Jesus Christ: Stages and Themes of the Reformer's Christology*. Translated by Edwin H. Robertson. Minneapolis: Augsburg, 1982.

Liere, Frans van. *An Introduction to the Medieval Bible*. Introduction to Religion. Cambridge: Cambridge University Press, 2014.

Light, Laura. "The Bible and the Individual: The Thirteenth-Century Paris Bible." In *The Practice of the Bible in the Middle Ages: Production, Reception, & Performance in Western Christianity*, edited by Susan Boynton and Diane J. Reilly, 228–46. New York: Columbia University Press, 2011.

————. "French Bibles c. 1200–30: A New Look at the Origin of the Paris Bible." In *The Early Medieval Bible: Its Production, Decoration, and Use*, edited by Richard Gameson, 155–76. Cambridge Studies in Palaeography and Codicology 2. Cambridge: Cambridge University Press, 1994.

————. "The Thirteenth Century and the Paris Bible." In *The New Cambridge History of the Bible: From 600 to 1450*, edited by Richard Marsden and E. Ann Matter, 2:380–91. Cambridge: Cambridge University Press, 2012.

Lotz, David W. "*Sola Scriptura*: Luther on Biblical Authority." *Interpretation* 35 (1981) 258–73.

Lubac, Henri de. *Medieval Exegesis: The Four Senses of Scripture*. 3 vols. Translated by Mark Sebane (Vol. 1) and E. M. Macierowski (Vols. 2–3). Grand Rapids: Eerdmans, 1998–2009.

Lüpke, Johannes von. "Luther's Use of Language." In *The Oxford Handbook of Martin Luther's Theology*, edited by Robert Kolb, Irene Dingel, and L'ubomír Batka, 143–55. Oxford: Oxford University Press, 2014.

————. "Theologie als 'Grammatik zur Sprache der heiligen Schrift': Eine Studie zu Luthers Theologieverständnis." *Neue Zeitschrift für systematische Theologie und Religionsphilosophie* 34 (1992) 227–50.

Luther, Martin. "Easter Monday (Luke 24:13–35)." In *The Complete Sermons of Martin Luther*, edited by Eugene F. A. Klug, translated by Eugene F. A. Klug et al., 6:18–31. Grand Rapids: Baker, 2000.

————. "Eighteenth Sunday after Trinity: Second Sermon: The Law and the Gospel, Christ (Matthew 22:34–26)." In *The Complete Sermons of Martin Luther*, edited by John N. Lenker et al., translated by John N. Lenker, 3/1:184–95. Grand Rapids: Baker, 2000.

Maschke, Timothy. "Contemporaneity: A Hermeneutical Perspective in Martin Luther's Work." In *Ad Fontes Lutheri: Toward the Recovery of the Real Luther: Essays in Honor of Kenneth Hagen's Sixty-Fifth Birthday*, edited by Timothy Maschke, Franz Posset, and Joan Skocir, 165–82. Milwaukee: Marquette University Press, 2001.

Maser, Peter. "Luthers Schriftauslegung in dem Tracktat 'Von den Juden und ihren Lügen' (1543): Ein Beitrag zum 'christologischen Antisemitismus' der Reformation." *Judaica* 29 (1973) 71–84, 149–67.

Mattox, Mickey L. "From Faith to the Text and Back Again: Martin Luther on the Trinity in the Old Testament." *Pro Ecclesia* 15 (2006) 281–303.

———. "Luther's Interpretation of Scripture: Biblical Understanding in Trinitarian Shape." In *The Substance of the Faith: Luther's Doctrinal Theology for Today*, edited by Paul R. Hinlicky, 11–57. Minneapolis: Fortress, 2008.

Maxfield, John A. *Luther's Lectures on Genesis and the Formation of Evangelical Identity.* Sixteenth Century Essays and Studies. Kirksville, MO: Truman State University Press, 2008.

McNutt, Jennifer P. "James, 'The Book of Straw,' in Reformation Biblical Exegesis: A Comparison of Luther & the Radicals." In *Reconsidering the Relationship between Biblical and Systematic Theology in the New Testament*, edited by Benjamin E. Reynolds, Brian Lugioyo, and Kevin J. Vanhoozer, 157–76. Wissenschaftliche Untersuchungen zum Neuen Testament 2/369. Tübingen: Mohr/Siebeck, 2014.

Minnis, Alastair J., and A. B. Scott, eds. *Medieval Literary Theory and Criticism, c. 1100– c. 1375: The Commentary Tradition.* Rev. ed., with the assistance of David Wallace. Oxford: Oxford University Press, 1988.

Minnis, Alastair J. "'Authorial Intention' and 'Literal Sense' in the Exegetical Theories of Richard Fitzralph and John Wyclif: An Essay in the Medieval History of Biblical Hermeneutics." *Proceedings of the Royal Irish Academy, Section C: Archaeology, Celtic Studies, History, Linguistics, Literature* 75 (1975) 1–31.

———. *Medieval Theory of Authorship: Scholastic Literary Attitudes in the Later Middle Ages.* 2nd ed., with a new preface. Philadelphia: University of Pennsylvania Press, 2010.

———. "The Trouble with Theology: Ethical Poetics and the Ends of Scripture." In *Author, Reader, Book: Medieval Authorship in Theory and Practice*, edited by Stephen Partridge and Erik Kwakkel, 20–37. Toronto: University of Toronto Press, 2012.

Moberly, R. W. L. "Christ in All the Scriptures? The Challenge of Reading the Old Testament as Christian Scripture." *Journal of Theological Interpretation* 1 (2007) 79–100.

Muller, Richard A. "Biblical Interpretation in the Era of the Reformation: The View from the Middle Ages." In *Biblical Interpretation in the Era of the Reformation: Essays Presented to David C. Steinmetz in Honor of His Sixtieth Birthday*, edited by Richard A. Muller and John L. Thompson, 3–22. Grand Rapids: Eerdmans, 1996.

Ocker, Christopher. *Biblical Poetics before Humanism and Reformation.* Cambridge: Cambridge University Press, 2002.

———. "Medieval Exegesis and the Origin of Hermeneutics." *Scottish Journal of Theology* 52 (1999) 328–45.

Olin, John C., ed. *Christian Humanism and the Reformation: Selected Writings of Erasmus with His life by Beatus Rhenanus and A Biographical Sketch by the Editor.* 3rd ed. New York: Fordham University Press, 1987.

Pilch, John J. "Notes and Observations: Luther's Hermeneutical 'Shift.'" *Harvard Theological Review* 63 (1970) 445–48.

Preus, James S. "From Promise to Presence: The Christ in Luther's Old Testament." In *Encounters with Luther, I: Lectures, Discussions, and Sermons at the Martin Luther*

Colloquia, edited by Eric W. Gritsch, 100–125. Gettysburg, PA: Institute for Luther Studies, 1980.

————. *From Shadow to Promise: Old Testament Interpretation from Augustine to the Young Luther*. Cambridge: Harvard University Press, 1969.

————. "Luther on Christ and the Old Testament." *Concordia Theological Monthly* 43 (1972) 488–97.

————. "Old Testament *Promissio* and Luther's New Hermeneutic." *Harvard Theological Review* 60 (1967) 145–61.

Raeder, Siegfried. "The Exegetical and Hermeneutical Work of Martin Luther." In *Hebrew Bible/Old Testament: The History of Its Interpretation*, vol. 2, *From Renaissance to the Enlightenment*, edited by Magne Sæbo, 363–406. Göttingen: Vandenhoeck & Ruprecht, 2008.

————. *Grammatica Theologica: Studien zu Luthers Operationes in Psalmos*. Beiträge zur Historischen Theologie 51. Tübingen: Mohr/Siebeck, 1977.

————. *Das Hebräische bei Luther: Untersucht bis zum Ende der ersten Psalmenvorlesung*. Beiträge zur Historischen Theologie 31. Tübingen: Mohr/Sie-beck, 1961.

————. "Luther als Ausleger und Übersetzer der H. Schrfit." In *Leben und Werk Martin Luthers von 1526 bis 1546*, edited by Helmar Jünghans, 1:153–278, 2:800–805. Göttingen: Vandenhoeck & Ruprecht, 1984.

Reinke, Darrell R. "From Allegory to Metaphor: More Notes on Luther's Hermeneutical Shift." *Harvard Theological Review* 66 (1973) 386–95.

Rendtorff, Rolf. "Must 'Biblical Theology' Be Christian Theology?" *Bible Review* 4/3 (1988) 40–43.

Reu, M. *Luther's German Bible: An Historical Presentation Together with a Collection of Sources, Fourteen Plates*. 1984. Reprint, Columbus, OH: Lutheran Book Concern, 1934.

Rowe, C. Kavin. "Biblical Pressure and Trinitarian Hermeneutics." *Pro Ecclesia* 11 (2002) 295–312.

Ruokanen, Miikka. "Does Luther Have a Theory of Biblical Inspiration?" *Modern Theology* 4 (1987) 1–16.

Rupp, Gordon E. Review of *From Shadow to Promise: Old Testament Interpretation from Augustine to the Young Luther*, by James S. Preus. *Journal of Theological Studies* 23 (1972) 276–78.

Sailhamer, John H. "The Messiah and the Hebrew Bible." *Journal of the Evangelical Theological Society* 44 (2001) 5–23.

Sasse, Hermann. "Luther and the Word of God." In *Accents in Luther's Theology: Essays in Commemoration of the 450th Anniversary of the Reformation*, edited by Heino O. Kadai, 47–97. St. Louis: Concordia, 1967.

Schild, Maurice E. *Abendländische Bibelvorreden bis zur Lutherbibel*. Quellen und Forschungen zur Reformationsgeschichte 39. Gütersloh: Gütersloher, 1970.

————. "A Translator Interprets: Luther's Prologues in Tyndale's New Testament." *Lutheran Theological Journal* 2 (1968) 149–60.

Schramm, Brooks, and Kirsi Irmeli Stjerna, eds. *Martin Luther, the Bible, and the Jewish People: A Reader*. Minneapolis: Fortress, 2012.

Seitz, Christopher R. *The Character of Christian Scripture: The Significance of a Two-Testament Bible*. Studies in Theological Interpretation. Grand Rapids: Baker, 2011.

————. "'In Accordance with the Scriptures': Creed, Scripture, and 'Historical Jesus.'" In *Word without End: The Old Testament as Abiding Theological Witness*, 51–60. Grand Rapids: Eerdmans, 1998.

————. "The Old Testament as Abiding Theological Witness: Inscripting a Theological Curriculum." In *Word without End: The Old Testament as Abiding Theological Witness*, 3–12. Grand Rapids: Eerdmans, 1998.

————. "Old Testament or Hebrew Bible? Some Theological Considerations." In *Word without End: The Old Testament as Abiding Theological Witness*, 61–74. Grand Rapids: Eerdmans, 1998.

————. "The Trinity in the Old Testament." In *The Oxford Handbook of the Trinity*, edited by Gilles Emery and Matthew Levering, 28–40. New York: Oxford University Press, 2011.

————. *Word without End: The Old Testament as Abiding Theological Witness*. Grand Rapids: Eerdmans, 1998.

Siggins, Ian D. Kingston. *Martin Luther's Doctrine of Christ*. New Haven: Yale University Press, 1970.

Simpson, Gary M. "'You Shall Bear Witness to Me': Thinking with Luther about Christ and the Scriptures." *Word and World* 29 (2009) 380–88.

Skarsaune, Oskar. "Schriftbeweis und Christologisches Kerygma in Der Ältesten Kirchlichen Schriftauslegung." In *Schrift und Schriftauslegung*, edited by Heinrich Kraft, 45–54. Erlangen: Martin-Luther-Verlag, 1987.

Slotemaker, John T. "The Trinitarian House of David: Martin Luther's Anti-Jewish Exegesis of 2 Samuel 23:1–7." *Harvard Theological Review* 104 (2011) 233–54.

Smalley, Beryl. *The Study of the Bible in the Middle Ages*. 1952. Reprint, Notre Dame: University of Notre Dame Press, 1964.

Steinmetz, David C. "Luther and the Two Kingdoms." In *Luther in Context*, 112–25. 2nd ed. Grand Rapids: Baker, 2002.

————. "The Superiority of Pre-Critical Exegesis." In *Taking the Long View: Christian Theology in Historical Perspective*, 3–14. Oxford: Oxford University Press, 2011.

Surburg, Raymond F. "The Significance of Luther's Hermeneutics for the Protestant Reformation." *Concordia Theological Monthly* 24 (1953) 241–61.

Thompson, Mark D. *A Sure Ground on Which to Stand: The Relation of Authority and Interpretive Method in Luther's Approach to Scripture*. Studies in Christian History and Thought. Waynesboro, GA: Paternoster, 2004.

Tsai, Lee-Chen A. "The Development of Luther's Hermeneutics in His Commentaries on the Psalms." PhD diss., University of Aberdeen, 1989.

Treier, Daniel J. "Proof Text." In *Dictionary for Theological Interpretation of the Bible*, edited by Kevin J. Vanhoozer et al., 622–24. Grand Rapids: Baker, 2005.

Vanhoozer, Kevin J. *Is There a Meaning in This Text? The Bible, The Reader, and the Morality of Literary Knowledge*. Grand Rapids: Zondervan, 1998.

Vischer, Wilhelm. *The Witness of the Old Testament to Christ*. Vol. 1, *The Pentateuch*. Translated by A. B. Crabree. London: Lutterworth, 1949.

Wahrig, Gerhard. *Deutsches Wörterbuch, Mit Einem "Lexikon der Deutschen Sprachlehre."* Rev. ed. Gütersloh: Bertelsmann Lexikon, 1978.

Wengert, Timothy. "Philip Melanchthon's 1522 Annotations on Romans and the Lutheran Origins of Rhetorical Criticism." In *Biblical Interpretation in the Era of the Reformation: Essays Presented to David C. Steinmetz in Honor of His Sixtieth*

Birthday, edited by Richard A. Muller and John L. Thompson, 118–40. Grand Rapids: Eerdmans, 1996.

———. *Reading the Bible with Martin Luther: An Introductory Guide.* Grand Rapids: Baker, 2013.

———. "The Rhetorical Paul: Philip Melanchthon's Interpretation of the Pauline Epistles." In *A Companion to Paul in the Reformation*, edited by R. Ward Holder, 127–64. Brill's Companions to the Christian Tradition. Leiden: Brill, 2009.

Werrell, Ralph S. "Tyndale's Disagreement with Luther in the Prologue to the Epistle to the Romans." *Reformation and Renaissance Review* 7 (2005) 57–68.

Whiting, Michael S. *Luther in English: The Influence of His Theology of Law and Gospel on Early English Evangelicals (1525–35).* Princeton Theological Monograph Series 142. Eugene, OR: Pickwick, 2010.

Wilch, John R. "Luther as Interpreter: Christ and the Old Testament." *Consensus* 9 (1983) 3–9.

Yeago, David S. "The New Testament and the Nicene Dogma: A Contribution to the Recovery of Theological Exegesis." *Pro Ecclesia* 3 (1994) 152–64.

Young, Frances. "Exegetical Method and Scriptural Proof: The Bible in Doctrinal Debate." In *Studia Patristica*, edited by Elizabeth A. Livingstone, 19:291–304. Louvain: Peeters, 1989.

24655076R00126